Cosmopolitan Business Ethics

In *Cosmopolitan Business Ethics: Towards a Global Ethos Manag*[illegible] Dahl Rendtorff maps the concept of global business ethics, related to sustainability and corporate governance, via an examination of the major theories of business ethics and the philosophy of management.

The book is based on the philosophy of Immanuel Kant and the European tradition, which is applied as the foundation for the analysis of the contemporary European and Anglo-American debate on business ethics in order to formulate an up-to-date theory of global business ethics. The book will compare the different schools of business ethics, corporate citizenship, and the philosophy of management and will address the modern-day issues of sustainability, business and human rights, corporate social responsibility, stakeholder management, and corporate governance, offering insights on how to deal with these international challenges of global economics, the development and protection of human rights, and the environment.

This book proposes a decision-making model for cosmopolitan business ethics as the foundation of management and leadership in dealing with the complexities of globalization. The case studies will address the efforts of businesses to work with global and cosmopolitan business ethics at the levels of maintaining corporate integrity. Both the theoretical argument and case studies presented in the book are based on exchanges with notable business ethicists, philosophers of management, business managers, and public policy-makers.

Jacob Dahl Rendtorff is Senior Associate Professor of Responsibility, Ethics and Legitimacy of Corporations at the Department of Social Sciences and Business at Roskilde University, Denmark. Rendtorff is Member of the Executive Committee of EBEN (European Business Ethics Network), a Member of the Academy of Management, and European Editor of the *Journal of Business Ethics Education*. He has been a visiting professor at universities in Europe and the United States and has published several books.

Finance, Governance and Sustainability: Challenges to Theory and Practice Series

Series Editor:
Professor Güler Aras, *Yildiz Technical University, Turkey; Georgetown University, Washington DC, USA*

Focusing on the studies of academicians, researchers, entrepreneurs, policy makers and government officers, this international series aims to contribute to the progress in matters of finance, good governance and sustainability. These multidisciplinary books combine strong conceptual analysis with a wide range of empirical data and a wealth of case materials. They will be of interest to those working in a multitude of fields, across finance, governance, corporate behaviour, regulations, ethics and sustainability.

For a full list of titles in this series, please visit www.routledge.com/Finance-Governance-and-Sustainability/book-series/FINGOVSUST

Sustainable Markets for Sustainable Business
A Global Perspective for Business and Financial Markets
Edited by Güler Aras

Sustainable Governance in Hybrid Organizations
An International Case Study of Water Companies
Linne Marie Lauesen

Transforming Governance
New Values, New Systems in the New Business Environment
Edited by Maria Aluchna and Güler Aras

Strategy, Structure and Corporate Governance
Nabyla Daidj

Corporate Behavior and Sustainability
Doing Well by Being Good
Edited by Güler Aras and Coral Ingley

Corporate Social Responsibility and Sustainable Development
Social Capital and Corporate Development in Developing Economies
Risa Bhinekawati

Cosmopolitan Business Ethics
Towards a Global Ethos of Management
Jacob Dahl Rendtorff

Cosmopolitan Business Ethics

Towards a Global Ethos of Management

Jacob Dahl Rendtorff

Routledge
Taylor & Francis Group
LONDON AND NEW YORK

First published 2018 by Routledge

2 Park Square, Milton Park, Abingdon, Oxfordshire OX14 4RN
52 Vanderbilt Avenue, New York, NY 10017

Routledge is an imprint of the Taylor & Francis Group, an informa business

First issued in paperback 2019

British Library Cataloguing-in-Publication Data
A catalogue record for this book is available from the British Library

Library of Congress Cataloging-in-Publication Data
Names: Rendtorff, Jacob Dahl, 1965– author.
Title: Cosmopolitan business ethics : towards a global philosophy of management / Jacob Dahl Rendtorff.
Description: Abingdon, Oxon ; New York, NY : Routledge, 2018. | Includes bibliographical references and index.
Identifiers: LCCN 2017014687 | ISBN 9781472447081 (hardback) | ISBN 9781315574400 (ebook)
Subjects: LCSH: Business ethics—Cross-cultural studies. | Management—Cross-cultural studies. | Corporate governance—Cross-cultural studies.
Classification: LCC HF5387 .R449 2018 | DDC 174/.4—dc23
LC record available at https://lccn.loc.gov/2017014687

ISBN: 978-1-4724-4708-1 (hbk)
ISBN: 978-0-367-88038-5 (pbk)

Typeset in Bembo
by Book Now Ltd, London

For Victoria and Arthur

Contents

Figures

Tables

About the author

Jacob Dahl Rendtorff, Ph.D. and Dr. Scient. Adm. is Senior Associate Professor at Roskilde University, Denmark. Rendtorff has a background in research in ethics, business ethics, corporate social responsibility, management philosophy, bioethics, information ethics, political theory, and philosophy of law. He has also been doing research in phenomenology and hermeneutics, and continental French and German philosophy. Since 1994 Rendtorff has been visiting professor at Bentley College, Boston, Markkula Center for Applied Ethics, Santa Clara University, and Stanford University (2001), Bard College, New York (2011), the University of Paris-Ouest-La defense (2012), University of Tübingen (2014), and Copenhagen Business School (from 2013). Rendtorff is Member of the Executive Committee of EBEN (European Business Ethics Network) and European Editor of the journal of business ethics education.

Rendtorff has written many articles and books on issues of existentialism and hermeneutics, French philosophy, ethics, bioethics, and business ethics, as well as philosophy of law, and he has been co-author and editor on more than ten other books: in particular, as author, *Responsibility, Ethics and Legitimacy of Corporations* (Copenhagen Business School Press 2009) and *French Philosophy and Social Theory: A Perspective for Ethics and Philosophy of Management* (Springer International 2014); as editor, *Perspectives on Philosophy of Management and Business Ethics: Including a Special Section on Business and Human Rights* (Ethical Economy No. 51, Springer International 2017).

Preface

This book presents an argument for cosmopolitan business ethics that sees ethics and social responsibility in the perspective of a global philosophy of management. The book summarizes my position on business ethics, corporate social responsibility, corporate governance, and legitimacy of corporations that I have developed during my research at Roskilde University in Denmark since 1999, but it also goes further back to my research on bioethics and law since 1993. The philosophical background of my views is the existentialist philosophy of Jean-Paul Sartre based on the idea of the individual's universal responsibility for the whole world (Rendtorff 1998). But I am also very much inspired by Paul Ricoeur's ethics of the good life, focusing on "the good life for and with the other in just institutions" (Rendtorff 2000). Important previous works and milestones on this process toward defining business ethics as cosmopolitan business ethics are our work on social development of global society (Rendtorff, Diderichsen, and Kemp 1997). The theoretical basis for ethics in this book is also developed in my work on bioethics and law (Lebech, Rendtorff, and Kemp 1997; Rendtorff 1999; Kemp, Rendtorff, and Johansen 2000; Rendtorff and Kemp 2000). With my research on ethics of organizations I have moved toward integrating this research on bioethics and law with broader approaches to business ethics, corporate social responsibility, and legitimacy of corporations. Here this work resumes, summarizes, develops, and updates my earlier research on business ethics and corporate social responsibility and corporate governance (Buhmann and Rendtorff 2005; Rendtorff 2007, 2009, 2010). It is correct to say that the book as a dissemination of research effort is a presentation of this research in a short form to be available to the generally interested reader. In particular, my previous work on the responsibility, ethics, and legitimacy of corporations has been essential for the argument in this book (Rendtorff 2007, 2009), but also later works on the philosophical dimensions of business ethics and stakeholder management are important (Rendtorff 2014a; Bonnafous-Boucher and Rendtorff 2014). The concept of a decision-making model for ethical decision-making was first presented in the context of ethics of organizations and the ethics of psychology (Rendtorff 2007, 2009, 2011b; Jensen, Rendtorff, and Scheuer 2013). Moreover, the idea of cosmopolitan business ethics has also been presented in earlier forms in these different publications (Baruchello, Rendtorff, and Sørensen 2016). Accordingly, with this presentation of cosmopolitan business ethics the reader faces an update and actualization of many years research on business ethics and corporate social responsibility, so I wish you good luck and enjoyment with the act of reading and I hope that the book will help to advance the knowledge and practice of business ethics and corporate social responsibility for the promotion of the good life and justice in institutions of global society.

Acknowledgments

Many people have during the years contributed to enrichment of my research on business ethics and corporate social responsibility. I wish to thank them all. Indeed, important institutions and organizations contributed to making the research project for the book possible. Roskilde University granted me research time to work on the book after my work as head of the research group on management in transition. The idea of the book grew out of a research project on Cosmopolitan Business Ethics in 2014, sponsored by the Carlsberg Foundation where I was visiting professor at the Center for Global Ethics at the Eberhard Karls University of Tübingen in Germany. The meetings of the European Business Ethics Network (EBEN) represented important contexts of presenting ideas for the book. I am happy that these institutions and organizations gave me the ideal context for writing the book. Moreover, I would like to thank Güler Aras and the Gower/Routledge Editors of the Finance, Governance and Sustainability: Challenges to Theory and Practice Series for doing such a good job with review and editing. Indeed, I am grateful to my wife Victoria for her strong support and help and inspiration during the hard times of the writing process. I would like with love and gratitude to dedicate the book to her and also to my son Arthur who was born during the process of writing the book and in his own remarkable way also inspires my ideas about cosmopolitan business ethics.

Introduction

This book is about responsibility and ethics of organizations in cosmopolitan business ethics. It is a book about business ethics in a global context that considers ethics as the basis of management, governance, and leadership. The background is that values-driven management, corporate social responsibility (CSR), organizational ethics and business ethics, ethical accounting and new values in public organizations, and private business in the context of new relations of responsibility between public and private, have become a top agenda issue of management in recent years.

As a part of making the public sector more efficient and providing a higher level of service, public organizations in the Western world are focused on stakeholder dialogue and service for citizens with social responsibility. In business corporations new ethical guidelines for compliance and good corporate governance are introduced. In connection with the general marketization and privatization of public institutions in the competition state, among others in the form of social partnerships with public institutions, private businesses are encouraged to show political engagement and CSR as globally responsible corporate citizens (Aras and Crowther 2009). At the same time, public organizations are increasingly influenced by private management methods.

Global inequality is increasing and businesses are getting more powerful. This was emphasized at the meeting of the World Economic Forum in Davos in Switzerland in 2017. World business leaders called for state regulation of the market to make better conditions, but they also asked business corporations to look inward in their corporations as that would be more responsible. In the aftermath of the financial crisis from 2007 there has been focus on ethics and responsibility in business worldwide, an agenda that is widely shared both by left-wing and right-wing governments in the Western world, both in Europe and the US, since governments have great interest in business contributions to the good of society. With the words of the new French President Emmanuel Macron cosmopolitanism means that we all must work to "make the world great again" instead of just following national or personal interest.

With this international development we can emphasize the close connection between ethics and responsibility when it comes to formulating a sustainable strategy for private business and public organizations in a globalized world (Crane and Matten 2016). However, it is not uncontroversial to define ethics, responsibility, and good corporate governance as a constitutive element for strategy, organization, and philosophy of management. In private business it is still a widespread opinion that formulation of strategy and management is still either purely an economic challenge of improving the competitiveness of the business organization and its role in the market, or an organizational issue of the technological development capability of the business, as well as its ability to plan production efficiently and to sell the cheapest and best products at the right time. In the public sector there is also focus on good planning and efficient production, and many public officials argue that competent economic governance and legal thinking is the solution to the management problems in the public sector.

To focus on responsibility and ethics in organizational development challenges such a traditional concept of strategy and management philosophy. We need to emphasize that there is a close relation between strategy and ethics (Paine 1997a, 1997b). Today, good and efficient economic and organizational governance depend on the values of the organization and its capacity to be responsible in society. Hence, it is therefore not possible to imagine good business governance without ethics and responsibility, and a business cannot seriously be socially responsible without a connection between this responsibility and the more or less directly formulated values and ethical conceptions of the business organization. The combination in this book of corporate strategy with ethics, responsibility, and legitimacy in the context of cosmopolitan business ethics therefore aims at clarifying the inner connection between these concepts in order to determine the changed conditions for good strategy, management, and governance in the context of the economic and social conditions in the globalized society of late modernity.

This book therefore deals with what is morally right and good for business to do in the global economy. It is a book about the global and cosmopolitan responsibilities of the business corporation as a global corporate citizen. This does not mean that this book does not prioritize the fundamental problems of strategic business economics. On the contrary, the focus is on the important issues of good management, corporate governance, and organizational development in globalization. It is a dominating idea that ethical reflection in connection with strategic and organizational abilities in economic governance, finance, marketing, production, innovation, and technological development constitute the basis for a coherent development of strategy. Strategic management and governance is not possible without technical and economic insight and knowledge, but it is the ethical reflection about different alternatives of action that is decisive for creation and development of a sustainable business corporation.

Themes for cosmopolitan business ethics

While morality and moral convictions are defined as the values, rules, norms, and moral convictions that we follow in our daily lives, ethics can be defined as the theoretical and practical deliberation and justification of why we should follow those norms and values. *Business ethics* is the theoretical and practical work of developing well-justified values and norms for the function of business in society. Seen in the cosmopolitan context, business ethics should take as its point of departure the idea of the business organization as world citizen and assume its global citizenship. *Values-based* or *values-driven management* can be considered as a general term for conscious management with values and is closely connected with business ethics, because it concerns the formulation of the correct ethical values that shall determine the strategy and vision of the business corporation and contribute to implement ethics in the business firm. In the context of intercultural and global management it is important to find common values for intercultural management. *Social responsibility* or *corporate social responsibility (CSR)* is in this context a part of business ethics and values-driven management that expresses the responsibility of the business corporation toward its external relations and stakeholders (Fischer, Lovell, and Valero-Silva 2013). Social responsibility is today global, relating to the cosmopolitan responsibility of a business organization. The following topics are important for cosmopolitan business ethics as a global philosophy of management for international business:

- Integrity, honesty, and fairness
- Corruption and conflicts of interests
- Dishonesty, manipulation, and fraud
- Business ethics for international markets (anti-monopoly legislation)
- Corporate governance in international business
- Stakeholder relations and global responsibility
- Shareholders and international investments
- Accounting ethics and finance ethics (corporate mergers, hostile takeovers)
- Globalization and cultural differences
- Business and human rights in the international community
- Socially responsible investments
- Ethics for the employees and employee rights (privacy, affirmative action, non-discrimination)
- Ethics of self-management and human rights
- The political consumer and fair trade in international business
- Ethical accounting, social accounting, and environmental accounting
- Public relations and international social legitimacy of business corporations
- Business responsibilities for local communities (help to developing societies)
- Corporate philanthropy in the global context.

With the focus on cosmopolitan business ethics this book will propose different conceptions of values-driven management, responsibility, ethics, and legitimacy in public and private organizations and discuss the possibility for developing a global theory of social responsibility of business that corresponds to the expectations of the modern globalized society. In particular, the book sheds light on stakeholder management, which makes the concern for the groups or stakeholders that affect the corporation a central concern for good management. On this foundation the book begins by presenting the central features of an ethical and values-driven business in globalization. Corporate social responsibility as global responsibility will be discussed in the tension between ethics and economics, which demands methodological considerations about the foundations of the study of values-driven management and social responsibility. After this, we will discuss the role of ethics in globalization. We determine the concept of cosmopolitan business ethics and discuss ethical principles from the perspective of globalization; in the book it will be emphasized that ethics is essential in a globalized market economy. The concept of value will also be discussed from this globalized perspective, because it is an essential for businesses when they wish to improve business ethics. In the discussion of values-driven management it is also important to decide about the criticism of values-driven management. What is the criticism and is it possible to overcome this criticism? What are the best empirical examples of good values-driven management? What are the commonly applied theories for understanding values-driven management?

In this context the book will also present important theories of business ethics from a cosmopolitan perspective, including utilitarianism, universalism, rights-based approaches, virtue ethics and the republican and cosmopolitan theory of the business corporation as a good corporate citizen. From this we move to the presentation of the historical and contemporary approaches to cosmopolitan business ethics as global philosophy of management. Moreover, an important question is how to define social responsibility in relation to theories of business ethics and in relation to different international declarations and value statements (codes of conduct). In connection with the internal and external relations of the business corporation the question is how corporate governance and stakeholder management can be decided not only in relation to shareholders and owners, but also in relation to other stakeholders such as employees, consumers, suppliers and the global and local community as an important stakeholder. Furthermore, this is also discussed in relation to the ethical and social accounting and reporting of the business corporation (Ertuna 2016).

In relation to the international discussion of cosmopolitan responsibilities of corporate citizenship about business ethics and the environment, it is important to consider how the connection between values-driven management, global responsibility, sustainability, and the triple bottom line is defined. How can we define sustainability as the foundation of the strategic activities of the firm, i.e. integrate economic, environmental, and social deliberations in the definition of corporate strategy? How do we legislate about sustainability, ethics, and responsibility in the different parts of the world, North America, South America, Europe, Asia, etc.? And how do we develop cosmopolitan norms about business ethics and human rights with the global activities of the United Nations? In this context, the book presents the American and European approaches to business ethics, values-driven management, and corporate social responsibility. Roughly, we can say that the US approach is based on a legal compliance approach, while the European approach is based on a social responsibility approach in voluntary engagement of corporations in business and society. The Asian approach (China, Japan, and South Korea), although we will not elaborate on it in detail, is also very important and it can be seen as attempts to reintroduce the Mandarin virtues of Confucian ethics in the contemporary business world. In this context we also discuss the relation between social values and CSR.

Finally, we will give a summarizing attempt to describe the conceptions of CSR with special emphasis on an institutional conception of good corporate citizenship as cosmopolitan or global citizenship in order to define the legitimacy of corporations in modern society. Here we can discuss the dimensions of institutionalization of CSR and cosmopolitan business ethics in international business and management. In this context, we will also present a decision-making model for cosmopolitan business ethics.

This book is intended primarily as a basic book on cosmopolitan responsibility of business and a global philosophy of management that is directed toward the generally interested reader, but is also directed toward "reflective practitioners" in private and public organizations who wish to be oriented toward the latest developments in business ethics and CSR. Moreover, the book can be used as introduction to strategy, management, and organization in business studies and social sciences at business schools and universities.

Cosmopolitan business ethics as future management science

A very famous researcher in strategy and management, Henry Mintzberg, in the book *Managers not MBAs. A Hard Look on the Soft Practice of Managing and Management*

Development (2004) has argued strongly for the importance of responsibility and ethics of business with a strong criticism of management education and leadership development at business schools in the US and in the rest of the world. The essence of his criticism is that teaching institutions in disciplines as marketing, strategy and management, business law, accounting, and finance teach the students scientific method, quantitative statistics, and analysis of business economics, based on theoretical models and a method of teaching that is very far from how businesses really work. The teaching of business education has been focused on "operations management" according to the strategy of "planning, budgeting, programming," i.e. focus on the technical production function of the firm, and the students have in particular learned analytical problem-solving according to Michael Porter's bestseller *Competitive Strategy* (1980).

Business economics has become a technical discipline, while real problems and questions of management, concerned with leadership and management in practice dealing with human beings, have been forgotten. On the basis of this criticism Mintzberg suggests rethinking management science and leadership based on the real practice of management. In such a management education ethics and responsibility should not only be added as some hours to help improve efficiency in the organization or give more value to shareholders (Mintzberg 2004: 42). Management science should focus on real problems of leadership in practice, where management deals with human beings and is not only concerned with economic models. Managers should not be considered as highly paid heroes that are supposed to save the organization by doing everything to create value for shareholders. Rather they need to be responsible human beings that, democratically and with the ability to listen and understand, include and give attention to their employees. Mintzberg emphasizes that management cannot only happen according to pure economic parameters, but that the social consequences of economic decision-making always must be taken into account in good management. Mintzberg's criticism of the greatness and fall of the technical science of management is the basis for this book. In the center of business economics stands not only technical ability but indeed also the ethical art to manage and lead with responsibility and concern.

In a recent report by the Carnegie Foundation, *Rethinking Undergraduate Education: Liberal Learning for the Profession* (Colby *et al.* 2011), it is argued that it is important to reinforce the importance of the humanities in management education. In this context, we can emphasize the importance of business ethics and philosophy of management for management education and for the future of management. Ethics and philosophy in humanistic management and liberal education contributes to create a deeper, reflective, philosophical, and ethical understanding of the organization (Rendtorff 2015b). In particular, a case study and practice-oriented approach to dilemmas of business ethics in organization contributes to such an ethical awareness in organization. Such a case-oriented approach contributes with an integrated analysis of the different ethical dilemmas of the action in an organization. Here, philosophy of management and business ethics contributes to form a critical ethical consciousness among the management profession which contributes to reform the profession with focus on practical problems of business. With its contribution to phenomenological and hermeneutical analysis of the case the case study provides a problem-oriented analysis of the practical and theoretical problems of action that companies are facing.

This case-oriented approach contributes to rethinking management with focus on standards of excellence of practical reasoning in business life. Philosophers like

Aristotle and Immanuel Kant contribute with a concept of practical judgment that can help to find the practical abilities of managing that Mintzberg is searching for. Immanuel Kant extends Aristotle's ideas of judgment as phronesis and distinguishes between reflective and determinant judgment (Rendtorff 2015b). The combination of ethics and philosophy of management with practical judgment contributes to enabling the manager achieve ethical and philosophical formulation competency that helps to solve particular problems of management in the practical life of organizations. Accordingly, with human sciences and philosophy of management, managers become leaders who are capable of facing ethical problems in complex practical situations (Rendtorff 2015b).

1 What is cosmopolitan business ethics?

Cosmopolitan business ethics aims at finding responsible principles and values that should guide the actions and strategies of public and private business corporations and organizations. Cosmopolitanism suggests that business ethics must be global. This must be realized in the social responsibility and engagement of business corporations. Now, we shall see why business ethics has become so important in contemporary society, discuss the possibilities to realize ethics and values in practice, and treat the question whether ethics can give the business corporation economic gain and competitive advantage.

Business ethics in private and public organizations

Today, business ethics, corporate social responsibility, values-driven management, and values in organizations have become the central focus of organization and management (Pedersen 2015). This is the case for both private and public organizations (Pedersen and Rendtorff 2010). There is an ever-growing understanding that organization theory should include the values and stakeholders of the business as a basis for organizational development, business improvement, and organizational culture and identity (McAlister, Ferrell, and Ferrell 2005; D'Anselmi 2011). This is the concern for both private and public businesses. This debate about business ethics originated at the beginning of the 20th century, and during the 1950s, 60s, and 70s social responsibility became important in the discussions of the aim of business in the US and Europe. A number of economic scandals in the 1980s and 90s made it clear that it was necessary with ethical guidelines for private and public organizations. During the early 21st century, culminating with the global financial crisis in 2007 and 2008 and onwards, this need for global business ethics became even more important (Bruin 2015; Ims and Pedersen 2015).

We can distinguish between different definitions of business ethics and CSR that circulate around notions of good corporate citizenship, global citizenship, stakeholder management, sustainability and the triple bottom line, corporate social performance, social engagement, and ability to respond to social issues. These approaches to business ethics have a different focus, and they emphasize different dimensions, for example profits, international relations, societal expectations, corporate communications and public relations, voluntary self-regulation of businesses as good citizens, and their good relations with stakeholders. These different dimensions should not be conceived as oppositional, but rather as approaches that mutually supplement and develop each other. Ethics also includes economic, ecological, and social aspects of the organization's relations with the environment, including those with stakeholders and partnerships in civil society. The increased focus on business ethics is not least focused on the bad reputation that business corporations have had in the contemporary global community (Aras and Crowther 2009).

If one asks a randomly selected person in the street about the aims of businesses and corporations, one is likely to get the answer that they never focus on ethics or shared values, but always on making as much profit as possible. Some even describe businesses as psychopaths, who, because their owners, the shareholders, have limited liability and economic responsibility in reality do not have any kind of moral responsibility or social obligation (Bakan 2004: 16). Businesses cannot be responsible, because only human beings and not organizations or things can have a moral responsibility. Therefore, businesses function as psychopaths who are characterized by a sick denial of their responsibility and lack of concern for morality and ethics in their actions. The ordinary conception of business therefore is that corporations only exist for profit and that this aim excludes any morality in these organizations. In addition to this the power of businesses has today become so big that it is stated that no one any longer really has control of their actions and activities in society. According to critical analysts the greed of business corporations is unlimited and their power is growing in the international community because of the decrease of state power (Korton 1995). This is confirmed by the fact that the biggest corporations in the world, i.e. WalMart, Exxon or General Motors, have annual turnovers that are bigger than the national products of many African countries or even of Scandinavian countries like Denmark or Norway (Ferrell, Fraedrich, and Ferrell 2005: 228) without any increase in engagement in society of these businesses.

The conclusion of this skeptical opinion is that the combination of business ethics and social responsibility should be considered as an oxymoron, i.e. a concept that represents a contradiction that can never be overcome. The consequence of this lack of focus on the connection between business and social responsibility is considered by the critical public as threatening and even fatal to the coherence of society. When businesses in the private market economy cannot contribute to the common good in society, then the economy cannot improve public goods, which is necessary to improve and develop society. By omitting certain social and environmental concerns, businesses risk becoming an expensive cost to society.

The tight interest of business in economic gain in a free market leads to the consequence that they are only concerned about their own economic costs without assuming responsibility for the social and environmental consequences of their production and other activities (Martin and Schumann 1998). Accordingly, there is a risk of externalization, which means making society take care of the social and environmental costs, whereby society becomes responsible for the payment of the human costs of employees and of the pollution of the environment. At the global level we can observe that such externalities are exported from developed to developing countries, for example traders selling garbage from the rich countries for disposal in poor countries. Global capitalism risks implying less responsibility and greater inequality, because businesses are not based on the laws of the nation states, but freely can move production from one country to another. The bad reputation of businesses and their potential psychopathic conception of morality and ethics is the basis for the international criticism of their lack of social responsibility. The Canadian journalist and writer Naomi Klein summarized the criticism in the book *No Logo. Taking Aim at the Brand Bullies* (2000) as a criticism of the big businesses that only care about protecting their brand value. This criticism was continued in Klein's work on neoliberal capitalism as the shock doctrine of modern society and on climate change as an ultimate challenge to disaster capitalism (Klein 2000, 2007, 2014). Law professor Joel Bakan continues this critical perspective in the book *The Corporation. The Pathological Pursuit of Profit and Power* (2004), followed by the documentary movie *The Corporation* that Bakan produced together with Mark Achbar and Jennifer Abbott. Bakan attacks the doctrine of limited liability of business corporations (i.e. the fact that owners and investors, although they may lose the money they have invested, do not have responsibility for the activities of businesses) as a clear expression of the psychotic situation of business corporations in modern society. The opinions can also be found to be held by many critical non-governmental organizations (NGOs) attacking the lack of social responsibility of businesses, like Greenpeace, which has made different manifestations against the pollution of the environment by corporations. Other critical NGOs that attack the global businesses for lack of social engagement have in the public sphere created greater focus on the global and cosmopolitan dimension of the social responsibility of business corporations (Crane and Matten 2004: 345). From time to time we face political consumers who critically direct their anger against specific corporations. Critical media with their global news stream have also implied that businesses cannot hide from the public sphere. Moreover, employees have become more critical and caring about the values of the companies they work for. They do not only want to work and earn money, but they will work for a business corporation that they think is good and gives their lives meaning in a moral sense.

Cosmopolitan business ethics and creation of trust

Creating trust and trustworthiness (Govier 1997; Rendtorff 2017) is a part of the ethics and values of corporations that need to be institutionalized with cosmopolitan business ethics in order to create social acceptance and legitimacy of business firms. High levels of trust within organizational cultures are important for coherence of interactions in the firm. These internalizations of common norms establish reciprocity and bounded solidarity in the firm, which will be the basis for enlarging the institutional network of the firm in confident relations with its stakeholders. Accordingly we can argue that trust and accountability is important for the process of dynamic establishment of good corporate citizenship as an embedded factor of civic relations in society, responding to social expectations of consumers and citizens.

Our focus on cosmopolitan business ethics demonstrates the need to see trustworthy business practices from the process perspective of creating good corporate citizenship and legitimacy with business ethics as the basis for trust and trustworthiness (DiPiazza Jr. and Eccles 2002; Rendtorff 2017). When we analyze trust as a process of reduction of complexity in the social world we say that business ethics is important for the creation of system trust as a necessary reduction of complexity in business institutions of the modern world. Here we say that the ethical culture of corporations creates good corporate citizenship that makes the business organization trustworthy. Trust is needed for institutional coherence both externally and internally in organizations. Trustworthiness and trust contributes to a process of reduction of complexity through sense-making by measures of ethical governance, values-driven management, and corporate reporting. As a dynamic movement of accountability and responsibility, creating trust through trustworthiness becomes an instrument for dealing with problems and complexity in business firms and organizations.

By communicating trustworthiness through corporate citizenship, corporations respond to social expectations and contribute to seeing themselves as good corporate citizens. Here, a firm creates trust and becomes trustworthy by responding to ethical norms and values (Bidault *et al.* 1997; Rendtorff 2017). This is the dynamic movement of ethical accountability, integrity, and responsibility where this relation is constitutive of authentic trust. This emergence of integrity contributes to the definition of trustworthiness as the result of the sense-making process in organization where organizational integrity emerges as a result of the efforts of making the corporation trustworthy. Social capital is created, since the business corporation becomes trustworthy through business ethics performance that becomes an essential element and condition of trust in complex business systems.

Accordingly, from the ethical perspective, trust, trusting, and trustworthiness are an integrated part of business ethics in institutions that functions as an effort to improve the social legitimacy of business corporations. Business ethics activities create trust and trustworthiness because the sense-making of the process of ethics includes focus on accountability, integrity, and responsibility, which in general makes the corporation a trustworthy and legitimate institution and organization according to social expectations of society.

Focus on global social responsibility

The requirement of corporate social responsibility is not only advocated by critical voices among consumers, media, and the organizations of civil society. In the 1990s and 2000s corporate ethics and responsibility were put on the agenda by governments in the US and Europe, and this agenda also became an important dimension of the efforts of the UN to improve the ethics and responsibility of transnational corporations in order to ensure social responsibility among developed and developing countries in the processes of globalization (Blowfield and Murray 2011). The basis of the demand by governments of CSR must be found in the process of globalization, where it becomes more and more difficult for nation states to manage the development and the activities of businesses. Therefore companies are encouraged to self-regulation. The US government enacted in 1991 the so-called *Federal Sentencing Guidelines for Organizations* that asked large corporations to have ethics programs as a part of their efforts to become good corporate citizens (Kaplan, Murphy, and Swenson 1993). After the Enron scandal of 2001–2, which implied that the large idealized company Enron had falsified accounts to make it appear that the company was in constant growth, congress enacted the Sarbanes–Oxley Act, which increased demands on good corporate governance in boards and rules of transparency for the accounts and reporting procedures of corporations. The European Union worked in the 1990s and 2000s toward improving the contributions of businesses to combat exclusion and ensure coherence in the European societies. This led in 2001 to a European Union *Green Paper* which was later followed up by communications about CSR, which asked European corporations to be greatly involved in the work of CSR (European Commission 2001).

The UN drafted, on initiative from Kofi Annan after the economic summit in Davos in 1999, the so-called Global Compact principles that constitute a foundation for ethical regulation of international businesses and that are based on sustainable development and respect for human rights. In Denmark this agenda of social responsibility was in particular developed in the 1990s, and later in the 2000s the Ministry of Employment did a lot to improve the social responsibility of employees in the form of private and public partnerships (Hardis 2004; Morsing and Thyssen 2003). In addition we can mention various efforts to develop different projects in order to improve attention to social integration of employees and the good life in the labor market (Copenhagen Centre 1998 and later). Today this has been extended to imply greater focus on the relation between social responsibility and globalization, where it is required that Danish companies operating in foreign countries are aware of their ethical and moral obligations.

Social responsibility in Scandinavia: The inclusive labor market

The Scandinavian and in particular the Danish model of social responsibility should be considered from the perspective of the future of the welfare state and its emergent change toward a neoliberal competition state (Rendtorff 2011a). There has been a movement from welfare to workfare, i.e. from passive economic support to active labor support and efforts to integrate people into the labor market. From the beginning of the 1990s, social policy in the welfare state has been changing from being rights-based subsistence support policy to be an activation-based employment policy, and today this is a major characteristic of the welfare state, which is moving toward the competition state. One can say that social responsibility was likely to emerge in a Scandinavian welfare state, combined with a stable and well-functioning labor market, characterized by a flexible-security model, where employees easily can be fired, but at the same time are captured by a social-security net. The social democratic government in Denmark at the beginning of the 1990s had an understanding of the role that social responsibility of business could play in such a redefinition of social policy to become labor policy. In connection with the development of the inclusive labor market, partnerships between private and public authorities have been decisive in order to create greater social dynamics between private interests and greater social concerns, where businesses work together with a common social goal. The Copenhagen Center for Corporate Social Responsibility was created in the 1990s with support from the government as a think-tank that should work to the improvement of social partnerships between public institutions, NGOs, and private businesses. Government supported this by channeling social support over the labor market by contributing economic support to different programs of flexible-security jobs in order to keep the weakest citizens in the labor market. Enabling the employment of the elderly or people with disabilities with up to half of their salary in state support has been a success and has made corporations assume a social responsibility and contribute to an "inclusive labor market." Accordingly, social responsibility in a late modern flexible society has gained positive acceptance from unions and employers. The creation of the human labor market can be combined with economic growth, which is one of the effects of satisfied employees. Social responsibility has become a part of a new employee policy founded on basic social values that aims at integrating private life and work life and avoiding human tragedies arising from work and working conditions. This policy implies creating better and secure working conditions, reducing sick leave and taking care of the ill, giving children's families more flexible possibilities, having a senior policy, creating learning and development at the work place and having a human resource policy that is based on personal development, diversity, integration, satisfaction, welfare, and wellbeing among employees (Mølvadgaard and Nielsen 2006a, 2006b; Rendtorff 2009, 2011a). Today this approach to social responsibility is considered an integrated part of the welfare state. However, with increased neoliberal focus on competition and the competition state this model is more and more challenged. So we cannot be sure of the future of this inclusive labor market model of CSR due to the attempts to abolish welfare state privileges.

In addition to the fact that it is necessary to take into account the critical voices in the public debate and rethink the role of private businesses in relation to employment and social policy, we can mention a number of fundamental arguments for the concern for the responsibility and ethics of business corporations from a global and cosmopolitan perspective. A classical argument is that business and ethics cannot be mixed (Schwartz and Gibb 1999). The retention of the dogmatic statement that "the business of business is business," i.e. that business should only be concerned with itself and only be interested in profits, represents according to this argument an old-fashioned conception of economics that does not have an understanding of the long-term interest of business. Instead it is argued that business without ethics and morality is bad business, i.e. "bad ethics is bad business." In order for something to be good business it must be based on a responsible ethical foundation where all implied parties can be satisfied. If one has such a conception of business ethics, one cannot consider social responsibility as something external to the business, but instead as a part of the core activities of a business corporation. Responsibility and ethics is rather a part of the existential foundation, i.e. the basis of the business corporation, its "license to operate" (Zadek, Højensgård, and Raynard 2001; Crane and Matten 2016). The argument is that social responsibility can be good publicity and branding and can give the business greater earnings and economic sustainability because society does not doubt that this company as a good corporate citizen will contribute to the improvement and development of a sustainable society (Cannon 2012).

These arguments for good corporate citizenship do not only concern private business. In the context of increased marketization of the public sector, business is also relevant for public organizations. There is a close connection between business ethics, organization ethics, and professional ethics. Private business and public organizations are struggling with the ethical problems and therefore there is increased focus on professional ethics and responsibility in public organizations, for example municipalities, public organizations, or state administration. Such public organizations should be less bureaucratic, be more service-oriented, and take into account the interests of citizens. In this process they face the same problems as private business corporations that also should be concerned with the stakeholders of the company and understand their place in society (Pedersen and Rendtorff 2003). In addition, ethics and values in the public sector can function as an important addition to mainstream forms of management because ethics and values can increase employee motivation at the same time as ethical reflection can come with the solution of problems of administration in municipalities and state administration. Solutions can imply recognition of citizens not only as customers and clients, but as real ethical and political co-citizens, and this cannot really be captured by governance methods like new public management or other economic or legal efficiency methods. When we, on principle, must refuse the idea that "the business of business is business," and refuse to consider organizations only from an economic perspective, it implies that the doctrine of the economic purity of the market, i.e. that economic actors only act from the perspective of their own economic utility maximization, in practice cannot make sense. Even the grand old man of the market economy, Adam Smith, did not only consider human beings as economic actors (Smith 1776). In his major work *The Wealth of Nations* he proposed the idea of the invisible hand implying that if everybody follows their own interests it will in the end lead to the common good for everybody. In his analysis of moral feelings in the book *The Theory of Moral Sentiments* he indeed emphasized that human beings always have moral feelings that affect all their actions (Smith 1759). Those two works do not exclude each other and Smith did not change his mind.

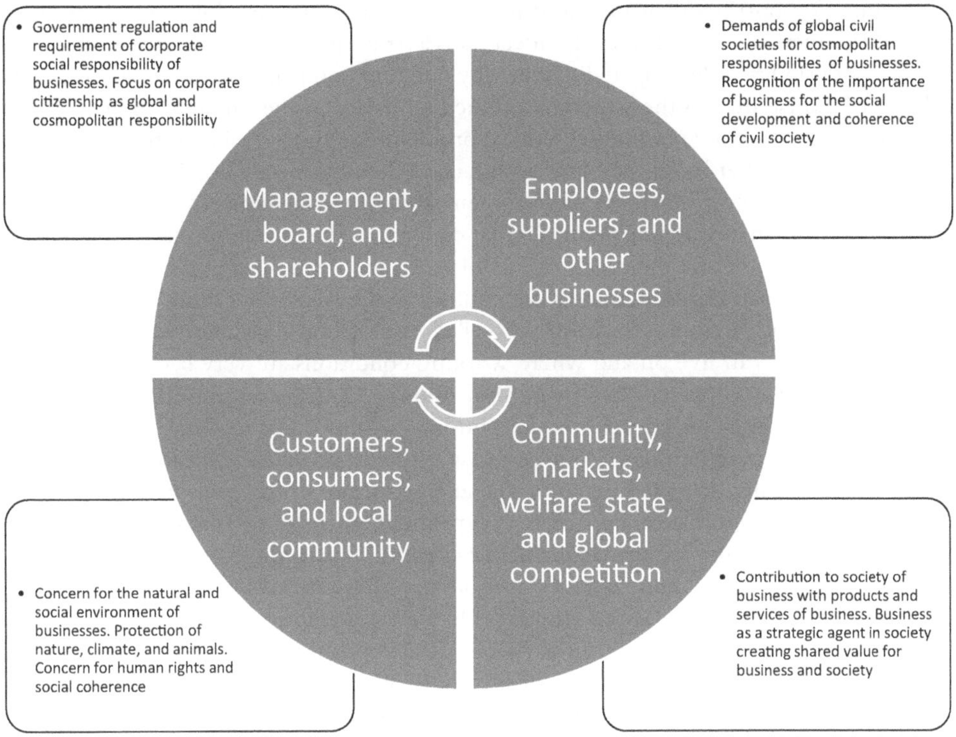

Figure 1.1 Business ethics and responsibility in global civil society.

Rather, he wanted to emphasize that there is a close connection between economics and morality. If this is correct, organization theory for both private and public organizations must combine economic deliberations with ethical approaches to organizations that can capture the interaction between different forms of values. We must move from a Tayloristic and bureaucratic concept of organization to values-driven management and we have to include a large number of implied stakeholders in order to understand the patterns of actions of organizations (Figure 1.1).

Business ethics in practice

In practice, many companies are conscious of the close connection between ethics and economy. In the pharmaceutical industry, businesses know very well that they have to convince consumers that they prioritize the health of patients before profits, because only in this way can they be sure of making a good profit. The Danish company Novo Nordisk (Novo Nordic) strives to make a good profit and to be sure to make a good profit. Novo Nordisk has a mission to combat diabetes, and the big American pharmaceutical company Merck has created a foundation for free donation of medicine to the poor and needy (De George 1999: 237; Rendtorff 2009). In the biotechnology industry, corporations like Monsanto have several times been criticized for the creation of genetically modified crops and seeds, and this has led to dialogue with stakeholders about respect for the environment. But the Danish biotechnological corporation Danisco (now owned by Dupont) has contributed to the work on social responsibility and respect for the environment at the global level. Indeed, it is a striking feature that business ethics and social responsibility is developed differently by different companies in different businesses. This is of course due to the structural differences between the different industries, but also to the fact that some businesses' ethical problems are more visible to the public than the problems of other businesses. For clothing and shoe businesses like Nike, H&M, and Levi Strauss it is not so much the environment, but rather the concern for human rights in their factories in developing countries that constitutes the most important ethical issue. Levi Strauss had to close their factory in Burma in the beginning of the 1990s because of the unfair human rights politics of the country. Nike has several times been criticized for the treatment of employees in the so-called "sweatshops," where workers only get a salary that they can live on and where working conditions are very bad (Paine 1997a, 1997b). For other companies like Body Shop and the Danish company Brdr. Hartmann A/S, which produces packaging products, business ethics is not so much crisis management in order to avoid criticism, but rather an effort of proactively creating for itself an image of a company that has a green profile and takes care of the environment.

In the public sector, business ethics is very much an issue of avoiding bureaucracy and ensuring better service management for citizens. This is the basic theme of values-driven management in municipalities and other public institutions and organizations. But we can also mention classical ethical problems of corruption and bribery that at the local level represent one of the most serious ethical problems in public organizations. In many countries we see examples of incidents of corruption and illegal administration practices, for example in relation to tax issues or immigration issues. A case of such illegal administrative practice from Denmark was the so-called Tamil case from the beginning of the 1990s where state bureaucrats in the government ministries followed an order from their minister to avoid reuniting refugee families even though this was illegal according to Danish law.

These examples illustrate how Danish, European, and global companies' responsibility and organization ethics represent a necessary approach to the study of organization and management. From an ethical perspective, business ethics is very important for how to govern business in practice. An important strategic concern in this context is a new ethical understanding of business economics and accounting. Profits should no longer be thought of exclusively from an economic perspective, but the company needs to operate with the triple bottom line (Elkington 1997; Idowu, Kasum and Mermod 2014; Crane and Matten 2004, 2016), that equally measures the social, environmental, and economic dimensions in the financial and other reports of the company. We need of course a surplus at all three dimensions in order to talk about an economical and profitable business firm. Nevertheless, ethics does not stop with the triple bottom line.

We also need to integrate values and ethics in the culture and identity of the business corporation. It needs to be an integrated part of the identity of the business to have its attention directed toward ethical concerns for its external stakeholders and internal environment. We can say that good corporate governance manifests itself in the moral integrity of the employees and management and through a set of coherent values that are in connection with the basic ethical principles and theories. In this context, business ethics is not first and foremost a question of following external rules, but rather an issue of making coherent values an integrated part of the culture of the business corporation (Driscoll and Hoffman 2000). Business ethics is therefore in practice also a question of developing the employees' and the managers' capability of judgment and ethical formulation competency so that they can make good and well-founded decisions in the complex context of action.

Business ethics in organization and management

Business ethics is considered by many people as a new discipline in organization and management, but one can also find ethical aspects of the organization theory of earlier times. In organization theory at the beginning of the 20th century there was a strong focus on the organization as a technological and rational machine. Businesses were first and foremost considered as factories, mechanical and rational production machines that on a production line have to deliver as much output as efficiently as possible. The machine is an apt metaphor for this conception and its ethics can be described as goal rational efficiency ethics. With the emergence of the humanistic and psychologically based conceptions of management from the famous Hawthorne experiments in the 1930s where it was stated that the employee's wellbeing was essential for increasing productivity, a new form of organization ethics emerged. This organization ethics emphasized the importance of the focus on employee motivation and engagement in work. Ethics later became central in human resource management, based on employee influence and work democracy. In the context of the increasing power of the unions, organizations were from the 1960s to the 1990s increasingly considered as the center of work conflicts between employees and management and capitalists. The Scandinavian economies were in this context characterized as negotiation economies, based on free negotiations between employees and employers. The ethics in this conception of the relation between management and business can be considered as a negotiation-oriented rationality that gets its legitimacy from what the German philosopher and sociologist Jürgen Habermas calls the "forceless force of the better argument" (Habermas 1981). The movement of the ethics and responsibility of business really started during the 1990s. This approach to organizations has been inspired by the development of the flat project-based organizations and an increasing focus on culture, quality management, and service organizations, and on values, identity, communication, and their legitimate public relations. But we can also mention self-management and liberation management. This approach puts ethics at the center of management of business corporations.

Is business ethics profitable?

The worried CEO, head of the board or manager in the public sector with responsibility for the economy of the business organization would rather ask what all this means for the future business of the corporation. Does ethical business really exist? Is there a business case for the social responsibility of business? To this we can answer that in addition to doing something right, there are also good business arguments for the fact that businesses should act ethically and responsibly. Business ethics ensures that the business appears trustworthy and responsible to the public and diminishes the risk of destroying its reputation and brand value in society. Furthermore, business ethics gives the business firm a foundation for dealing with problems that can reduce the risk of the business receiving legal suits and being judged responsible for having committed illegal actions.

In addition, an ethically sound strategy gives the company greater economic sustainability in the longer term, since there are durable values that strengthen the company's place in society. As we know, business ethics also reinforces employees' motivation, if they feel that there is a meaning to their job in a company that rests on good values and principles. All in all, this will create a better brand for the company, which will be able to use its values and social responsibility to raise its profile in relation to its competitors. There are good theoretical arguments for how social responsibility strengthens competitiveness, although studies of the relationship between social responsibility and profit and competitiveness are not very reliable because of the complexity and difficulty of measuring something like that (Capron and Quairel-Lanoizelée 2004: 95; Crane and Matten 2016). In addition, common sense says that goodwill in the environment also makes it easier to run the company. However, one can also ask more critical questions about a company's social responsibility. What actually are the boundaries of these ethical requirements? Will the requirements not be infinite and unattainable, and move the focus from the economic earnings, which in itself can be severe enough for some unrealistic requirements beyond the scope of business activities? What about stakeholders and all the parties involved? Is it not utopian to believe that one can make them all happy? They can have such different interests that they will always come into conflict with each other.

Moreover, one can ask whether this implies a dangerous politicization of the company, moving the focus from economics to politics, while forgetting that the company itself is undemocratic, when ownership depends on the financial resources and not on individual rights where each participant has a voice. It is claimed that businesses use the new situation to seize power from the state. The criticisms aimed at the interfaces between the new public and private, market and state are not only positive, but also can affect democracy negatively, so that people lose their power to influence the interest groups, because decision-making is opaque, and special interest groups are always closer to the real decisions than individuals. Nor is it certain that corporate social responsibility involves a "win–win" situation for communities and businesses. One could argue that companies will guide the development to their advantage and take power over the processes in a way that is not in the state's general interest. The problem is also whether ethics and social responsibility can solve all the problems and dilemmas. Moreover, it is a big question whether CSR should be voluntary or forced through legislation and what role governments should actually play in the development of corporate ethics and social responsibility. In addition, critical organizational theorists have proposed skeptical arguments for the discourse on CSR. In view of the late modern organizational theory, inspired by the French author Michel Foucault's theories of power and politics, in addition to other post-structuralist criticism of capitalism, it can be argued that attempts to use business ethics to humanize the market by means of ethics-sensitive vocabulary hides deeper economic power structures where ethics is used to suppress and dominate the market (Hardt and Negri 2001). Here, ethics and responsibility represent a form of "governmentality" rationality (Vallentin and Murillo 2012). According to this post-structuralist thinking, modern society's management installs rationality by a number of mechanisms of self-management and self-control. Foucault's theory is based on the English philosopher Jeremy Bentham's idea of a "panopticon," which is a model prison, consisting of a watchtower in the middle, surrounded by cells. The idea is that all cells are transparent and open, so that the guard in principle only needs to watch to keep track of all the prisoners. The thinking behind the panopticon, according to Foucault, runs through the whole of society, which has developed a multitude of panopticon systems with the power mechanisms of self-control and self-control that comes to apply everywhere: in schools, factories, media, legal systems, businesses, etc. Talking about business ethics and social responsibility is just another example of this power of management rationality, which is a new disciplining tool that cleverly helps to control companies and discipline employees (Hatchuel *et al.* 2005).

The point is to look at business ethics and social responsibility in the light of the above critical conditions. We must ask the question, "What is business ethics?" It is important to discuss the main theoretical approaches to business ethics in the context of practical analysis of individual issues and focusing on the relationship between leadership and business ethics. When discussing the relationship between ethics and CSR, one cannot avoid considering the relationship between profit maximization and ethics. The questions are, first, what the integration of ethics and responsibility in the discussion of corporate strategy means for our understanding of economic markets. Second, how we can really define the social responsibility of the business corporation?

The central focus for analyses of ethics and responsibility in both private and public organizations is accordingly professional ethics and the requirements for good custom rules, norms, or "codes of conduct," i.e. codes of ethics in both private companies and various public organizations and institutions. How do rules and values of business ethics contribute to the development of ethical organizations? How should the tension between economics and ethics be understood in the public sector? And what role should values play in development of organizational cultures in private companies? In connection with the development of enterprise ethics, it is important that business ethics should focus on the role of values in the organization and look at the comparative relationship between values-driven management and responsible development that contributes to realizing ethics through various tools of values-driven management, storytelling for example: that is, the values-driven management based on employee's perceptions of their own work, mediated through narratives, that is, stories about the company. Additionally, one can refer to the dialogical forms of management, i.e. democratically oriented conversations about the company's future strategy. If it must make sense to talk about social responsibility, the discussion about the social responsibility must form part of the company's integrated strategy for ethics and values-driven management. We are therefore particularly linking values-driven management and ethics to stakeholder theory as a tool to identify the values of the various parties involved in the company (Ballet and Bry 2001; Freeman *et al.* 2010; Rendtorff 2009; Crane and Matten 2016). Stakeholder management or stakeholder theories are important in practice to develop organization values and ethics as the basis for the company's external and internal identity. This forms the basis for the formulation of ethics and values related to different fields of business ethics, in relation to both internal and external stakeholders and the environment. As well as research on value management in the practical application of the strategic methods, values-driven management must be combined with the development of instruments for measuring values through alternative reporting systems in the firm. Here social and environmental reports of the firm are combined with the financial accounts.

So it is important to emphasize that research and analyses of values-driven management has great significance for the practical work of business ethics. Good programs for ethics and values-driven management proves to have a solid theoretical footing.

Values-driven management, also called values-based management, when referring to a more controlled process in an organization, must be regarded as a strategy that combines economic and ethical considerations of business development and planning. Values-driven management therefore represents a visionary basis for the strategic development of organizations. It is strategic thinking, which, in interaction with production, innovation, and marketing, makes ethics, social responsibility, and corporate governance basic to the company's financial performance. Combined with values-driven management the company's own interest and profit maximization proposes a broader societal perspective, which develops corporate welfare, while ensuring that the company is accountable to society. With values-driven management and ethics programs arises the possibility that the company becomes a responsible moral agent. This strategy and leadership are used to create economic value while simultaneously developing the ethical identity as the basis of the firm's contribution to society as a good citizen corporation.

The purpose of the programs for ethics and values-driven leadership

1 Solving management problems within the company
2 Development of common values and visions
3 Resolving internal problems in the company
4 Handling of ethical problems in relation to stakeholders
5 Environmental issues. Ethical rules for ecology and sustainability
6 Finance and investment ethics, ethical investments, etc.
7 Marketing ethics in late modern society
8 The involvement of consumers in management
9 Solving problems of discrimination and oppression
10 Protection of employees' privacy (right to privacy)
11 Ethical issues related to corruption and bribery
12 Ensuring transparency and openness in the company's accounts
13 Development of criteria for product safety
14 Working with honest and ethical employee behavior
15 Improving the working environment and health at work
16 Proactive management of crisis situations

2 Business ethics in the age of globalization

We live in the age of globalization, which is also a condition for business ethics (Rendtorff 2009: 29–46). We will now look at the changed situation of ethics that arises with globalization's strengths and weaknesses, as well as examining the possibility of establishing universal principles and ethical guidelines for corporate activities in the global market as a condition for cosmopolitan business ethics. There is indeed a close link between the need for corporate social responsibility and the increased process of globalization (Blowfield and Murray 2011).

Ethics and globalization of the market economy

The current globalization process makes business ethics and CSR even more relevant (Pedersen 2015). Globalization means that companies are free to move beyond the nation states' borders and operate across the globe in different countries and different contexts (Beck 2000: 164). Thus the question of what standards are applicable for corporate actions does not have a set answer. The companies find themselves both in national and transnational contexts, and it is important to formulate coherent standards of corporate responsibility and ethics that go beyond the limits of the nation states and can be applied internationally. Therefore globalization processes increase the pressure on companies to make ethics and social responsibility key dimensions of their visions for management and organization. The process of globalization has been described as universalization of the free market economy (Giddens 1999; Beck 2002; Blowfield and Murray 2011). The driving force in globalization is that the market economy will apply anywhere in the world. The philosophy of globalization is that the development of a global free market, liberalization of the economy toward a global laissez-faire condition, will be good for all of us and lead to growth worldwide. Therefore, activities of international organizations like the World Bank and the International Monetary Fund (IMF) in order to break down trade barriers contribute to creating the basis for worldwide growth. Table 2.1 is an attempt to describe the change from a modern industrial economy to a post-modern communication and network economy (Boyer 2001: 32). Market globalization of the economy may be regarded simultaneously as the driving force behind cultural globalization, where values from different cultures are mixed universally and internationally (Giddens 1999). Since the market is the driving force of globalization, the companies are key players in the creation of the new values in a globalized society. This makes it necessary to have even greater focus on business ethics and values-driven management in the globalized market economy. However, this is also the possibility for businesses and companies to help to shape the world and create a more democratic society (Boyer 2001) as the aim of cosmopolitan business ethics.

Table 2.1 From industrial economy to a globalized market economy

Industrial economy	*Network economics in hypermodernity*
Manual work	Immaterial work
Geographical space	Cyberspace
Structure	Process
Industrial capitalism	Cultural capitalism
Fixed capital	Circulation
Property legal logic	Connection logic
Individualist	Community
Strategy for market	Strategy for network
Scale economy	Time economy
Production/sales	Value creation
Market/discontinuity	Customer time/space
Law/legal regulation	Ethics/values

Companies contribute here to the formulation of standards and codes of conduct for international business ethics (Enderle 1999; Blowfield and Murray 2011). They help to create the values that form the basis of an informal world law, which should be followed, no matter where they operate in the world. In fact, the United Nations in cooperation with a number of different companies, states, and NGOs already are in the process of formulating these standards. We have already mentioned the UN Global Compact principles and the UN Development Goals for Sustainability, but there are also the Universal Declaration of Human Rights and the codes of conduct enshrined into force by the International Labour Organization (ILO) standards for workers, as well as various international value codes of conduct prepared by various business organizations, companies, and associations of businesses.

In addition, regional value guidelines and codes of conduct, for example, the OECD principles for multinationals and the World Bank's work in the 1990s and 2000s contribute to making social responsibility a part of corporate life in developing countries. On the whole it is a challenge for international companies to create a framework for values-driven management in a cross-cultural context, where many different standards meet and come into conflict with one another. In this context, corporate work with values and ethics would help to clarify the ethical standards on the transnational level as an important response to globalization's lack of national government and global governance of international economic life.

The changed conditions for corporate activities imply that businesses in the cosmopolitan community are no longer controlled as strongly by national government legislation rooted in the changed international relations after the Cold War. We have moved from a bipolar international community toward a society that is both unipolar and multipolar. The international community seems to have gone back to something resembling the situation in the 18th century, when globalization was not determined by world domination of a particular state, as in the colonial era and the Cold War years, but an increasing internationalization of all social relations (Søndergaard 2003; Rendtorff 2016a). The same is true in the contemporary globalization of trade due to the removal of trade barriers and because of increased private interaction when globalization first and foremost is economically reflected in the development of the global economic market. Only after economic globalization comes cultural globalization.

One of the factors that have enabled globalization is the rise of communications and computer technology that makes it easy to transcend national state borders (Castells 1996; Rendtorff 2016a). Globalization is manifested in the emergence of a number of global specialized digital communication networks based on computer and information technology. This technology makes it easy to move economic investment from country to country via the Internet in a few seconds. Information technology is a critical component for businesses opportunities to operate transnationally, because it makes communication between continents easy and fast. The globalized communication society also expresses a movement toward the cosmopolitan society (Kemp 2005, 2011), where companies can act as world citizens as global agents have the option to help to create global solutions to global problems.

Neoliberalism, competition states, and globalization

Since the beginning of the 21st century there has been increased development of neoliberal structures in the world economy. In particular, economic and fiscal policies of states have moved in the direction of neoliberalism, focusing on new public management and the marketization of the state in relation to society. Neoliberalism has become a historical term to define our contemporary economic system between hypermodernism and biopolitics (Bidet 2016; Rendtorff 2016a). Different governments seek to strengthen their place and capacity of competition in the globalized world economy by ensuring an effective and healthy competition in the economic market. The values highlighted by many governments are higher productivity, greater transparency, and clearer rights for shareholders, consumers, and businesses. In addition, efforts to strengthen the financial sector include encouraging more foreign investment, marketization, and liberalization of public services, greater cooperation between the public and private, and ensuring better education and research. In Scandinavia, neoliberalism was combined with a dynamic labor market, based on flexible security with state support for unemployment with a publicly funded labor insurance system. With such a growth strategy, governments in the global society strive for a private economic streamlining and strengthening of the free market, and this involves a conflict with a heavy and inefficient public sector, attempts to help business with the simplification of bureaucratic rules on labeling of products, and efforts to avoid protectionist barriers to trade both nationally and internationally. In combination with tax reduction on work, governments use the private market to increase employment, by training and increasing labor participation among immigrants, and also by unleashing entrepreneurship, in order to make it easier to start and run a business. Highlights of this policy are more openness, better use of knowledge and resources, effective competition, and intensified use of the possibilities of globalization. Here many governments emphasize the free-market opportunities inspired by the classical and neoclassical economists like Adam Smith, Friedrich Hayek, and Milton Friedman, who viewed the market's invisible hand as a precondition for shared economic growth, where everyone seeks to maximize performance and personal use.

With emphasis on competition and market, the global competition state realizes that its future depends on dynamic and fair competition between actors that comply with market principles within the laws of society and culture. But at the same time, this growth strategy expresses an attention to necessary prerequisites for the market economy. It is important to strengthen the values of civil society in the market, as social capital and knowledge constitutes the prerequisite for economic growth. This focuses the government's growth strategy on the need to improve what the Indian economist Amartya Sen terms the market economy's institutional basis (Sen 1999). It goes beyond a narrow economic context and establishes a policy and social framework for the market, where we can talk about openness, absence of bureaucracy, creditor and shareholder rights, corporate governance, enforcement of competition law, the involvement of citizens as customers with free choice rather than as clients, and finally, strengthening of consumer security. One can say that this growth strategy requires new values in business and gently but unambiguously calls for healthy competition as the basis for a fairer society.

Against this background, it is legitimate to ask what values the businesses need for business ethics in the cosmopolitan society, and how the legislator can contribute with an ethical value policy that supports community development trends. In a liberalized and globalized cosmopolitan society with emphasis on private initiative one should, as stated in this book, strengthen the ethical virtues of honesty, high moral integrity, and loyalty to the community in business as the most important framework conditions for effective and sound market economy. The French economist Thomas Piketty shows in his important study *Capital in the Twenty-First Century* (2014) how inequality has increased in economic development in history. The process of globalization leads to more inequality because of the accumulation of capital by the rich because of inheritance and little redistribution of wealth due to weak taxation by governments. In order to ensure more global equality we need stronger taxation regimes and a stronger interventionist policy by governments (Rendtorff 2014b).

Strengths and weaknesses of globalization

The necessity of the aforementioned cosmopolitan setting emphasizes globalization's cultural contradictions. Although globalization as an economic phenomenon offers many opportunities for community growth and earnings, it is not harmonious because it simultaneously leads to culture clashes and cultural conflicts between the world's different countries and civilizations. Just as globalization allows international solutions to societal problems, it also contributes to worsening of global problems that require transnational solutions (Kemp 2005, 2011). This applies, for example, to the environment, with global warming and the destruction of the ozone layer, and international crime, with trafficking in women for prostitution and drug trafficking across national borders. In addition, not all are equally enthusiastic about the growth opportunities of globalization. Critics argue that the market economy of globalization leads to a cultural impoverishment and regimentation. They talk about McDonaldization and about the emergence of a global Disney World, where all the cultural differences dissolve in the market economy, based on mere material values. Sociologist Zygmunt Bauman belongs to those who are skeptical about the human consequences of globalization. In his analysis of globalization, Bauman argues that globalization is dominated by a global biopower, where a gigantic "panopticon" has taken over the power from the Earth's citizens (Bauman 1999: 49; Rendtorff 2009). The idea of a panopticon prison strains as previously described by Bentham, and Bauman now claims, inspired by Foucault, that the panopticon technology has become dominant globally. Using this technology, those in power globally can monitor the Earth's population, who are nailed to their TV screens by a proliferation of global media shows such as competitive sports or cultural events. From this perspective the globalized and cosmopolitan world does not lead to freedom and emancipation, but to more inequality, where the global market economy creates greater distances between the rich tourists traveling for their enjoyment, and the poor vagrants, that as refugees and immigrants are forced to travel to where they have greater possibilities of survival. Bauman does believe that globalization has provided greater opportunities for ethics and responsibility. Instead, the consequence is a global uprooting where companies have completely lost their social responsibility and sense of community (Bauman 1999: 58). With world trade liberalization it has without much effort been possible for the company to escape from its local responsibilities, since it can just move to where the possibility for profit is greatest.

The British sociologist Anthony Giddens has a somewhat different view than Bauman. He looks at globalization's democratic possibilities and argues that economic globalization also requires democracy around the globe (Giddens 1999: 44; Rendtorff 2009). Giddens also proposes critical reflections on the relationship between globalization and risk. For him, the greatest threat of globalization is an uneven economic distribution of risk between rich and poor countries that makes poor countries rely heavily on the rich society. However, globalization implies at the same time a liberating potential. According to Giddens it leads toward a global civil society and a liberation from tradition-based constraints to local cultural traditions that are standards determined by a given society's more or less contemporary moral standards. Although economic globalization is undermining the traditional ways of life, the movement toward a cosmopolitan and democratic world contains, according to Giddens, also a possibility to combine globalization with democratization and emancipation. The central premise for this is the globalization of the economy, including corporate opportunities to operate freely in global markets because a market economy in order to function must demand democratic and flexible political institutions to support the free-market values of fair competition, absence of corruption, and freedom from bureaucratic state control. Globalization thus implies that capitalism and the free-market economy have emerged as the most efficient form of organization to ensure global growth, progress, and innovation. But what is capitalism really, and what values should we require of actors in a functioning capitalist economy? It is here that business ethics is important. We have already mentioned Adam Smith's "invisible hand" as an important element of the market economy. In *The Wealth of Nations* the invisible hand is considered to be the driving force of competition between nations. The concept of the invisible hand expresses that free competition between nations is important for creating growth and wealth (Smith 1776). With free competition is included fair competition, where people are struggling to sell the best products at the lowest prices without external intervention in pricing. This idea of free competition is the central element in the economic understanding of development. Proponents of globalization refer to the economic discussion by Smith to demonstrate effectiveness established by the free-market mechanism. Schumpeter's reflections on the importance of innovation as creative destruction and Hayek's remarks on the importance of individual choice for optimal market economy contribute to this understanding of the free market in globalization. According to Hayek, the knowledge held by individual players is far greater than what can be gathered under the command and control of the economy (Hayek 1973 II: 9–11).

One can, however, also point out problems that create greater inequality in the globalized market economy. Grass-roots movements and anti-globalists emphasize the ecological problems and the depletion of nature as a result of globalization's lack of regulation of free-market activities. They also believe that globalization leads to less social responsibility, as companies are no longer tied to a particular country or community. Companies do not shy away from moving or using corruption or bribery when operating in developing countries with lower legal standards and requirements for wages and working conditions than their own. Globalization therefore leads to higher profits, social inequality, speculative investments, uneven standards for dangerous products, and an intensified "corporate cannibalism" where companies as the world's strongest organizations and economies are becoming increasingly more greedy (Korton 1995).

Social responsibility as risk management

Large international companies such as Novo Nordisk, Royal Dutch Shell, and Johnson & Johnson are among the companies that have learned the need to work with values to carve out a considered place in society. Novo Nordisk was in the 1970s close to going bankrupt due to huge criticism regarding potential health hazards from its enzyme products, a situation in which Novo had no systematic resources to respond. Since then, Novo has done everything to be up to date with bioethics and to engage in dialogue with stakeholders, which was an advantage in the public debate on easy access to medicines in Africa in the 2000s. Royal Dutch Shell initially remained arrogant and indifferent to criticism of both the dumping of the company's Brent Spar oil platform in the North Sea, and when Shell failed to intervene when the Nigerian government shot an environmental activist who fought the construction of an oil refinery in an environmentally vulnerable river delta in Nigeria. The harsh international criticism of these events has led Shell to reformulate its strategy first and foremost to be based on the triple bottom line, where people and ecological sustainability are on a par with economic profit. Johnson & Johnson, an American pharmaceuticals company, in 1982 decided to recall the entire stock of a pain-relief product from the market after some of the bottles were found to contain cyanide as a result of external tampering. This action, which expresses great honesty and accountability, has since become a textbook example of ethically based business management.

Values and globalization

The Indian economist Amartya Sen argues in *Development as Freedom* (1999: 168) that we can avoid globalization problems by ensuring stable social and political institutions as a basis for the free-market economy. According to Sen, it is true that free capitalist markets are conditions for economic development, but we must also realize that democracy and respect for human rights are prerequisites for stable economic development.

This is also Francis Fukuyama's point of view; in his great book *Trust. The Social Virtues and the Creation of Prosperity* (1995) he stresses that strong relations of trust are a prerequisite for a well-functioning market economy. For Fukuyama, social capital is created through trust. Social capital refers to the economic potential that is determined by a society's social cohesion and ability to collaborate across local differences. By examining the relationship between strong and dynamic cultures and economically disadvantaged communities one can observe that the weak community does not have particularly good trust relationships and especially that it has a large degree of distrust of strangers outside the family and the close community. According to this view, Protestant belief is also characteristic of the powerful moral obligation that at the same time includes an openness and trust toward the foreigners one has to deal with. One can say that this shows that there are always moral feelings and values behind the economic rationality, so that the players in the financial markets are never completely free from being affected by moral conditions. In the end it is the moral consciousness that lies behind the actors' self-understanding and actions. Therefore, one refers to a market ethic that in a more or less invisible way imposes certain limits to greed and defines the rules for the players' actions in the financial markets. Behind the egoism, violence, and self-interest there is a more or less mutual understanding of the actions that can or cannot be allowed in trade and production in order to participate in the game. In other words, there are moral limits on the rules of the game in the market economy. In interaction with civil society, companies are key actors that help to influence which values should prevail in the market economy. It is with an eye for the corporate and social policy and institutional function of the market that we can argue that a focus on values-driven leadership and business ethics can help to draw attention to the local, national, and global challenges posed by the market in globalization and at the same time provide relevant solutions. Values-driven leadership and business ethics can make a special contribution to supporting the market economy through well-functioning social institutions. From this, business ethics is in the globalized society justified both from corporate self-interest and from companies' social obligation to ensure "fair competition" and support the social basis of the market economy. The already-mentioned international legal and political initiatives to promote corporate social involvement, i.e. the US Federal Sentencing Guidelines for Organizations, the EU Green Paper CSR and the UN Global Compact principles as well as the UN Development Goals for Sustainability, reflect governmental and societal support to the initiatives for integration of ethics and values, including human rights, in corporate vision and mission statements that have already been started in many businesses. In this context, values and value statements function as a strategic vision and mission for the company, but also as a basis to improve the image, identity, and public relations. Through companies' work with values in an intercultural context, human rights are contextualized between the local and the universal. This means that the work with values-driven management helps to find the right cosmopolitan corporate citizenship with cosmopolitan value principles applicable in the interaction between the individual company and the global community.

International codes of ethics and codes of conduct

Human rights declarations and conventions

Important international rules and codes that can help determine corporate actions primarily include human rights. In the 1948 Declaration of Human Rights, foundations were laid for the later conventions on political and social rights. Also declarations on cultural and social rights contribute to the constitution of an international regime for respect for human rights. International codes of conduct to regulate international companies include guidelines formulated by international organizations as the UN, OECD, and the World Trade Organization. The International Labour Organization has formulated rules to protect workers all over the world. The UN health agency, WHO has developed such guidelines for health and health products. We can also mention the OECD guidelines for multinational companies or the UN Global Compact principles from the summit in Davos on world economic conditions. Moreover, the global business and human rights initiative contributes to focusing on human rights in international business (Cuilla, Martin, and Solomon 2007; Rasche and Gilbert 2012).

Codes of conduct and guidelines formulated by businesses and their organizations

Here we can mention, for example the Global Sullivan Principles. This is a classic set of ethical guidelines for international companies. These guidelines have been important in creating awareness of apartheid in South Africa. They were formulated by the black pastor Leon Sullivan, who later was a member of the General Motors' board of directors. A further example is the so-called Caux Round Table Principles, which were the initiative of a number business leaders who in Caux in Switzerland adopted some principles of business ethics, based on respect for human dignity. The Caux Principles have been important as sources of inspiration for our regulating measures such as the EU's Multi Stakeholder Forum on CSR and international guidelines. In this way they contribute to the creation of reflexive proceduralization of CSR and business ethics (Buhmann 2014).

Measuring and reporting instruments for assessing corporate ethics and social responsibility

The Global Reporting Initiative is an accounting and certification instrument, which aims at sound sustainability reporting from UN standards. The SA8000 Standard documents whether the company complies with international standards for the protection of human rights. Danish Industry and the Centre for Human Rights' CSR compass also measures similarly human rights and CSR (Buhmann 2006; Buhmann 2014). Recently, the universal human rights regime has been increasingly cemented with the global standards for human rights and business. The UN "Ruggie Framework" "Protect, Respect and Remedy" is a powerful instrument for business compliance for protection of basic human rights. This reflexive law framework functions as a compliance pull that motivates businesses toward protection of human rights and sustainability (Ruggie 2013; Buhmann 2014).

International business ethics as a first dimension of cosmopolitan business ethics

International business ethics deals therefore with formulation of ethical standards and guidelines that may apply to international and globalized companies doing business in different countries. One can ask the following questions: What should really be the basis of these norms and values? What standards can we find for international justice that can apply across cultures? Should businesses follow the standards that apply in their own country, or should they comply with the standards of the foreign country in which they trade?

International business ethics revolves primarily around the problem of unequal distribution of environmental risks and safety in the world community. This is documented by the fact that there have been a number of cases of heavy pollution and environmental disasters in developing countries. A characteristic example of such a disaster is one of the worst ever accidents to have been caused by the activities of enterprises in developing countries, namely the large Union Carbide disaster in India in 1984 (Hoffman *et al.* 1994). Here a cloud of toxic gas leaked from a pesticide plant, with the result that more than 3,000 people died in the surrounding area within a few days and around half a million more came to suffer from exposure to the gas. Another problem is the issue of social security and equality in the world community. It is alleged that some companies, such as Nike, let their production take place in factories, the so-called sweatshops, with underpaid staff working under such miserable conditions that they can only survive for a few years (Post, Lawrence, and Weber 2002: 570–572).

Therefore the international public requires that companies are more aware of taking into account human rights and generally live up to their social responsibility in developing countries. A good example of the cultural contradictions between the South and North is Nestlé's tragic marketing of milk products to poor women in Africa (Crane and Matten 2004: 300) in the 1970s. Nestlé marketed the milk products in such a way that the women thought that the artificial milk was better than their own. But when the milk powder was mixed with impure water, their children caught diseases which they would not have been submitted to if they had only been breastfed. When the women could not afford to buy milk powder products and used their own milk again, they could no longer breastfeed, and children had to starve. One can also mention the problem of corporate responsibility to consumers in countries which do not have the same legal limits as their homeland. Here we can for example mention Philip Morris, which today sells more cigarettes in overseas markets than in the domestic market, where there is great awareness of the risks of smoking. Philip Morris is very conscious of the fact that their strategy depends on operating in countries where the company knows that there is less skepticism about smoking than in the West (Post, Lawrence, and Weber 2002: 538). The principal issue behind international business ethics is the question whether a company operating in a developing country must remain in the country and continue sales and production, even though it is ethically problematic, or whether it would actually do more good by leaving the country and respecting international human rights standards. Often a cynical economic argument is that the company will do well with its operations in developing countries despite lack of social responsibility. It is claimed from a utilitarian and pragmatic point of view that as long as a low level of respect for human rights and sustainability is tolerated as an acceptable local standard, and as long as the company can be said to do more good than harm, the low level of ethical sensitivity may be regarded as a necessary evil.

The philosopher and business ethicist Richard T. De George sharply argues against that attitude in the book *Competing with Integrity in International Business* (1993), when he argues for the need for high integrity in international business ethics. De George emphasizes integrity as a commitment to values and principles and as an ability to act in line with these values and principles (1993: 234). De George puts an integrity strategy against a number of common perceptions of international business commitments. The first can be called the myth of the immoral activities. This refers again to the view that "the business of business is business." It is argued that the company's main obligation is to ensure economic profit and efficiency and not to meddle in politics. Globalization shall create a free market and allow enterprises to operate freely, and there can be no requirement that the market should be regulated from random social standards in developing countries. In view of the emphasis of business ethics on the link between economics and ethics this view appears as absurd, and it can also be dangerous because it does not involve the company's political and social function in society. The second view that De George mentions is described as "when in Rome do as the Romans do." This view assumes that companies just have to follow norms and rules in the countries in which they operate, even if these standards are different from the countries that they come from. This view is based on a kind of ethical relativism, which claims that all standards are relative. That view may be rejected based on the argument that ethics instead of being relative involves taking a moral position from a coherent integrity point, and here ethical relativism cannot be consistent. This does not mean that the opposite view, which De George calls "Act in the American way" is more accurate. This view consists in a sort of reverse ethnocentrism, based on universalization of the values in one's own culture. This means that Western companies uncritically must follow their own Western values when operating in other countries. The problem with this view is that the idea to follow one's own values without a hermeneutic openness to local values and other traditions is at risk of being cultural imperialism, which ignores the other cultures' local values.

Integrity in international companies can be defined as the effort to find the right balance between cultural relativism and naive universalism. To appeal to the notion of integrity as a company's ability to follow their own standards is to highlight that the company must be developing a consistent set of values that is coherent with international rules and codes of conduct. Such a focus on integrity must, however, be based on human ethical judgment, that is, our ability to think and put ourselves in the place of others and thereby apply general moral standards to specific conditions.

Richard De George summarizes the background for his theory in a set of principles for international corporate strategy (De George 1993) that can be paraphrased as follows:

1. Companies must not knowingly cause direct damage.
2. They need to do more good than harm for the host country.
3. They should contribute to the host country's development.
4. They should respect their employees' human rights.
5. To the extent that the local culture respects ethical standards, international companies must respect the local culture and work with it and not against it.
6. Multinational companies should pay a fair share of taxes.
7. They must work together with local authorities to develop and support community institutions.
8. Multinational companies are responsible for providing adequate compensation for any damage that they may cause, directly or indirectly, intentionally or inadvertently.
9. The management of the company has the ethical responsibility for its actions or errors.
10. If an international company builds a dangerous factory, the obligation to ensure that it is made safe is essential. If dangerous technology is transferred to developing countries, these international companies are responsible for properly designing this technology so that it can be safely administered in the host country.

With these ten principles to ensure corporate social and ethical responsibility, we have a basis to formulate guidelines and codes of conduct for international business ethics. Basically, we must highlight the need for a cosmopolitan approach to business ethics, based on a universal understanding of ethics and aiming to protect human rights and strengthen universal ethical standards for multinational companies' activities. But at the same time, companies cannot bypass the many complex ethical problems that arise when the international norms come into conflict with local conditions. Therefore, we can distinguish between three basic levels of development of a strategy for multinational companies' activities (Donaldson 1989: 170):

1. Basic respect for human rights, i.e. labor rights, political freedoms, and social rights: at this level the company cannot compromise on its own principles, even if there should be different standards that apply in the community.

2 Contributing to business development and community welfare in poor countries: at this level the company needs to help to make society better and improve forms of economic and social initiatives, such as trade, ensuring sustainable production, transfer of know-how, etc.
3 Ensuring the right balance between the local and universal: at this level it is a challenge for cosmopolitan business ethics to find the moral standards of the local culture that should be respected for their own value, despite the fact that they differ from the company's own standards.

International business ethics must therefore, as a cosmopolitan approach to globalization, address issues based on universal ethical principles; at the same time it is a challenge for companies to handle cultural differences and diversity with an open and constructive attitude so that they become productive for the company's strategy and economic development. Strategic planning for multinational companies thereby combines economic considerations with respect for societal values.

Caux Round Table Principles: Guidelines for global ethics

The Caux Round Table Principles is a set of guidelines for multinational companies. They were established in 1986 and therefore they have foundational values for the development of international business and protection of human rights. Also they have been updated continuously and combine strategy and concern for ethics. There has, for example, been an update of the Caux Principles in 2010. These principles were the result of several years of discussions between entrepreneurs and business managers from the East, especially Japan, and from the Western countries (Enderle 1999). They agreed a set of guidelines for companies dealing with their relationships with customers, employees, owners and investors, suppliers, competitors, and local communities. The Caux Principles are considered as a benchmark for the design of values-driven management in multinational companies. The principles emphasize the necessity of respect for customers' dignity, fairness, and high quality of its products and services, both in marketing and consumer satisfaction. It is important for a high level of health and safety, environmental quality, and respect for customers' integrity and culture.

Businesses are encouraged to have a high level of responsibility with regard to how they treat employees. Concern for the dignity of employees involves caring for their social welfare and for their specific working conditions, including protecting them from diseases, but also treating them with dignity in conflicts and in negotiations. Respect for human dignity entails rejection of any type of discrimination, as well as care for the disabled and socially vulnerable. As for owners and investors, the Caux Principles emphasize the importance of return and profit, and they highlight corporate obligations to make corporate governance based on trust and responsibility with a competent and fair treatment of investors' deposits, and the principles also stress that it is important to respect investors' requirements. Suppliers are considered as equally important as investors. The relationship with subcontractors must be based on freedom, mutual respect, and fairness. The Caux Principles emphasize the importance of long-term relationships with suppliers, based on value, quality, and reliability. It is emphasized that it is important that subcontractors have work conditions that respect human dignity and human rights. The Caux Principles emphasize competitors as important stakeholders. Companies should together ensure that they all contribute to the wealth of nations by respecting the free and open markets and a competitive behavior that does not destroy the environment. In addition, companies should have mutual respect for each other's intellectual rights. The emphasis on society as a stakeholder in the Caux Principles is to see the company as a cosmopolitan world citizen respectful of human rights and democratic institutions by recognizing the corporation's legitimate obligations to the government. The company's good citizenship (good corporate citizenship) on the international level would therefore entail a contribution to sustainable development and to provide health and social welfare of all citizens in society; likewise, the integrity of local cultures must be respected.

3 What are values?

The following describes the relationship between business ethics and values-driven management in the experience and authenticity economy (Pine and Gilmore 1999; Pine and Gilmore 2007; Lipovetsky and Serroy 2013), which is a strategic communication and management tool, which focuses on ethics and social responsibility. We discuss the role of values in today's society and how values must be defined and analyzed within the company's culture, communication, and organization theory (Rendtorff 2009: 55–89). Indeed, we can argue for a close connection between values and business ethics where personal and collective values are regarded as the foundation of ethical action in business corporations as a characteristic feature of the global economy (Fischer, Lovell, and Valero-Silva 2013).

Values in the late modern society

How then actually to define the concept of value in the globalized market economy era? On the cultural level, globalization in late modern society is combined with post-modernism, which dissolves morality and claims that the grand narratives are dead, and that everything is relative. In this context, it is difficult to defend objective values or assert that there is a meaning beyond economic materialism. On the other hand, morality and ethics become more and more prevalent in our society, and more and more people are concerned with corporate social responsibility and community involvement. The French philosopher and sociologist Gilles Lipovetsky is extremely precise in his description of the concept of humanity in the movement from modernity to the late modern, post-modern, or hypermodern community. His thinking may help us to understand the paradox why there will be more ethics in a time where nihilism and relativism are the prevailing philosophies of life (Lipovetsky 1983, 1992, 2006; Lipovetsky and Serroy 2013; Rendtorff 2014a). With Lipovetsky, we can argue that the post-modern morality involves an opinion on moral issues, implying a pragmatic approach to ethical issues. One can say that the late modern morality balances between the virtues and self-interest. Lipovetsky sees charity as an "existential supplement" to the individual self-expression of the person (Lipovetsky 1992: 15). There is, in fact a relation between a giver and a receiver, where the donor through the experience of charity also get great pleasure out of the generous and philanthropic gift. This explains the great benevolence that followed the tsunami of 2004 that occurred in the Indian Ocean, for example, and other recent international catastrophes of war, earthcrakes, storms causing human misery and disruption arising from various charity events around the world, or the humanitarian organizations that depend on individual contributions. The individual's sense of being a good person is not unimportant for philanthropic and generous efforts. It provides individuals with personal reasons for being moral and it is not only based on the mere duty to obey the moral law. The concern shown by disinterested corporations for philanthropy and generosity is also an example of how management's and employees' need for personal moral self-expression and the sense of doing something good in the world through charity becomes an integral part of its business.

An action is of moral value if it is both in one's own interest and at the same time a virtuous activity that serves the common good. This characterizes especially business ethics that always asks whether a good action is also economic and serves an economic purpose (Lipovetsky 1991). One can therefore say that the values and the morality of the late modern society are carried out by a realistic ethics of prudence that prioritizes the individual's own wishes and rights. The post-modern ethics in the zeitgeist is characterized by the fact that one should act responsibly in a situation where one is aware of one's own moral limits. Achieving happiness is the sole purpose: "Le bonheur sinon rien!" (Happiness or nothing!). Therefore, self-control and the central slogan "Consommez avec modération" (consumption in moderation), or one could also say "sustainability morality," is the hallmark of contemporary morality without obligation or sanction.

According to Lipovetsky this late modern society is characterized by individualization and personalization of the individual's work and leisure. It has become fashionable to take into account the workers' right to self-realization. Capitalism has been given a "human face," and it is therefore fully in accordance with the late modern society to refer to ethical companies and to the global importance of CSR. The problem is, however, that this humanizing and individualizing business approach also reflects a new form of oppression, as an increased requirement of originality, release, or flexibility in reality can be a sophisticated form of disciplining of workers. Despite this risk, we should not ignore the fact that the cult of the individual and of the personal is central in the late modern society's attractiveness. The personality cult is found in the body cult, in the renewable quest to be "natural," relaxed, physical, communicative, and flexible at work and in private life (Lipovetsky 1983: 10). With this focus on individual expression and personal creativity, ethics is, according to Lipovetsky, not contrary to the late modern community values. Its strength and appearance can, however, be understood as a consequence of the emergence of the experience society and experience economy, where individual self-realization is at the center of the economy.

It is important to emphasize that in the late modern society ethics is not an old-fashioned ethics of duty to ban and impose limits as part of a higher morality and for morality's sake. Rather, globalization and the late modern societal ethics is a combination of a pragmatic utility morality with a personal virtue ethics and value morality that bases the ethics of the individual on self-fulfillment and on the quest for the good life. The new morality revolts against traditional values of family, work, and the homeland. The family and work are based on luck and not on duty, likewise the homeland has diminishing importance in the globalized era. Also in policy, we focus increasingly on individual rights rather than on mutual virtues.

For Lipovetsky post-modern society means, paradoxically, that the smaller the duty, the more the need for values and unwritten rules – ethics becomes a democratic and realistic ethics, which combines gain and profit, celebration and joy with ethical action. It is, for example, expressed in the new environmental consciousness where ecology and ecological awareness are considered to be part of the human personality development, since the individual attaches great importance to the body and health as part of self-realization. One can say that the return of ethics and the ethics effect in the late modern community follows the slogan: "A morality without obligation or sanction" (Lipovetsky 1992: 60; Rendtorff 2014a). This manifests itself in companies and their working life, where we can observe a movement from disciplined work toward "flexible man." Today, one works for one's own sake and not for the sake of society. Self-organization and creativity are key words for our present work culture. The company must through human resource management make sure of the development of the whole person, so the personnel policy is fundamental for personality formation and self-development of the employee. From this perspective, corporate values, ethics, and morality are no longer a foreign body in relation to a more comprehensive policy or ideological ethics, but illustrate the new function of ethics in the post-modern and globalized era. Business ethics is precisely the expression of a pragmatic value ethics where ethics and self-interest are combined. It can be said that "ethics pays" because there must be a moral contract created between the company and employees, where the company's moral values contribute to overall strengthening of both the employees' and the managers' personalities and the position of the business enterprise in society.

Business ethics in experience society

Developments in the late modern society are moving toward the hypercomplex society, knowledge society, or consumer society of second-degree, "la société d'hyperconsommation," hypermodernity as Lipovetsky calls it (2006: 35). Most recently, business theorists have also started to name this community the experience society, where the industrial society and consumer society economy is transformed into the experience economy (Pine and Gilmore 1999, 2007; Schulze 1995, 1999, 2003; Sundbo and Sørensen 2013; Lipovetsky 2013; Rendtorff 2014a). Critics argue that this reflects the market economy's absolute dominance over man's subjective reality. With Karl Marx they emphasize that the whole world is now turned into a commodity, where even our most intimate experiences can now be bought and sold. The experience economy fits well with the personality cult in the late modern community. We have a relationship with ourselves and our values as something we can choose and construct as we wish through strategic buying and selling experiences. Where experience previously was something that just happened, the experience economy now changes experience into consumer choice, which one can control in advance through selective buying behavior.

The experience economy is society's aesthetics. It is art, creativity, and innovation that replaces the industrial society's view of companies as industrial production machines. It implies the search for authenticity by consumers who in experience society really just want to have and live an authentic life by any means (Pine and Gilmore 2007). The question is, what does this mean for ethics? In relation to the critical voices that claim that there is a contradiction between experience society and ethics, our analysis of values in post-modern society shows that the experience economy and the ethical values precisely because of the increasing focus on the individualization and personalization can easily be combined. The experience industry involves such a large degree of democratization of the right to have experiences. At the same time, companies have to create values and stories in their brand if they are to be successful in the experience society (Jensen 1999; Jensen 2013; Sundbo and Sørensen 2013). This shift toward a dream society implies increased focus on the individuality and identity of the consumer (Jensen 2013). The expressive or aesthetic company incorporates ethics as a dynamic element of self-expression. In the experience economy, meaning and symbol production manifests as the company's ability to position itself as ethically and socially responsible and to have a good reputation in a dynamic movement of self-realization. A good example of the new attitude to consumption and experience is charity as an ethical ideal in the experience society. Giving a gift creates a reciprocal relation between giver and receiver. Rolf Jensen has emphasized that the visibility of the gift produces in the giver a great experience of joy from the act. This is exploited among other things by humanitarian organizations, such as the Children's Foundation when they personalize the gift relationship by asking people to donate to a particular child in Africa to help with living and education. Through the personal relationship with the child the charitable gift becomes visible, and the giver gets an experience of that gift and this kind of charity becomes widely popular. In this sense, we can trace a close correlation between experience economy and ethics and social responsibility as visibility of social care becomes an important parameter of experience.

Values in business organizations

If we understand values and values-driven management on the basis of the late modern society diagnosis, it becomes clear that values must be central in management and business development. We can define values-driven management as an instrument to articulate the values that realizes the company's ethics in practice. Values and business ethics express the company's changing status in a globalized post-modern and cosmopolitan context. Companies can no longer be understood as purely economic organizations, because values have become central to understanding the organization's function, meaning, and purpose. At the same time organizations are characterized by many different values. Thus we must ask the question, how we can distinguish between the different types of values? What is for instance the ratio of economic and ethical values?

In a sense, values have always been present in businesses, which allowed themselves to be determined by the different cultures, norms, and strategies. Being conscious of a company's values and values-driven management means that one has a more considered concept of the values and norms to be applied in the company. At the same time values-driven management and focus on the company's values implies a conflict with a purely economic understanding of the business organization. Therefore, employees, management, and shareholders must relate to the values that really need to be applied to their business. Values may, however, be defined in many different ways. Sociologists, philosophers, and theorists of organization operate with many different perceptions of values. A post-modern definition could include that values express a subjective view of an objective reality. There are different preferences, requirements, and expectations to persons and organizations that are expressed in actions and beliefs. Values express assumptions in different worldviews, and they are yardsticks for attributing negative and positive evaluations. Values are particularly visible in value conflicts in which we become aware of our values whenever they are criticized, when we doubt them, or when we ask ourselves about what we really perceive as really good in itself and most worth striving for in our lives. Values are an expression of the individual's or collective's prioritization of meaning and perception of the good life in society, and as such, values emerge in an organization's culture and norms, often as ideals and visions that are more or less implicit in the company's actual actions. Values affect the company's history and social position. These values are relative to the environment of the business organization. The outside world affects the company's values, which in turn affect the outside world. Managers' and employees' values affect the company and the outside world by acting in accordance with these values. Values and value performances thus operate at many various levels of the organization, such as organizational culture, in the relationship between management and employees or in relation to consumers and suppliers.

Values are found in all parts of the organization and they also have influence on the normative decisions which constitute the actors' implicit and explicit ideas about their actions. The values should be understood here both as psychological and social, since they function as the basis of the actors' world understanding, beliefs, actions, and judgment, and also cause them to pursue specific goals. Values are therefore at once cognitive and normative influences on the participants in the company, which means that they are both descriptive and evaluative.

The US business ethicist William C. Frederick in his book *Values, Nature and Culture in the American Corporation* (1995: 7) has argued that organizations and businesses have original values that can be traced back to three groups of values, which are about economizing, increasing power, and adaptation to the outside world. From a historical and naturalistic perspective, these values are the real values. These values characterize business organizations, which function as mechanisms that work to economically increase their power in the constant adaptation and interaction with the outside world. Economizing (being economic) expresses the activity that characterizes the company as a player in an economic market. Economizing is based on cost–benefit calculations, and this value refers to the company on the bottom line. Increasing power (power aggrandizing) refers to the company's effort to develop and increase its power and position in the world. This type of value refers to the internal and external quest for power in organizations. Power is both a fact and a representation in human consciousness. Power refers to the company's hierarchical structure and reminds us that the company is based on economic power and ownership. Adapting to the environment (ecologizing) refers to the interaction between a company and its surroundings. The company aims at achieving a good relation to the environment in order to survive as an organizational unity, and this is done with a constant adaptation and development relative to the surroundings of the business corporation.

Values-driven management as a strategic management communication

Values-driven management can be defined as the practical realization of business ethics. It is characteristic that ethics is formulated through the companies' written description of their vision, mission, or values. The ethics of value development is largely a matter of communications, verbalization or articulation of corporate purposes and understanding ethics through these value formulations. Therefore you can argue that the strategic management of communication first and foremost is ethical communication (Bordum and Hansen 2005; Rendtorff 2009), which develops into strategic CSR communication dealing with dissemination of the company's commitment to social responsibility (Morsing and Beckmann 2006). The formulation of the company's values and goals is extremely important to develop the organization and get the ethics integrated in the company strategy. Communication of strategy for ethics, values, and social responsibility is thus aimed at both internal and external conditions of communication. Internally, it deals with getting employees engaged in value development and getting them to understand that the business can make a positive difference in the world with its activities in the economic market. Externally, the issue of communication, values, and ethics is closely related to the involvement of the company's stakeholders in the formulation of the corporate strategy and mission statement. Bordum and Hansen (2005) carried out an analysis of the strategic management of communication in the 50 largest Danish companies. While most of these companies have formulated their values, only about 60% publish them. Of the obligations of companies mentioned in the declarations can be emphasized: "manufacturers, partners, children, supplier, colleagues, authorities laws, management-directors themselves, members, people, consumer, shareholder-owner, environment, society-world-public, others, customers, employees, staff, generally" (Bordum and Hansen 2005: 227). Among the themes, the focus of value statements can be mentioned:

> mood, self-moral vigor, skilled-professional rights, proud community-professional-ethics-democracy, fair-security-ambition-reliable optimization, return-open-focused stability, confidence-care, content-friendly, largest-results-expertise-use, sustainable, dedication, improvement, best-competitive initiative-attractive-health, needs-honest dialogue position, competence-effective-economy-credible-impact, better knowledge, success-security, respect effort, growth, desire, innovation-energy, useful, quality leader, cooperation, active, community, responsibility, service, development, environment, value.
>
> (2005: 214)

These are the words that are used most often in the statements. This thorough analysis of value statements shows that the concept of value is understood broadly and combines basic ethical representation with other kinds of values. It is also characteristic that companies are trying to integrate values in a communicative and pluralist understanding of the community of the business firm. Also interests of stakeholders are seen as important for the dissemination of the company's values, ethics, and responsibility (Bordum and Hansen 2005; Morsing and Beckmann 2006; Rendtorff 2009), since it is a prerequisite for successful value development that the involved stakeholders understand the company's message.

Values and values-driven management

Frederick's description of the original values of the business corporation can be seen as a description of the factual values affecting businesses. But facts do not justify legitimacy. Values-driven management, which is defined as the practical realization of business ethics poses here the question of the relationship between the company's original values and ethical values. Values-driven management can be seen as a way in which the company can adapt to its environment, achieving integrity and respect its stakeholders. This means that values-driven management is needed to develop the organization as well as to create and influence the organization's values and ethics. A particular company or organization embodies a particular group of values and perceptions of ethics, and values-driven leadership is an instrument for the development of these values. One cannot, however, overlook that there is a certain tension between the ethical values and the company's original values: economizing, increasing power, and adaptation. At the same time the original values will always affect the ethics of business. It should also be taken into account that values-driven management is often introduced in situations where organizations are in a moral crisis regarding the systemic whole, coherence, and integrity of the organization. Mette Morsing (2001) has brilliantly categorized some basic strategies for value management, which she describes as religion, democracy, control, and illusion. The religion strategy sees the company as a church where the values are given religious authority. The democracy strategy creates values to aspects of an open and democratic dialogue on corporate strategy. The control strategy tries to use values as rules for management and control of employees. Finally, the illusion strategy uses values as a tool to improve branding and marketing in the world of images of self-representation. These basic strategies can be seen as visions for business planning and decision-making. However, they may also be an expression of ill-considered features of the organizational culture, in some cases requiring new strategic discussion in order to review and change if they hinder the organization's optimum operation.

Mette Morsing (2001) has established a categorization of the different strategies, described in Table 3.1, which illustrates some of the extremes in the development of values-driven management, and also shows the risk of using values in companies. Fundamentally speaking, it is perceived as a description of some possible ways to use values-driven management. Values-driven management should thus be seen as a way that individuals and organizations can be helped to act ethically. The individual actions are considered in relation to the organizational level in order to achieve a comprehensive understanding of the organization's shared values. This is about engaging people in their organization to improve the organization's systemic integrity. Good values-driven management adds values to employees' own inner values that affect their actions and commitment to the organization, which will be integrated into the entire culture of the organization. It is important that this does not happen by manipulation and brainwashing, but by virtue of an open dialogue with the workers where they will be able to self-develop values on their own and relate critically to them. This we can see in Table 3.1 (Morsing 2001; Rendtorff 2009).

In contrast to the values that an organization already possesses, values-driven leadership is built on an explicit formulation of the company's strategic values. This is done through development of various types of missions, credo and vision statements, ethical codes of conduct, and principles that formally apply both to the employees and to the organization as a whole. Ethical issues should be discussed at the organization's management board meetings and be an integral part of the themes for the daily management and governance. It can be a big challenge for the organization to formulate the right balance between the individual and the common goods of community. The initiative to work

Table 3.1 Different conceptions of values

	Strategies for values-driven management			
	Religion	*Democracy*	*Control*	*Illusion*
Values are:	True	Process	Transparency	Marketing tool
The purpose of values is:	Dialogue	Normative	Control	Profiling
Key players are:	Leaders	Employees	Management	Customers
Evaluation procedure:	Job engagement	Active involvement	Measurement	Customer image studies
Strengths:	Commitment	Participation	Uniqueness	Free
Weaknesses:	Inertia/hypocrisy	Complexity	Demotivation	Unveiling

with values-driven management can be seen as an effort to create a collective identity and mission for the organization.

In this way value self-awareness is manifested in the organization, thus creating the organization's corporate culture. The organization is oriented toward gaining knowledge about the company's internal and external aspects.

Against this background, the organization begins by describing the ethical problems and dilemmas that it faces. This contributes to opening ethical reflection at all levels of the organization. The institutionalization of such a culture of shared values means that employees become much more involved in the activities and goals of the organization.

Such learning, however, is not necessarily the only process of values-driven management that should be undertaken. A proper ethics program should also include procedures for evaluation, reporting, and accounting. These evaluations can be considered as important as the organization's financial accounts, and help to formalize the ethical culture of the company. With this definition of values-driven management, ethics must work as the integrating force in the company's activities. Thus the organization moves from being determined by bureaucratic structures and economic goal rationality toward social responsibility and is determined by an effort to find the right balance between individual and organization, and between business, society, and political democracy.

Requirements for an ethical culture in the organization

1. There should be a focus on the manager's ethical role.
2. There should be a formulated objective (vision).
3. There should be a formulated objective of the ethics of the organization (mission).
4. This should include a description of the company's values (values statement).
5. There should be a code of values-driven leadership.
6. There should be designated an officer responsible for ethics in the organization.
7. This should be able to report to senior management or to the organization's ethics committee.
8. The company should have a strategy for external and internal communication ethics.
9. The company should provide ethics training to employees.
10. There should be goals to deal with ethical issues in crisis situations and the need to develop strategies for ethical issues to daily at work.
11. Ethical behavior should be rewarded and lack of ethics exposed for sanctions.
12. There should be developed systems for measuring and analyzing ethical issues.
13. These should be subjected to periodic evaluation by ethics committees, management, etc., and there is need to develop a reporting system that involves employees and those who are responsible for ethics.
14. There should be formulated strategies for implementing ethics programs, in the specific context so that ethics moves from rules to virtues, according to the company's specific identity and culture.

Values-driven leadership, ethics, and organization theory

Values-driven management and ethics must necessarily be rooted in organization theory. In this regard include can be mentioned applied business economics in strategy theory, which seeks to develop businesses and companies strategically and rationally, i.e. decide about a coherent organization and then implement it in life, for example, by the use of a SWOT analysis, i.e. an analysis of the company's strengths and weaknesses, opportunities, and threats. The idea is that the business through the strategy implements a rationally justified mission and vision. Such a rational theory of the business is widespread in mainstream organizational analysis and can as such also be used to develop the company's values if one is aware of its limitations. Strategy analysis represents the dominant paradigm after World War II according to which it was considered possible to manage organizations from rationally defined objectives. This neoclassical theory is based on the notions of fair competition and full information, rational and independent decisions, well-defined products, and the concept of a homogeneous market, where businesses are free to enter or leave. The non-cooperative game theory (i.e. the players do not cooperate but selfishly follow their own interests) of business management is a variant thereof, wherein it should be noted that it is possible to obtain economic equilibrium in a market where each player follows the strategy that is the best answer to the others' strategy (Knudsen 1991). Later this rational business paradigm was expanded with the economic principal–agent theory and transaction cost theories that consider companies as cost-reducing devices in the hands of their owners (principals) that optimize financial gain. For transaction cost theory, the company is a knot of contract relations, determined by the individual utility maximization and property rights.

Already the behavioristic conception of the company by March and Simon (1958) challenges this approach to business strategy. The company should not be understood as a closed mechanical and hierarchical system, but as an open "political system" that constantly is in interaction with its complex surroundings. When the organization is understood as a social system of simultaneously interdependent actors who at the same time take care of their own interests and are included in the strategic and political coalitions with each other, the practical reality of organizations is not determined only by profit and property rights; because of the political coalitions there is a shift toward inclusion of values and broader cultural factors in decision-making processes. From this perspective, we do not always face rational and ideal outcomes but we are also adapting the requirements and conditions that apply specifically in the organization. The result is a potential ambiguity in the decision-making and we can say that decisions are made based on a "garbage model," a "bricolage" of existing opportunities, by which one can say that the strategic rationality is always "bounded rationality," i.e. that the actual decisions are subject to an impact and consequence logic, which is conditional upon that there is always complete safety or full knowledge, and that one must choose between limited options. Strategic rationality is thus determined by the limited situational political conditions in organizations. In addition, the strategy is determined by some requirements on procedures for legitimacy that need to be respected so that the strategy can be implemented. The result is, as Henry Mintzberg (2004) has highlighted, that very few of the company's overall strategic objectives will be implemented in the manner that management originally intended. Furthermore, the company and not least the public organization is not only perceived as a system of contracts, but as a kind of economic-political system, where management also have to deal with the company as a kind of senior management of a constitutional system, which will also contribute overall procedures and values to the organization of the company.

Code of conduct for leadership in the public sector

In addition to the discussion about values-driven management in private business there is also focus on values in public governance, i.e. ethical guidelines for management in the public sector. This can be seen as a response to the many changes and reforms that are underway in the public sector. In late modern welfare states, public organizations are less bureaucratic and more service-oriented and focused on economic efficiency and earnings in market conditions. This requires improved public governance. Eva Parum, in *Strategic Communication about Management. A corporate and public governance perspective* (2006), analyzes developments in corporate governance in both private and public companies. She stresses here nine recommendations for chief executives, built on challenges to public governance at macro, micro, and individual levels:

> 1. Clarify your managerial space with the political leader. 2. Take responsibility for ensuring that the policy objectives are met throughout the organization. 3. Create an organization that is responsive and can affect the world around the organization. 4. Create an organization acting as part of a coherent public sector. 5. Require that organization to focus on results and effects. 6. Possess vision and work strategically with the development of your organization's tasks. 7. Exercise your right and duty to lead the organization. 8. Display professional duty and personal integrity. 9. Safeguard the public sector's legitimacy and democratic values.
>
> (Parum 2006: 28–29)

These recommendations express a series of important issues for public management, which take into account both politicians and employees, as well as the citizens as stakeholders in democratic societies. They can be summarized in some overarching requirements: (1) to engage in constructive dialogue with political leaders about the organization's strategy, values, and ethics; (2) to ensure the organization's efficiency in policy implementation and confident contribution to society; (3) to establish transparency in relation to the public through effective and honest communication; and (4) to help the organization's development and visions for the future of the public sector (Parum 2006). This focus on leadership in the public sector must be seen in the context of values-driven management as an effort to adapt the public sector to today's challenges by focusing on organizations' ethical mission and vision.

With the description of organizations as open economic and political systems by Simon and March we arrive at values-driven management as the strategic response to the company's status as an open political and economic system. Here it is important to combine system theory and practice philosophical reflection about the functioning of organizations in order to define the role of ethics in modern organizations. By becoming aware of its ethical norms and values it is possible to improve communication and information sharing much better in the company. Ole Thyssen (1997, 2009) has helped to develop a system theoretical analysis of the function of ethics in modern organizations. He views organizations as systems controlled by communication as a generalized symbolic medium. Ethical communication makes the organization more open to the world and in turn it contributes to clarifying the purpose of organizational development. Ethics is considered simultaneously as a reflexive management mechanism, since the organization basically seen is controlled through coercive forms, such as pure economic governance and goal rationality. This means that society's functional systems, for example, economics, law, and policy, from a system theoretical perspective, are often foreign to morality. Although the sharp division between ethics, power, and economy can be problematic because power also expresses an ethic – namely power ethics – it is important in organization theory to examine how people in functional systems occupy roles and masks, which become compulsory forms and impede the ethical communication. In many organizations requirements to persons to follow the general constraint of growth and profit are intensified (Thyssen 1997, 2009). This exercise of power, however, has consequences on the individual level, where individualization and atomization in mass society can make individuals increasingly lost and lonely when they are not part of functional systems.

This means that the harsh organizational logic of modern systems cannot fail to challenge systems of human coherence in the organizations. Ethics must therefore be about how to find human solutions that can overcome dehumanization in modern organizations. An organization can be defined as a well-ordered processing system that produces output and reduces the complexity (Thyssen 1997, 2009). Organizations act on decisions that are processing information. It is here that ethics must be integrated into the system logic. When solving problems of organizational ethics and political questions and conflicts between stakeholders, system logic can no longer be based on system-immanent rational planning, i.e. a rationality that is within a narrow economic, legal, and organizational bureaucratic framework. Rather it must look at the system from the point of view of ethics. Ethics appears as a new tool in the communication process to resolve the different types of conflicts between stakeholders in the organization, and ethics helps to formulate a strategic vision for the company's development. This applies both in the case of a public institution or a private company. Ethics is, in values-driven management, a vital component to clarify: (1) decision-making (democratization); (2) good arguments (broader values-driven foundation); (3) decision legitimation (involvement of several groups of employees); (4) decision preconditions (visibility of the implicit agenda of decision-making). By including these terms, management can base its technical expertise on broader values and have an ethical basis for the decision-making of the company.

Organization, perceptions, values, and ethics

In *Images of Organization* (1996), Gareth Morgan describes some of the most common perceptions of organizations. The book's metaphors for organization can (freely after Morgan) also be considered in the light of business ethics:

- *Machine metaphor:* in the understanding of the organization as a machine, ethics is forgone in favor of functional systems. Ethics is needed to ensure that the mechanical organization will not get caught in function and utility rationality.
- *Organism metaphor:* in an organization that can be considered as an organism, ethics is central to contributing to the organization's adaptation to the outside world. The values serve as communication with the outside world.
- *Brain metaphor:* the organization based on knowledge management needs ethics and values to make it easier to share knowledge and communicate across the different centers of knowledge in the organization.
- *Culture metaphor:* when an organization is understood as a culture, ethics and values emerge as the pillars of this culture. Should one go deep into the cultural development, one must involve the company's ethics and values.
- *Policy metaphor:* the political organization functions by confrontation between different sets of values and ethics perceptions that clash and in interaction form the organization's development.
- *Psychic prison metaphor:* here, the values and ethics primarily function as repressive mechanisms that capture employees in the organization and determine the applicable standards.

- *Flux of change metaphor:* here, values-driven management is a tool to consolidate and develop the processes of change. Values may be used to teach employees to operate with ambiguity and act in turbulent surroundings.
- *Power metaphor:* in the organization understood as power and oppression, values-driven management can be used as a management tool that helps to discipline employees.

These different perceptions of values and ethics are certainly at play in different organizational forms. It is also a challenge for ethical and values-driven management not to let oneself be dominated by unethical forms of organization.

In modern organizations, democratic communication is an important ethical component. Management should recognize the employees' importance for decision-making. According to the German philosopher and sociologist Jürgen Habermas (Habermas 1981), we can say that values-driven management must be based on a domination-free communication and on the necessity of the "force-free force of the better argument." Democratic communication between employees and management is central to the post-conventional leadership ethics that sets limits on pure power demonstrations and avoids charismatic management ethics built on personal branding and appearance. It is for the common good that decisions are justified in a deliberative policy, i.e. in a common democratic deliberation.

One can, with Ole Thyssen, say that the concept of "values-driven management" in modern management makes values – unlike pure function-based solutions – the key components of management decisions in modern private and public organizations. Values should be understood as an inclusion of general ethical and normative components of decision-making that improves the organization's sensitivity and flexibility. Values-driven management is not simple and straightforward, but integrates questions about justifications of values, premises, and the need to distinguish between basic and instrumental values. In concrete decision-making processes we also face a compromise between different conceptions of values (Thyssen 1997: 135, 2009). Values-driven management can on this basis be understood as a negotiation-based rationality that as an ethical management instrument aims at the common good. The necessity of values-driven management is due in particular to the fact that the societal basis of rationality, manifested in organization's decisions, is no longer unique. Values are expressed on many different levels in modern society, both externally and internally to the organization. Values in organizations may be more or less clearly established. One can distinguish between declared or actual values, rhetorical values and principles, as well as values that are in conflict with the organization's other goals concerning power and money. One can say that values-driven management has to realize which values an organization follows and whether these values are those it wants to follow in the future. Such values are not only based on pre-given goals, but also depend on employees and different lifestyles and subcultures of society. Values are enshrined in the community of citizens' life conceptions and are manifested in their tastes, lifestyles, intuitions, behaviors, and attitudes to life. Values express personal life and beliefs of agents, players, and stakeholders. Values-driven management can be said to constitute a basic ethical approach to ensure cohesion in organizations with people who have many different private attitudes to life. Values have meaning in relation to shareholders, employees, and management in order to create social harmony in the organization. This implies responsibility, trust, and commitment to a common code of values in the company. Impairment and reporting of values enshrines this. Here one can include dimensions such as tradition, stakeholders, user surveys, and external values to ensure optimum ethical organization. The ethical considerations are involved here in the measurement of technical efficiency in relation to the overall objectives of the organization. Central to this view of organization theory is the integration of ethical considerations in a theory of strategy and management. The idea is to make ethics an integral part of organizational development.

Different theoretical approaches to values-driven management

The national and international debate on values-driven management as a concrete tool for change and development of enterprises is characterized by a number of basic positions which are more or less in contrast to each other. They can be summarized as follows:

- *Values instead of rules.* According to this approach, values are perceived fundamentally in contrast to the rules and laws. Values come from within and are motivating and inspiring, while the rules come from the outside and are authoritarian and restrictive. Rules belong to a former management paradigm, which was based on the notion of the hierarchical organization and the strong chief, while values require a dialogical and create meaning management (Paine 1994a, 1994b; Jensen 1997; Rendtorff 2002a; Petersen 2003; Rendtorff 2009). This approach considers values-driven management as an instrument for self-organization in companies (Petersen 2003).
- *Values as dialogic democratization.* According to this approach, values are first and foremost an expression of the democratization of the company that makes it possible to involve a wide range of stakeholders so that they may be heard in the management process (Freeman 1984). Values-driven management must be used to democratize and develop the organization in close connection with stakeholders. This approach considers values in the framework of policy-making in organizational development (Thyssen 1997, 2009; Pruzan 1998).
- *Values as an ethical point of reference for management.* This view combines elements of the previous two opinions, but emphasizes the concern for ethics as the central focal point for the development of values in companies and organizations (Driscoll and Hoffman 2000). The ethical approach perceives values and rules as basically complementary and agrees with the importance of democratization, but integrates consideration of individual stakeholders in an overall focus on ethical principles and the good life (Rendtorff 2003a, 2003b, 2009).
- *Values as strategic management instrument.* This approach considers values as fundamental for the company's strategic direction. Values help to clarify the long-term sustainability and purposes of the company (Paine 1997a, 1997b). They help to focus on relevant targets for planning and to integrate the company's various decisions with respect to a single purpose. Values-driven management is thus an instrument to develop and think through the business context, identity, and integrity.

4 Values-driven management in practice

Values-driven leadership stands as an instrument for development of companies which also makes the company more democratic and opens the firm to cosmopolitan business ethics. With a discussion of values-driven leadership as change management we will illustrate values-driven management in practice with some concrete examples. For this we have chosen a private and a public Danish organization, Novozymes and Aalborg Municipality, and as an illustration of values-driven management in an international business, we have selected the US Corporation Lockheed Martin.

Values-driven leadership as change management

In order for organizational changes to function, it is necessary to create a strong vision for the company which is tied to values. This vision will motivate employees to understand the need of organizational change, because the change is going to stand for an opportunity for better organization rather than being exclusively motivated by economic efficiency. A values-driven transformation may combine economic and values-driven management, so that there is formed a new self-awareness and collective identity of the company, contributing to open ethical reflection at all levels of the organization (Hildebrandt and Brandi 2005). This approach to values-driven management emphasizes that values in opposition to rules are not pushing the world into a fixed framework (Jensén 1997; Petersen 2003; Beyer 2006; Rendtorff 2009). Management by values recognizes that the world is open and unpredictable – as opposed to the bureaucratic perceptions of the organization that will maintain a certain standardized image of reality. One can say that values-driven management is able to be critical of fixed structures and circumstances.

In continuation of culture and learning theory, as well as quality and knowledge management, values-driven management is based on an understanding of the post- or hypermodern community's flexible framework with changing working conditions and persistent restructuring of organizations. Values-driven management can be understood as an instrument to deal with the terms of ecologizing, i.e. adaptation in a post-modern project economics, where organizations continue to develop and adapt to their environment. Values-driven management aims at integration and cooperation and ensures the development toward new forms of thinking in open interaction with the environment, where it is recognized that action takes place in a space of complexity with many possible solutions, which together constitute a challenge to traditional economic approaches. Such a focus on values-driven management as part of the change can be said to document how the shift from hierarchy, rules, and solid structure to dialogue, values, and flexibility are central to the understanding of new requirements for management of companies and public organizations. Niels Åkerstrøm Andersen and Asmund Born (2001) have described this shift in public organizations as a development from the bureaucracy obligation concepts to more personal concepts such as love and personality. If one analyzes the discourse on change and conversion of public organizations in municipalities and regions from these concepts, it can be concluded that values-driven management in addition to new public management contributes to improving the efficiency of the public sector. New public management includes a market-oriented, goal-rational contract and a quality-based strategic perception of the target public organizations. This can be implemented by means of values-driven management, which emphasizes values, dialogue, and self-management. It combines focusing on efficiency and financial bottom line of the new public management with the development of the company's ethics and values through methods of collaboration and staff development in values-driven management (Beyer 2006). Perhaps that is why values-driven management has been so central to the municipal mergers and the market of the public sector. The different roles of employees in values-driven management can be seen in Table 4.1 (Rasmussen, Jagd, and Rendtorff 2006).

Table 4.1 The employees' role in various forms of values-driven management

	Community and dialogue	*Democracy and criticism*	*Management and control*	*Branding on values*
Basic problem focus	Value resolution and lack of common values in society and organizations	Challenging authority-based management styles, missing participation from employees	Problems with rule-based management in decentralized organizations where employees have to consider new problems	Problems of visibility of the company as different in the market
Goal of the values work	The goal is to involve all stakeholders	To create a reflective and debating organizational culture	To ensure uniformity in the organization's basic values	To create a true image, wherein the description of the values is reflecting the organization
Definition of organizational values	Management initiates a process in which employees participate actively in defining organizational values	Defined in a value process where employees participate and are authorized by management	Is defined both by the management and employees	Defined by management, possibly with input from employees
Implementation	Managers and employees contribute together to implement the organizational values	The values are implemented partly through definitions, partly when used actively by employees	The employees accept values as their own	The values are communicated by management to employees, and to customers

(Continued)

Table 4.1 (Continued)

	Community and dialogue	*Democracy and criticism*	*Management and control*	*Branding on values*
Use of values in everyday life	Values express a common understanding, taken for granted on a daily basis	Values are used as a reference in discussion and for reflection	Conduct deviating from the values, can be described as "wrong"	Used to give a total (ideal-) image of the organization to the world

We can say that values-driven management has become a key instrument to develop employees in the public sector from being bureaucrats to being service-oriented, dedicated, and responsible exponents of the company's values. The combination of respect for the financial bottom line and ethical value change, which manifests itself in the use of values-driven management as tool for change may seem like cynical discipline and manipulation of employees to work in even more stressful working conditions. This concern should be taken very seriously. At the same time we hope that focus on the chaos and self-organization in complex frameworks of organization is so pervasive that a process of good values-driven management indispensably will bring in the necessary radicalism and creativity in thinking, which can help to overcome a reduction of values-driven management to be a new organizational imperative and bureaucratic imperative, and contribute to a quantum leap toward social responsibility and participation, an effort to find the right balance between individual and organization and between business, society, and political democracy.

Case 1: Novozymes

The Danish biotech company Novozymes, which produces enzymes, has been working with values-driven management in a cosmopolitan perspective (www.novozymes.com). Novozymes' use of values-driven management is a good example of an attempt to create a vision of social responsibility and ethical values that is the core of the company's strategy. In the description of itself on its website and in its Annual Report and in various information about the company, Novozymes emphasizes that the company's efforts to develop biotech enzyme products should be seen as a part of the creation of a balance between business, environment, and human welfare. The otherwise controversial industrial biotechnology research and development of enzymes and microorganisms should be used to improve and develop biological solutions that are also economically viable. The company predicts that growth in biotechnology business, and the organization will in this context be responsible and find environmentally and socially responsible solutions based on universally valid perceptions of sustainability. This is why the company wants to support relevant international conventions and guidelines and agreements, such as human rights declarations, conventions on biodiversity, and international agreements on sustainable development. The company emphasizes that its values should be in accordance with the international agreements and values (www.novozymes.com).

In the company's daily work it emphasizes values by financial, environmental, and social responsibility. These values also represent its objectives. Financial and economic responsibility implies management of the business's economic development and living up to international standards. Environmental responsibility means to improve the corporate environmental profile and meet international environmental standards, e.g. regarding sustainability and biological diversity. Social responsibility deals with values, which include respecting workers' rights and health. When Novozymes tells us how it lives up to these obligations, it tries to present the company's ideal values and personality. It has to be creative, curious, quick, enterprising, and innovative in order to find new perspectives. Another ideal is passion and commitment to the company's values by virtue of a fascination with the fantastic and with innovative ideas. Transparency, integrity, and trust are also highlighted as fundamental values, and so it is stressed that the company stands for a passion for science and technology, looking for opportunities for society and community. Novozymes therefore highlights the following values as fundamental: "Accountable," "Ambitious," "Responsible," "Engaged with Stakeholders," "Open and Honest," "Ready for Change" (www.novozymes.com). These values imply an invitation to be trusted by society and each other within the organization. Ambition means to ensure the highest standards in everything the company does. Responsibility means to ensure economic, environmental, and social responsibility in all business activities. Engagement for stakeholders assumes that the company is open to dialogue with the parties which affect or are affected by its activities. Flexibility and innovation builds on the company's values to create a learning and knowledge culture, ensuring advances and new business opportunities.

In its knowledge management strategy, Novozymes has tried to translate these values in a series of "Fundamentals," a set of doctrines disseminated to employees that aim to express the corporate values in practice and make sense of what is expected from the company and its employees. Novozymes therefore emphasizes that the company's units constantly must strive to achieve better practice and higher quality. There must be clear definitions of responsibilities and decision-making skills. There should be planning to improve activity and operations in all parts of the company. All employees must be able to get opportunities for competence development and feedback on their performance. There must be development plans for individuals as well as for teams. In addition to these standards of excellence, managers must ensure that they comply with relevant laws and codes of practice nationally and internationally.

Employees should be service-minded toward customers, and it must be ensured that corporate units serve customers in the best way. Novozymes combines these values and standards of excellence with a strategy for corporate social responsibility (www.novozymes.com). The strategy for social responsibility is to increase respect for human rights and contribute to ensuring social welfare as an integrated part of the company's daily operations. This must be done at local, national, and international levels. Social responsibility means to follow relevant laws and guidelines and ensure "best practice" standards and to be open to its stakeholders and relate closely to the communities where it operates. Social responsibility therefore implies respecting international human rights and labor standards, including non-discrimination. Labor and product safety should in this context be essential, and the company strives to report honestly about its performance in the social field.

The importance of values for the company will also be highlighted in the area of environmental protection. Here it is emphasized that Novozymes works with bioethics and that the company's scientific responsibilities include protection of the human genome. To work for an improved environmental profile is characterized as key to the company's efforts to integrate environmental and bioethical considerations. Especially this must be done by finding new solutions that can eliminate polluting technologies and by identifying areas where environmental performance can be improved. In this context, the company highlights the importance of being open to stakeholders and collaborating with suppliers, subcontractors, and public authorities in order to be environmentally and bioethically responsible. This happens not least by reporting openly and honestly about the company's environmental activities. Novozymes has also worked to incorporate values into the organization structure. It has set up a strategy group for values and sustainability, and they have established a small group working on improving the company's values and efforts to meet to its value standards. This strategy group reports directly to the management, and the responsible working group is responsible for implementing and highlighting the values in the organization.

Ethics and bioethics in biotechnology companies

In a project undertaken by the Danish National Consumer Agency at the beginning of the 2000s, I helped to develop some ethical principles for the work of biotechnology companies. These fit very well with the values of Novozymes. The starting point was the ministerial consultancy BioTIK Committee's principles: utility, autonomy, integrity, and speech and discourse ethics. To this was added principles of sustainability, dignity, and protection of the vulnerable (Rendtorff 2016b). These principles have been well defined philosophically and politically, but now we are left with the difficult task of concretizing them in relation to research in biotechnology companies. Here one can distinguish between some fundamental ethical applications:

1 *Research ethics:* issues of scientific responsibility and criteria for scientific fraud in the biotechnology area.
2 *Business ethics:* questions about business decency in relation to the purchase and sale of biotechnology products and inventions, including employee relations and social responsibility.
3 *Environmental and animal ethics:* questions about the proper treatment of nature, animals, and of the environment.
4 Last, but not least, the issue of *the company's legitimate treatment of the public:* public relations, dealing with the correct communication of company activities to the general public, including issues of secrecy versus open communication of company activities.

The analysis of these principles of concrete practice is based on the analysis of ethics in specific companies in order to contribute to a model for the establishment of the general ethical principles. This is based on the following model for analysis: (1) stakeholder analysis – definition of the parties that have an interest in the company; (2) examples from model companies, such as ethics programs in Novozymes and Novo Nordisk; (3) description of the ethical dilemmas that companies face, put in relation to the ethical principles. This review of the ethical principles and concrete analyzes of stakeholders and ethical dilemmas could result in a short list with the following points:

1 Ethical biotech companies work determinedly with "early warning" of ethical dilemmas and potential conflict areas.
2 Values become the company's core strategy.
3 Ethics and responsibility are communicated as part of a good image.
4 Ethical dilemmas and tension are brought to light.

5 The management and employees pay attention to conflicts of interest between stakeholders.
6 Management and employees discuss ethics, also with their stakeholders.
7 Businesses are involved in the community.
8 The company contributes to the public debate on sensitive biotech issues.

Case 2: Aalborg Municipality

In the article "Values-driven management – a response to the challenges to public organizations and institutions?" I, together with John Storm Pedersen, have described a process of working with values-driven management in the mayor's department of Aalborg Municipality (Pedersen and Rendtorff 2003: 163). The reason for the municipality's focus on values-driven management was the internal and external challenges that public organizations and institutions face in late modern welfare states. Briefly, the problem is that fiscal resources are less, while users and taxpayers require even more services and products increased user influence, etc. Therefore, the public administration faces increasing demands on efficiency and service-oriented work. This was also the case for Aalborg Municipality, which at the end of 1990 saw the necessity of changing from a bureaucratic management to being a values-driven organization that uses values as conscious management tools for promoting the employee's inner sense of responsibility and motivation, as opposed to external management by rules and bureaucracy. The mayor's administration in Aalborg Municipality is a part of an organization which in 2000 had to administer a city of 160,000 inhabitants, with around 15,000 employees and an annual budget of about 9 billion Danish Crowns. Employees work in public institutions such as schools, day-care centers and home care. The mayor's management unit is the central joint management of the corporation with five major administrative officers and a number of offices. There were 450 employees in the mayor management (Pedersen and Rendtorff 2003: 164).

Work on values-driven leadership was about making this type of management the foundation of a bottom-up process of the administration which could give employees and managers greater motivation and service readiness. Values-driven management was also introduced as an alternative to new public management, which had otherwise been a popular tool for the renewal of the public sector. Citizens' expectations for greater service from the municipality through increasing marketization were an important reason for working with values-driven management. At the same time, this work was in response to a demand for greater customization of a heavy and inflexible public organization (Pedersen and Rendtorff 2003: 166). In contrast to the sociologist Max Weber's bureaucratic form of organization and to the industrial form of production of Fordism and Taylorism based on planning economics and hierarchical models for budget and organization, values-driven management represents a new flexible and dynamic management system, which aims to engage employees from below in a bottom-up process.

In contrast to rigid organizations that dissolve in conflicts and rivalries, values-driven management enables service-minded and socially responsible relationships with users and clients, which are also economically effective. Values-driven leadership is namely based on the responsible involvement of employees to ensure the organization's credibility to stakeholders in order to withstand the external and internal cross pressure on the organization. One can say that we face the case of a reflective and more sophisticated self-observation of the organization in relation to its own organizational processes.

The process of values-driven management in Aalborg Municipality was built around a series of dialogue sessions with employees and the professional teams that, from preliminary interviews with various stakeholder groups, were involved in the formulation of values. From a longer process organized by the department of organization and staff, a consensus was reached after much discussion where 44 values were reduced to six core values of the organization:

1 We are responsible and take responsibility for what we do.
2 We are open and honest.
3 We treat others with respect and show others trust.
4 We are professionally good and competent.
5 We cooperate with each other.
6 We have a great community – and we are proud of it.

These core values were subsequently marketed and disseminated to employees, after which they were finally adopted and approved by politicians. In addition, a working group was set up to maintain and develop the values, first and foremost in relation to the company middle managers (Pedersen and Rendtorff 2003: 172). The centerpiece of the use of values-driven management in Aalborg Municipality is that values help to improve consistency of reflection about the interpretation of what were right decisions. Unlike rules, the scope for interpretation in values helps toward a better understanding of the values locally in the organization and it helps to focus on dialogue and discussion in relation to implementing the right initiatives for municipal clients and stakeholders.

Based on the core values, a number of key leadership values were formulated, which would ensure open debate and discussion about decisions in the organization. These values are formulated in a number of principles that were enshrined in a code of values-driven management. In particular, middle managers were among the leader's key persons to ensure that the values were carried out in practice, and there was therefore a greater focus on middle managers' position in the organization. The result of the process was that top management was responsible for the framework decisions while middle managers had to make specific implementations. The values helped to provide clarity and credibility in decision-making, and there was more open discussion about the decisions.

This was shown by a recent evaluation and further formulation of the decision-making process. In Aalborg Municipality, values-driven management was an important instrument for improving the efficiency of the organization, and values-driven management may be recommended if it happens in a democratic bottom-up process with a focus on motivation, flexibility, and stakeholders. It also aims to formulate concrete values-driven measures of good management, shown in Table 4.2, which were the result of the process in Aalborg Municipality (Pedersen and Rendtorff 2003: 175).

Case 3: Lockheed Martin

A controversial example of values-driven management is the multinational and US company Lockheed Martin, which manufactures advanced technology systems, military aircraft, helicopters, missiles, and other defense equipment and computer technologies, with among others the US government as a customer. Because of the importance of the production for the United States, but also due to the controversial activity of producing

Table 4.2 Values as a basis for management in Aalborg Municipality

Value	*Achieved by:*
1 A good manager supports personal and professional development	• Giving the staff personal and professional challenges at work • Giving positive feedback • Showing personal interest in the wellbeing of the staff
2 A good manager exercises visible management	• Creating relevant criteria of success • Giving appropriate information • Involving the staff in relevant decision-making • Promoting the team in and outside the administration of the Mayor • Promoting the administration of the Mayor in positive ways • Creating networks in and outside the administration of the Mayor
3 A good manager creates dialogue	• Involving the staff in setting goals and in achieving these • Trusting the staff • Solving problems and personal conflicts when these emerge
4 A good manager is well skilled and competent	• Showing outlook and insight • Ensuring relevant competencies in the staff
5 A good manager is stakeholder oriented	• Involving the stakeholders in the production of services • Developing new ways of problem solving and production
6 A good manager involves all the important partners	• Developing projects in co-ordination with relevant partners in the organization
7 A good manager is goal oriented	• Setting goals for the team • Communicating milestones and their accomplishments
8 A good manager is conscious of the limitation of the resources	• Utilizing the resources in best possible ways • Involving the staff in the utilization of the resources

weapons, Lockheed Martin began in the midst of the 1980s to develop a well-functioning program for ethics and values-driven management. Among other things, the US government had called for this, since it was not satisfied with product quality or morality in the defense industry. Lockheed Martin combines a program of values-driven management with a number of organizational structures and procedures in line with the US Federal Sentencing Guidelines for Organizations from 1991 (Terris 2005: 65; Rendtorff 2008). The company highlights the following values: "Ethics, Excellence, Can-Do, Integrity, People, Teamwork." This includes the following interpretation of company values: Honesty (to be faithful to the objectives, be honest and upright toward each other and in relation to customers, communities, suppliers, and shareholders); Integrity (to say what we think, do what we promise, fulfill our commitments, and stand for what is right); Respect (to treat each other with dignity and fairness, appreciating the diversity of the workforce and every employee's uniqueness); Trust (to build confidence through teamwork and open direct communication); Responsibility (to take responsibility for our actions, say things openly without fear of retribution, and report on conditions in the workplace, including breaches of laws, regulations, or company policies, and seek clarification if in doubt); Citizenship (to obey the laws of the countries where we do business, and play our part in improving the communities where we live and work) (Lockheed Martin 2005a). Lockheed Martin has developed a series of structures that develops the company's ethics program. The organization has assigned responsibility for ethics programs to members of senior management to ensure that ethics is a high priority in the strategy and organizational development.

There has been established an ethics program with a variety of documents and exercises that communicate the organization's values to employees through education and training. The employees are also informed regularly about areas that require high ethical awareness, such as bribery and corruption, conflict of interest and disqualification, occupational safety and environmental protection, prohibition of personal gain, fraud and cheating, discrimination and sexual harassment. They are also taught about the possibility of maintaining their ethical integrity as part of their professionalism, for example in connection with the local community and the customers of the business.

To ensure transparency the organization has also established an ethics office and an "ethics hotline" through which employees can contact the ethics office and without reprisals talk about ethical problems or report if they see anyone in the company do something illegal (Paine 1997a, 1997b). Lockheed Martin's ethics program can be said to combine values and rules. The goal is to avoid employees committing offenses while working for the company. At the same time, the program aims to make the employees do their best for the company and thus not just follow the rules, but meet the company's ethical values. One can say that the initial aim of the ethics program was to improve the company's operations in the market by ensuring the employees' ethical behavior.

Next comes the focus on top management's responsibility and issues in relation to the business's social responsibility for profit and products. Lockheed Martin has also worked on developing a decision model, so that employees can have a better basis for taking informed decisions in specific situations. The model includes the following: (1) Evaluate information and facts; (2) decide how your decision affects those affected; (3) decide what business values and ethics principles are relevant; (4) select the best action. To determine whether there are ethical problems in a specific action or case the company has compiled a short list of danger signs (Lockheed Martin 2005b):

- "Well, just this one time does not matter!"
- "No one will come to know anything about it!"
- "It does not matter how just it is done!"
- "All others do it!"
- "Shred this document!"
- "We can save it!"
- "It will not hurt anyone!"
- "What do I get out of it?"
- "This will destroy the competition!"
- "We did not have this conversation!"
- "This is a non-meeting!"

In addition to identifying these danger signals that can make employees aware that they are coming out in a gray area between right and wrong, the company has developed a "Quick Quiz" with questions that an employee should ask him or herself in connection with his or her actions (Lockheed Martin 2005b):

1 Are my actions legal?
2 Am I fair and honest?
3 Will my action stand the test of time?

4 How will I feel about myself afterwards?
5 How will it look in the newspaper?
6 Will I be able to sleep well tonight?
7 What would I tell my child to do?
8 How would I feel if my family, my friends, and neighbors knew what I did?

Criticism of values-driven management

The example of Lockheed Martin is provocative enough to many because it combines ethics and weapons. This gives rise to reflections on the relationship between values, power, and manipulation. There has also been a lot of criticism of values-driven management as a strategic tool for organization and management. Here are some of the most common critical views (Rasmussen *et al.* 2006; Rendtorff 2009):

Pseudo-values-driven management

Values-driven management is a new and more sophisticated form of manipulation of employees. It leads to a new "iron cage" – not a release as it is claimed. The new roles in modern businesses require autonomous and self-motivated employees – exactly what values-driven management is helping to create. Employees are manipulated in good faith to submit themselves totally to the company.

Values-driven management as ideology

Values-driven management gives employees a false impression of serving the common good, but serves really no purpose other than to strengthen the company's financial bottom line. As long as the matter of inequality and lack of democracy within the company does not come into focus, one cannot get out of values-driven management as an ideology. Values-driven management creates the illusion that the company is the only meaningful thing in the employee's life, and that the employee lives for the company, as if he or she was a religious disciple.

The ethics of sensitivity

Kirsten Marie Bovbjerg has shown that soft values are used as harsh disciplinary tools (Bovbjerg 2001). Values that emphasize autonomy and self-development are a way to ensure that employees internalize their obligations to the company, but thus the soft values in reality are hard values that oppress employees of the company.

The flexible human being

The modern employee has to be flexible; to have willingness to switch project, work, and workplace (Sennett 1998). Each employee becomes his or her own fortune. Work ethics is based on each employee's initiative, responsibility, commitment, and personal values. Values-driven management aims to ensure employee identification with the company under the new conditions and thereby it becomes a new form of a non-transparent exercise of power.

Deconstruction of morality

The French philosopher Alain Etchegoyen has pointed out that we live in an ethical crisis where many particular forms of values supersede universal morality (Etchegoyen 1991). Values-driven management is a desperate attempt to reconstruct ethics in a time when it no longer is possible. The new values are not ethics, but an intensified form of Taylorism that use values as an ideology of oppression and discipline.

Values as the company's instrument of power

Values-driven management is used as an instrument of power to make the community's values and ethics into something that the individual must abide under. This makes values-driven management an instrument to ensure power over employees by management as they are imposed on employees in terms of the values and the ethics that are perceived as "our ethics," i.e. the governing rules of the organization (Pruzan 2001).

From bureaucracy to the project capitalism

Luc Boltanski and Eve Chiappelo (1995) describe the evolution from the traditional organizational forms of project capitalism characterized by temporary forms of organization and change. The new forms of management and business ethics appear in the new-age ideology, where the soft forms of management replace more hierarchical management theories. Project Capitalism is an expression of that rotation of management, where employees' project are organized in such a way that it strengthens corporate power over them.

5 Theories and principles of business ethics

In this chapter we will review the theoretical basis and principles of business ethics that are behind the search for cosmopolitan business ethics. First, we highlight the understanding of the relationship between business, market, and society that lies behind business ethics, as it can be seen in the light of institutional theories of economics, politics, and society. Then we discuss important theoretical approaches to business ethics, to ethical principles, and to ethical judgment.

A new business understanding?

When we examine company values, we analyze the company not only as a strict economic unit, but largely as a social phenomenon. In addition to the original description of company values that combine economizing with increasing its power and ecologizing, we can highlight that the post-modern understanding of business entails a broader understanding of the business. The company is not just an economic instrument to ensure shareholders' economic interests but must also take into account a wide range of stakeholders, including its shareholders, managers, employees, suppliers, customers, the community, and the nation state.

We move toward a broad view of the company as a moral and legal person with extensive rights and duties. There is no longer a liability which restricts management's major obligations to apply only to shareholders and owners. By contrast, we are heading toward an inclusive and broader understanding of responsibility, as evidenced by the law on companies and firms in the US and EU since the 1980s. The American Law Institute has, among other things, formulated guidelines for public companies, involving a number of obligations to a third party, so that the company's interests do not always mean the owners' immediate economic interests, but also can mean broader consideration for the environment, consumers, or communities (Schans Christensen 1992: 35 ff.; Rendtorff 2009).

This values-driven concept of business analyzes the company's role in society from the point of view of economic sociology, and stresses the importance of focusing on business ethics and social responsibility. This values-driven management includes a new way to understand the company's role in society. This new business understanding is in conflict with the so-called neoclassical paradigm that argues that social responsibility and ethics should be perceived as nothing more than instruments to provide greater economic profit in the long run (long-term shareholder value). There is an institutionalization of a new set of standards with a closer link between economics and ethics, which has led to a change in the value orientations of the company (Mac and Rendtorff 2001: 73; Mac 2005; Crane and Matten 2016).

This approach rejects the neoclassical paradigm, stressing that the company is an instrument for profit maximization and economic efficiency and that public organizations must be like private companies. At the same time this reorientation of corporate value understanding is skeptical of the capitalism-critical attitude that considers values-driven management as another clever management instrument of mastery of the employees of private companies in order to contribute to the dissolution of the welfare state through efficiency and marketization of the public sector.

The new business understanding of the complex post-modern society can be thought of as a third way, which breaks the contradiction between supporters of capitalism and their critics. We live in a time, it is claimed, where the world is changed in a way that problematizes traditional contradictions between left and right, public and private, organization and environment. This happens with institutionalization of norms, where both private companies and public organizations and institutions engage in dialogue with their environment and stakeholders through more flexible management and organizational forms.

One can therefore argue that the values-driven organization involves a break with the neoclassical view of ethics and responsibility. The company's embedding in the social world creates another ethical obligation than merely focusing on economic competition. The obligation to safeguard not only shareholder interests, but also those of stakeholders – through dialogue and involvement of company stakeholders in management, strategy and the development of the company's values – has become a legitimate economic activity. Such a focus on the good life and social responsibility gives rise to understanding the company as more than an economic efficiency contract. In contrast to the dominant mainstream economic paradigm, the so-called neoclassical view of organizations and companies, this new business understanding implies a turn toward the company's social responsibility and corporate citizenship, where it is claimed that companies can and should be oriented toward the common good of the economy. The American sociologist Amitai Etzioni highlights in *The Moral Dimension. Towards a New Economics* (1988: 1) that the economy has been given a moral dimension, where the new economy expresses a critique of a selfish conception of human beings.

Within this mindset, we must recognize that the market system is a subsystem of the social system, and we must understand that our social standards of the good life and the common good in the end apply as the real basis for economic growth. The new business understanding therefore implies that the purpose of the economy is that people can realize their life projects together with others, and that the company, when it realizes its social responsibility by taking into account the common good of its stakeholders, contributes to realizing the common good in the market as a good citizen.

Corporate ethics and institutional theory

Institutional theory is an approach in social science that looks at the institutional aspects of social action and the interaction between actor and social institution (Nielsen 2006). Institutional theory can be considered as an important methodological and social theoretical prerequisite for understanding the role of business in society. A distinction is made between a number of different theories of institutional theory, each of which affects the understanding of organizations and interaction between values, ethics, social responsibility, and companies and organizations.

- *Historical financial institutionalism.* Historic and economic institutionalism, also called "old institutionalism," goes back to the 19th century and was developed by German economists, who were inspired by the German philosophy of history (Hodgson 1994). This theory was later defended by the Norwegian-American economist Thorstein Veblen. The theory is that the economy is influenced by historical and cultural factors, and it determines the economic standards. This theory can easily be combined with ethics because of its attention to the social importance of social relations for economic development.
- *Institutional political science.* Typical representatives are March and Olsen. Institutional political science, following the historical school, highlights the importance of institutions for social action. Institutional political science also contains positions which criticize the historical school, since they stress that action in an institution is based on individual rational choice and the quest to maximize its own interests. However, opposed to this, the institutional political sciences following March and Olsen criticize utility maximization on a hermeneutic basis and understand institutions as horizons of meaning that should be interpreted in order to understand the background for acts in political institutions (Torfing 2005a).
- *New institutional economy.* This approach investigates the importance of institutions for economic action and activities. New institutional economy uses insights from institutional political science in order to understand the economic action. This refers to economists like Williamson (1989) and North (1992). New institutional economy disagrees with the historical school on the rationality that characterizes economic development. It is based on an economic rationality which uses the concept of utility maximization, and there is a tendency to consider institutions like rationality-limiting frameworks that make it impossible to perform ideal economic operations. Ethics is, from this perspective, a transaction cost, which puts constraints on economic action.
- *Institutional sociology* is about how actor's cognition, perceptions, and values are shaped by institutions. Powell and DiMaggio (1991) are representatives of this. The institutional sociology has a different approach than institutional economics, as it recognizes that institutions are important for shaping the interpretation and understanding of value without going into the economic rationality concept. Instead it describes the social reality more or less as a social construction based on the players' implicit expectations.

This approach must indeed be combined with the ethical theory's emphasis of the significance of history and culture for the development of the organization's legitimacy and position in the external environment. The actions of the business corporation are conditioned by the symbols and context of meaning that also determine the point of view of the actors (Mac 2005). The institutional approach to business ethics and CSR looks at these dimensions of organizations from the point of view of institutional theory (Campbell 2006). Institutional theory looks at the institutional basis for corporate citizenship (Jeurissen 2004).

Institutional theory and business ethics

The institutionalization of new values and standards for businesses can be explained by the institutional theory in sociology, political science, and economics. The economic sociology emphasizes the importance of social institutions for individual actions and examines the effects of institutions for individual actions. The institutional sociology of DiMaggio and Powell highlights how companies are embedded in social and institutional conditions in their outside world, and describes how these social issues conditions the company's value orientations (Powell and DiMaggio 1991; Rendtorff 2009).

It is the changes in social institutions that affect the normative changes of value in the companies, and this also affects the economic relations between companies and their environments. This discussion leads us back to the debate on corporate social legitimacy. Institutional sociology points out that legitimacy depends on internal and external expectations of the company and determines the company's relations to the environment (Powell and DiMaggio 1991). The institution-based conception of legitimacy also highlights the contribution to the common good as a way to improve the company's social legitimacy.

Institutional economy also takes a broader perspective than neoclassical economic theory, since it claims that it is necessary to involve social transactions and relationships in order to obtain information about economic actions and operations. Economic science cannot settle for formal calculations, but should involve social and institutional conditions in order to understand the economic operation. In continuation of institutional theory, the US business ethicist John Boatright (1999a) claims that we can develop ethics in order to create the right conditions for the institutional markets. It is not only individual judgment, but also the institutional conditions for actions which are important for the development of the values and norms of companies and organizations. It is at the level of the market that ethics is central, and we must have an institutional and structural perspective on business ethics.

In this context, we can emphasize that the current changes in corporate value orientations reflect changes in the institutional norms in the financial markets. The concept of the common good at the level of society combines with concern for personal integrity and with general market logics. Traditional institutional economics had a historical and social view of the economy and highlighted how the economy would be seen from the society's general values and cultural norms. New institutional economy rather considers business as the starting point for the analysis (Boatright 1996: 218). Ronald Coase, in "The nature of the firm" (1937), questions why companies exist, and answers that companies are social constructs that can help to reduce the transaction costs of production and trade. This view was followed up by Oliver Williamson who, in his books, considers the company as a "nexus of contracts" between different individuals. We can consider this opening to involve social conditions in economic considerations as an opening toward ethics (Williamson 1989). As a knot of contracts the company can unleash a broader perspective that goes beyond a monistic view of the company as merely a tool for its owners.

Also Boatright (1996, 2003) argues for an ethical point of view of the role of the company in new institutional economics in the new economy. The company, understood as a knot of contracts, is an instrument for profit maximization, but this does not imply, as mentioned, a broader conception of the contracts. Thus, contract theory, though it is limited, may not be so far from stakeholder theory, which relates business to a wider number of stakeholders. I would argue that we can combine the two perspectives when we seek to understand the company's changing role in society. Institutional economic theory should not be neglected, but must be included in the ethical considerations of business, although there may sometimes be tensions between the economic and ethical perception of the company. Tensions, because there are different concepts of human nature where contract theory has not quite overcome the hedonistic selfishness, while business ethics primarily emphasizes the interests of the common good as the guiding principle for economic markets.

Existentialist basis for corporate ethics

Existentially, we can justify the need for business ethics out of man's search for recognition and efforts to achieve the appreciation from society that underlie our work in organizations and social institutions (Rendtorff 2009, 2014a). Individual managers and employees strive to become themselves as human beings with their ideal personality by doing something good at work. It is necessary to have an existential commitment behind good management and corporate governance. When we talk about business ethics in institutions, we must not forget the manager's personal motivation and driving force behind the actions. If we ask for an existential dimension in management, we can, with Soren Kierkegaard, emphasize that management and decisions at the workplace take place on an existential basis. In the provocative but also thoughtful book *Kierkegaard and Management,* Kirstine Andersen (2005) highlights so courageously poetics, dialogue, commitment, confidence, and the concrete meeting with the other person as existential dimensions of ethics, management, and governance. With Kierkegaard we can see the relationship between employees at work as part of human existence, where individuals are required to take decisions with responsibility for other people. This relationship with work is essentially an existential relationship where people must find themselves and meaning in life and existence. In this context, human beings choose themselves in relation to their work situations, and this choice is an existential choice of the meaning of life, which also has an ethical dimension, since, with Kierkegaard, it comes to choosing what is ethically right by virtue of the infinite individual responsibility.

With regard to good management the employee also needs to be himself, and thus management has an ethical dimension, which is to choose oneself in the authentic interaction with the other person. This means that the existential dimension in business ethics emphasizes that the starting point for good management is respect for the individual person's particular dignity and integrity as an employee in the organization. The existential perspective indicates that the individual never can be dissolved in structures and institutions. Existential management is based on the specific existential meeting between the manager and an employee, both of whom face each other as people in an open and personal dialogue. By virtue of this existential meeting with the other, management is based on practical wisdom and existential commitment. Ole Fogh Kirkeby (1997, 2000) has, with his theory of leadership in management philosophy from a radically normative perspective, positioned himself close to this position. He emphasizes human freedom and experience of contingency as the central basis for management, where the good manager does appear as a part of a subject–object relation, but works in a subject–subject relation to employees. Here the good leader is determined by his virtuousness and the ability to go into a situation with virtues such as respect, care, trust, commitment, values, and visions. Any good leadership is fundamentally ethical and normative, and Kirkeby ends up saying that leadership is a "cross" because the good leader greatly must sacrifice himself for the good and fight hard for his cause. Kirkeby (2003, 2006) combines this with a phenomenological organizational philosophy inspired by classic philosophers and by a kind of event philosophy, where management is considered as the leader's ability to capture the meaning of the situation and be energetic and action oriented.

The classical theories of business ethics

Apart from the institutional and existentialist approach to corporate ethics and responsibility we can highlight the ethics of utility, duty ethics, and virtue ethics as classical ethical theories that form the basis for the development of business ethics (Desjardins 2014). Here we can distinguish between a teleological approach related to the good of the aim of business (Sternberg 2004) and a deontological approach (Arnold and Harris 2012). These theories cannot stand alone, but must be integrated in a republican business ethics, based on considerations of the common good (*res publica*) in a society with a well-developed representative democracy (Figure 5.1). This also forms the basis for the basic ethical principles of concern for the human person, including human autonomy, dignity, integrity, and vulnerability. The ethical reflective judgment aims at giving the ethical theories and principles an understanding of ethical problems and dilemmas in specific situations.

Utilitarianism and consequentialism

Utilitarianism or consequentialism, also called utility ethics, which is one of the classic ethical theories, considers the good as determined by individuals' subjective preferences (Kappel, Petersen, and Ryberg 2003; Crane and Matten 2016). Ethics is a calculative effort to weigh the pros, cons, and total utility of different possible actions and benefits in light of the various preferences. The objective is to achieve the greatest happiness and usefulness, and the greatest good. The British philosopher Jeremy Bentham (1788) developed such a utilitarian calculus where the good action was the one that created the greatest good for the greatest number. The utility and good consequence of an action

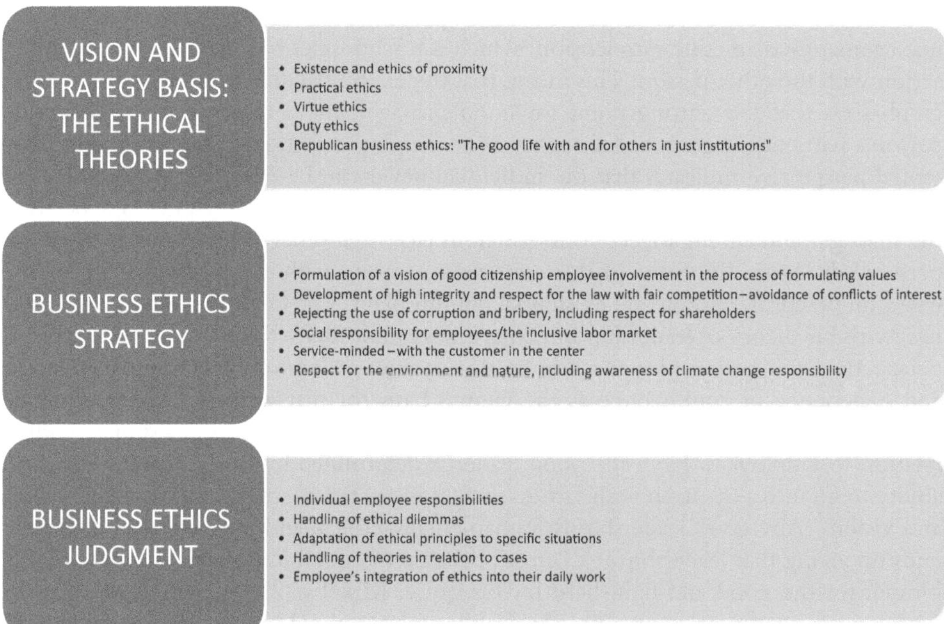

Figure 5.1 The company as good corporate citizen.

should be seen in light of the individual's preferences, and modern consequentialism builds on this by highlighting that ethics is based on accounts of individuals' basic preferences and weighing of those in the overall calculation of desire and dissatisfaction, pain and pleasure, usefulness and uselessness. While utilitarianism and consequentialism have been the ethical basis for modern welfare economics, this ethical theory has, however, also been criticized for its relatively simple character. A basic question is, how one can measure an action's benefits and happiness? It can be argued that the pros and cons, suffering and happiness are often closely linked, and therefore it is difficult to calculate these conditions. Also it can be difficult to judge what is meant by "benefit" and "cost" in a "cost–benefit" analysis that balances the relationship between benefits and costs of specific actions. There is, among different people and communities, disagreement about what are the disadvantages and advantages of certain actions and policies. Most good depends on the values that it is built on. It therefore becomes a problem whether non-economic benefits, such as life, liberty and equality, health and beauty, at all can be assessed using a single economic utility calculation (Velasquez 2002). Moreover, utilitarianism and consequentialism have been criticized for not being able to integrate respect for justice and rights of individuals in their theories. It is alleged that the utilitarian cost–benefit calculation does not respect basic human rights because it balances everything out of pleasure and pain. Thus utilitarianism forgets that respect for human dignity and the sanctity of life is the foundation of social justice and that there will be injustice of sharing burdens when you only talk about benefits (Velasquez 2002). The result is a great risk that the weakest become victims of the need to increase the welfare of the majority, and their utility and happiness. Utilitarianism can reply to this criticism by claiming that the utilitarian benefit calculation is not unlimited, but limited by the outer frames from the perspective of a so-called rule utilitarianism, i.e. the view that we should begin by respecting fundamental rights and then make utility maximization within areas that do not violate the dignity and sanctity of human life. It is therefore argued that the calculation of utility must not violate respect for basic human rights.

Duty ethics and contract theory

With this reduction of utilitarianism, we have reached contract theory or deontological rights theory, which has its basis in the moral philosophy of the German philosopher Immanuel Kant (1785, 1797). From this we can propose Kantian business ethics, focusing on dignity and the meaning of work from the perspective of Kant's philosophy (Bowie 1999a, 1999b; Arnold and Harris 2012). Kant defined the so-called categorical imperative as the basis of ethics. The categorical imperative is considered as characteristic of a universal moral law that protects basic human rights. The categorical imperative involves the following basic dimensions: (1) An act is moral if it can be made into a general application and a universal law. (2) A moral action is to treat humans not only as a means, but also always as an end in itself. (3) The righteous community is described as the kingdom of ends in themselves (this means a community of people who in mutual respect live up to the basic principles of morality), i.e. the rule of law and a society where all are recognized as free human beings with human rights and duties. The basis of ethics is not primarily utility and pleasure and pain, but respect for the fundamental rights of citizens. Rights are justified by our moral sense. They are assigned to every individual unconditionally, and they cannot be lost. Rights can be a person's rights to his or her own body and spirit, or it may be basic property rights. This contract theoretical approach to ethics can be said to form the basis of the Universal Declaration of Human Rights 1948, highlighting a number of fundamental rights that all must respect. Among these rights are counted the right to life, protection of privacy, political rights, and social rights, including the right of workers to freedom of association, etc. Rights are formulated in this context both as negative (refusing actions) and positive (accepting actions). They express basic protection concerns which are required by states or companies in relation to their citizens or employees.

The American philosopher John Rawls' Kantian-inspired contract theory about a just society in *A Theory of Justice* (1971) and in several later works can be considered as a modern justification of rights and contractual ethics. Rawls claims that a number of sensible people in an original situation, a consultation meeting behind the "veil of ignorance" in order to reach a social contract, where they do not know their own place in the future society, would choose a number of fundamental rights as basic in a just society. Rawls also believes that the rational choice as the basis for a social contract must consist of the choice of two principles: (1) freedom principle, which involves the principle of equal freedoms for all; (2) difference principle, which implies that inequality can only be justified if it is to the weakest's advantage. These underpin the notion of "fair opportunity," i.e. that everyone should have equal opportunities (Rawls 1971, 1985, 1993). Following his justice theory, Rawls also distinguishes between distributive justice, retribution justice, and compensatory justice as ways that can rectify inequality and create a fair distribution of wealth in society. This rights-based foundation of ethics combined with the notion of a social contract can be said to establish a series of formal requirements for contracts between companies (Velasquez 2002: 94–96). Such a contractual basis for institutions could consist of: (1) complete knowledge among the contract's parties; (2) bans on cheating with facts; (3) no compulsion to enter into a contract; (4) the contract cannot bind the parties to immoral acts. The central dimension of rights and contract theory is thus the concern for fairness and fair play in companies and organizations. Ethics is built on respect for human dignity and aims at ensuring fair treatment of the parties, partners, and stakeholders by taking them into account and letting them make their voices be heard in a fair way. In the economic market this is about ensuring a fair distribution of benefits and burdens. This implies, in a sharp interpretation of contract theory, that it is part of corporate social responsibility to ensure fair distribution of benefits and services, and thus define limits to the legitimate economic inequality in the market and in society.

Virtue ethics and communitarianism

Virtue ethics comes from the Ancient Greek philosopher Aristotle (1999). The concept of "virtue" refers to human endeavor to do one's best where the good refers to the norms and virtues, defined by the community as a basis for good deeds (Sison 2008). Aristotle talks about how human beings train their moral character by following their moral judgment and the appropriate middle ground between the extremes. Virtue ethics as business ethics puts emphasis on seeing the company as a community and as a way of life. The company considered here is primarily an expression of a community, based on that the people together, through their work, create a community and a practice that aims to be the best. Modern virtue ethicists such as Alasdair MacIntyre and Robert Solomon have tried to develop their virtue ethical performance as a basis for the modern business corporation. It is important here that the company's moral character develops from a search for the good life in the integrated community (MacIntyre 1981).

The virtue ethical or communitarian approach to business ethics is therefore based on the virtues of friendship, honor, integrity, and loyalty, which are important for business ethics (Sison 2008). Corporate citizenship is a matter of virtuous corporate culture and a good social practice in order to achieve common social goals. Robert Solomon has developed this virtue ethical approach in the book *Ethics and Excellence. Cooperation and Integrity in Business* (1992). The virtue ethical approach is a departure from the utilitarian concept of man as "*homo economicus*," since virtue ethics claims that economic growth is not primarily a result of selfish greed, but of cooperation and joint quest for the good life in fair institutions (Solomon 1992).

The market should not be understood as an abstract and amoral market, but rather as a result of a virtuous practice which is commonly striving for the common good. The market must therefore be considered as a way of life that is controlled by a practical sense, a virtuous prudence, a practice form with its own rules, goals, and role models for the actors at the market. This virtue ethical approach perceives the human individual and the joint realization of the efforts to achieve the good as central to the understanding of company activities. Leadership is, for the virtue ethicists, a matter of good practice and of the ability to make the right decisions in the specific situation. The main leadership virtues are integrity, fairness, and good judgment, as well as individual character that is shaped by practical judgment in concrete situations. Judgment and prudence is the ability to make the right decisions to ensure the organization's integrative wholeness and the individual's overall integrity and good life.

In this sense, one can trace a connection between virtue ethics and ethics of care, since for an individual with high moral integrity it is an important virtue to care for the other person's otherness as a person needing care and concern. The ultimate goal of a business as a social practice is to view the company as a good citizen and as a part of a larger whole of meaning. Justice in the organization's life is also at the center of the communitarian approach. Equal should be treated equally, and unequal should be treated unequally, as has been stated since Aristotle (1999). Communitarians stress that various factors, such as merit, performance, risk, and uncertainty, must be involved in the concrete assessment of fairness. However, it is also important to emphasize that for the virtue ethical approach to business ethics it is commitment, engagement, and sense of belonging to the organization that is perceived as the core of the development of the organization's values.

Republican business ethics and ethical principles

When the core of the new business ethics is the good life in the economic market, we must also formulate a corporate ethical paradigm corresponding to that view. Therefore, the notion of good corporate citizenship is central to business ethics (Ulrich 1998). If this is understood as republican business ethics, i.e. an orientation of the company's activities and values in the direction of the common good (*res publica*), the most obvious approach to business ethics can be a combination of the utilitarian, ethical, and community perceptions of the company. This is in line with the French philosopher Paul Ricoeur's thinking, when talking about the basis of ethics as "the good life with and for others in just institutions" (Ricoeur 1990: 202). We can thus say that the communitarian approach to business ethics articulates the vision of the company as a community and as a way of life. This vision is the basis for the company's values. It is a contract-oriented approach to business that ensures that the organization and management help to protect and defend human dignity and the individual rights of individuals. To this contributes also the utilitarian and consequentialist ethics. However, it is important to emphasize that this always happens in the context of a target of the good life and of the protection of individual rights, so the utility-oriented ethical pragmatism will not be put ahead of the consideration of the individual dignity of the human being. With republican business ethics, targeting good corporate citizenship, is it therefore important to talk about an integrative view of the ethical theories, based on a theoretical mix and functional division of the different views.

In this context one can highlight the social contract approach to business ethics (integrated social contract theory) as an attempt to mediate between respect for rights and contracts in the light of the interests of a particular political culture of a society. This view is developed by Thomas Donaldson and Thomas W. Dunfee in *Ties that Bind. A Social Contracts Approach to Business Ethics* (1999), where they argue that business ethics emerges in the tension between the particular and the universal in the global community.

By building on the combination of the vision of the good life and protection of specific rights, the concept of the company as a good citizen can easily be combined with fair competition in a free market, as long as the market can be seen as being to the advantage of the weakest in society. The key to this development is that corporate activities in the financial markets contribute to society's social integration. Furthermore, we can highlight a number of fundamental ethical principles as basic considerations to be integrated into the social responsibility of business. We can emphasize ethical principles such as respect for autonomy, dignity, integrity, and vulnerability, which are ethical concerns that play a major role in European societies, as described in the book *Basic Ethical Principles in European Bioethics and Biolaw* (Rendtorff and Kemp 2000; Rendtorff 2016b). These principles were originally developed for the protection of the individual human person in the Barcelona Declaration of 1998, where a number of researchers on the basis of the research on the ethical principles in Europe emphasize how these principles function as key ethical concerns in Europe.

The principles were defined as "middle-level" principles with the person as a pivot, but they can also be used as important indicators in organizational ethics and thus as a measure of a developed stakeholder dialogue within democratic corporate ethics. The principle of autonomy thus expresses the interests of the company in doing "self-regulation" in a liberal market economy. Dignity refers to respect for people and employees at the workplace and in organizations, while integrity refers to the organization's unity and moral identity. Lastly, the word vulnerability designates the condition of individuals in the competitive market conditions, thereby also emphasizing the need for concern and consideration of the vulnerable with regard to individuals as well as the companies, which breaks down in the competition of the market.

The ethical principles

In a report to the European Commission from a large European research project the ethical principles were defined in the following way (Rendtorff and Kemp 2000; Rendtorff 2016b):

1 Autonomy should not only be interpreted in the liberal sense of "permission"; instead, five aspects of autonomy should be put forward: (1) the capacity of creation of ideas and goals for life; (2) the capacity of moral insight, "self-legislation" and privacy; (3) the capacity of rational decision and action without coercion;

(4) the capacity of political involvement and personal responsibility; (5) the capacity of informed consent. However, autonomy remains merely an ideal, because of the structural limitations given to it by human weakness and dependence on biological, material, and social conditions, lack of information for reasoning, etc.

2 Dignity should not be reduced to autonomy. Although originally a virtue of outstanding persons and a virtue of self-control in life – qualities which can be lost, for instance by lack of responsibility or in extreme illness – it has been universalized as a quality of the person as such. It now refers to both the intrinsic value of the individual and the intersubjective value of every human being in encounters with others. Dignity concerns both oneself and others: I must behave with dignity, and I must consider the dignity of others. I must not give up civilized and responsible behavior, and others should not be commercialized and enslaved. Human rights are based on this principle of dignity.

3 Integrity accounts for the inviolability of the human being. Although originally a virtue of uncorrupted character, expressing uprightness, honesty, and good intentions, it has, like dignity, been universalized as a quality of the person as such. Thus it refers to the coherence of life, which should not be touched and destroyed. It is coherence of life being remembered from experiences and therefore can be told in a narrative. Therefore respect for integrity is respect for privacy and in particular for the employee's right to self-determination and non-interference in personal projects of life. Integrity is the most important principle for the creation of trust between people, because it also indicates the moral virtue of commitment and engagement in a personal vision of the good life.

4 Vulnerability concerns integrity as a basic principle for respect for and protection of human and non-human life. It expresses the condition of all life, that it can be hurt, wounded, and killed. It is not integrity as completeness in any sense, but the integrity of life that must be respected and protected as vulnerable. Vulnerability concerns animals and all self-organizing life in the environment, and for the human community it must be considered as a universal expression of the human condition. The idea of the protection of vulnerability can therefore create a bridge between moral strangers in a pluralistic society, and respect for vulnerability should be essential to strategic decisions in corporations and policy-making in the modern welfare state. Respect for vulnerability is not a demand for perfect and immortal life, but recognition of the suffering and finitude of human life.

Judgment and moral thinking in management

To actually make decisions in this complex interaction between social theory, ethical theories, and ethical principles within the framework of a republican business ethics, we have great need for moral thought and moral judgment. Aristotle (1999) describes judgment and prudence as the practical sense or the ability to find "the right middle" of the situation as a basis for action. For Kant (1790), however, judgment and prudence are based on the ability to combine them with understanding of the rules and the specificity of the situation. Kant distinguishes between the reflective and determinant judgment where the reflective judgment must find new principles for new cases, while determinant judgment uses existing rules in relation to agreed facts. When judgment must combine general ethical theories, ethical principles and facts in reflection, the relation between the individual judgment and the conflict between institutional responsibility and personal values become significant. The focus is on the individual human moral dilemmas and their choice of good and evil as an important ethical dimension of judgment and prudence in decision-making. This is emphasized by Joseph L. Badaracco Jr. in his book *Defining Moments: When Managers Must Choose Between Right and Right* (1997), where the personal perspective on business ethics is analyzed. It is about "defining moments" and "right versus right dilemmas." Badaracco illustrates this with an example from the book by Kazuo Ishiguro, *The Remains of the Day* (1989), which was filmed with Anthony Hopkins in the role of the butler Stevens, who looks back on his life (Badaracco 1997). The key is how the main character has not been able to act ethically, but has always been guided by his role as butler. The tragedy in the film is that Stevens' moral judgment has failed in crucial moments (defining moments), as when he discovered that his master was a Nazi sympathizer, or when he chose duties over being with his dying father in his final hours. Managers and employees are confronted constantly with such tensions between personal values and organizational requirements. The question in these "right versus right" dilemmas, on the border of ethical theory and principles, is whether the individual keeps his or her integrity and dignity when having to make hard decisions that involve other people. Perhaps it is precisely these choices that testify to the necessity of ethics and ethical reflection in management. They shape the moral identity; they show the values applicable to the organization; and they challenge business theories. The ethical theories and principles are also important in these "right versus right" situations, but they can never be sufficient. There is always a tension between principles and concrete situations. There is no "morality machine" with which one without thinking can deduce the correct answers. At the same time we cannot ignore the need of the individual's judgment to create the right synthesis between ethical principles and facts in the moments that become "defining moments," where it is essential for a leader to make good and right decisions.

Ethics and economics. What is the connection?

The debate on the relationship between economics and ethics is about the nature and limits of economic responsibility, as well as its relation to the debate between egoism and altruism (Sen 1987; Caillé 2000; Salmon 2002; Priddat 2007, 2010; Rendtorff 2010; Friesen and Wolf 2014). In the ethical correction of the economy, the economic person is a subject who makes a financial calculation, extending it to include the other person and integrating it in justified moral norms. Aristotle (1999) emphasizes that wealth and money are not sought for its own sake, but as a means to something else. The economy was initially perceived as a "moral science," not only as a mechanical science, but as part of the "good art of government." Adam Smith (1759) emphasizes that the personal utility maximization is only one among many virtues (such as diligence, fairness, generosity, and public emotion). Although modern economy and organization theory have tended to regard themselves as ethically neutral, ethics is still present in the economy and organization and it can be considered as a task of organization ethics to make this connection more visible.

In this context, business ethics is based on the idea that the economy is not morally neutral, but already has an ethical basis. Mainstream economics generally has, as its fundamental basis, been referring to a selfish utility-maximizing individual who rationally seeks to satisfy his preferences. Amartya Sen criticizes for example, the modern economic theory of focusing only on the individual's benefit and thus forgetting the common interest's importance to the economy. Alternatively, business ethics is founded on another kind of economic anthropology, where ethics becomes a critical correction of *homo economicus* that considers utility maximization as the sole ethical standard.

Ethical theory's vision of "the good life with and for others in just institutions" is considered as what underlies any legitimate economic activity. In addition, we can mention respect for the universal duty or rule of ethics that requires taking into account the rights of all human beings in addition to the need to maximize as much as possible benefit and good to the greatest number. Only then we can justify the principle of individual utility maximization as the basis for action, but this must be done within the framework of the other ethical theories. Often there is a fundamental tension between ethics and economics, but there may also be a convergence between ethics and economics, where the economic arguments may seem like a designer of ethics. There can in some cases be an encounter between selfishness and altruism, where ethics and economics overlap. Many economic considerations can also be ethical, e.g. fair competition, resource awareness, and utility and profit maximization. Business ethics integrates economics and ethics in a mutually interdependent arena in which the two disciplines mutually form, determine, and develop each other. Ethics can be said to be the basis for the normative needs of the economy. The economic calculation with respect for the individualist, utilitarian, and liberalist paradigm is framed by an ethical responsibility, in which the economic actor enters into a relation of responsibility with the other person with rights and duties. With this vision of an ethical economy we are now able to move from the analysis of the ethical theories to the presentation of the historical foundations of cosmopolitan business ethics.

6 Historical foundations of cosmopolitan business ethics

Before we look at present concepts of cosmopolitan business ethics on the basis of the presentation of the theories of business ethics, we will in this section discuss the historical foundations of cosmopolitanism (Kemp 2005; Brown and Held 2010; Kemp 2011; Taraborrelli 2011; Rendtorff 2012). The concept of cosmopolitan norms is that they, as ethical norms, go beyond the legal order of the state, but they are also based on the positive norms of state sovereignty. The cosmopolitan norms indicate the right to have rights and at the same time they refer to the right of universal hospitality. There is also a close link between cosmopolitanism and human rights (Rendtorff 2012). In this sense, the cosmopolitan norms shape the rights of the republican state, although they come from outside this republic and as such do not have any formal legitimacy in the republic. The idea of cosmopolitan business ethics situates the business corporation as a good corporate citizen that becomes a cosmopolitan citizen as a good international citizen supporting the responsibility in the cosmopolitan legal order.

How was cosmopolitanism defined historically?

We need to define cosmopolitanism from its historical origins to the present day. Already in the philosophy of Immanuel Kant this project of cosmopolitanism implied both a "*Weltbürgerrecht*" with a duty of hospitality on the one hand and the right that governs the relation between nations on the other (Kleingeld 2012). Kant argued that the law of "World Citizenship" shall be limited to conditions of "universal hospitality." By this he meant that it is important to protect individuals in the development in the law of nations in relation to conditions of perpetual peace for an international order of power between states in the world of his time which consisted of the political and legal order among the states in Europe (Westphalian legal order).

But how should we define cosmopolitanism? One simple definition is the following: "Cosmopolitanism is the idea of the whole world as a frame of human life; the idea that it is more important to think in the name of humanity than in its parts: nationalities, ethnic groups, cultures." Belonging to a specific community is conceived as of secondary significance in relation to the basic fact of being human. Cosmopolitans say "Human first and after this citizen." In this sense the concept of cosmopolitanism is both a moral and a political category related to human rights, to diverse moral, political and religious systems, to the UN and EU, to globalization and multiculturalism, and to a number of proposals to reform international relations and to educational programs in states and in the international community (Sørensen and Thorup 2004: 7; Rendtorff 2012).

Cosmopolitanism makes us think of the city of cosmos, the cosmo-polis in the world community. The cosmopolitan is a citizen of the world society. We can say that the cosmopolitan is no longer submitted to the distinction between friend and enemy, them and us, outside and inside, citizen and stranger, but is supposed to mediate and transcend these dialectical double edges in the creation of the norms of the international community. Historically, we can mention two important origins of the concept of cosmopolitism. It was an ancient idea in Stoic philosophy, the culmination of the reflections of antiquity, and it was also proposed by the Roman Empire as a kind of justification of its universal power. What is important in the ancient idea is the universalization of the dignity of the human being beyond a specific community (Nussbaum 1997; Rendtorff 2012).

As cosmopolitanism plays an important role in the natural rights tradition, the concept was taken up by Kant and used in his reflections on the international state system in his defense of cosmopolitanism as a movement toward eternal peace. In fact, we must not forget that the concept of cosmopolitanism in Kant is double-edged in the sense that it appears in the context of the discussion of international law of sovereign states. Moreover, there might be a limitation to the Kantian concept of cosmopolitanism because he reduces the cosmopolitan right to the right of the individual to hospitality. At the same time, the concept is mobilized as Kant's criticism of his contemporary society dominated by colonialism and the force of the strongest.

Today, Stoic and Kantian conceptions are indeed very present in the debates about globalization, liberalization, and human rights. We may ask the question, what really is the relation between globalization and cosmopolitanism? In fact, sociologists such as Ulrich Beck and David Held emphasize that cosmopolitanism and globalization represent difficult challenges to the social sciences (Held 1995; Sørensen and Thorup 2004: 15; Rendtorff 2012). For example, in the process of creation of the European Union, we can perceive some version of the project of combining globalization with new political structures. The formation of Europe contains all the problems of cosmopolitanism at what we may call a "regional level."

In this context, a fundamental element of the concept of cosmopolitanism is the idea of tolerance. It is argued that the concept of hospitality in the idea of cosmopolitanism implies the recognition of the "otherness of the other," a fundamental right to be as one wants to be in a society with many forms of life. The importance of tolerance as a fundamental element of cosmopolitan society is that we have to deal with differences of cultures and nationalities in a world that becomes more and more globalized.

Here many people often talk about the cosmopolitan identity as a way to express a tolerant lifestyle. But is tolerance the only content of cosmopolitanism? Or does it give meaning to imagine cosmopolitan individuals who live in the world without a particular identity? According to a sociologist like Ulrich Beck it is indeed a paradox that we live in a European society with cosmopolitanism as a fundamental project while Europe at the same time is a society of nation states, based on nationalism so strong that we encounter many nation states that defend their values on nationalist grounds.

So maybe the European Union is after all very far from cosmopolitanism. We can argue that even though cosmopolitanism is a part of the European project, little has been done to integrate and develop Europe in cosmopolitan terms. Europeans still think in terms of the nation state and, for example, in Denmark the nationalist political movement is so strong that many Danes vote for movements and parties that are against the European community at times of election for the European Parliament. So it is indeed a challenge how to conceive Europe, not from the point of view of a federation, but in terms of cosmopolitan principles. This is, for example, the argument of Ulrich Beck, who thinks that we should try to be European in a cosmopolitan way. According to him, Europe should overcome the double edge and Europe should be reconceived not as the community of nations but as a cosmopolitan project!

David Held has a more global approach to the double edge of cosmopolitanism. He argues for a global transformation toward political cosmopolitanism (Held 1995; Thorup and Sørensen 2004: 27). According to him, we need a political transformation toward a political cosmopolitanism in the global community. The idea behind this is that in the present world we no longer have only "national communities of destiny" but we have "overlapping communities of destiny" where there are issues of climate change, economy, culture, communication, war, etc. At the international level we are more and more connected and connecting people in a cosmopolitan community. Therefore, we need to put something more into the concept of cosmopolitanism than hospitality. We need international political structures and also international market structures; here, corporations and businesses can contribute to the establishment of a cosmopolitan legal order.

David Held argues that when we deal with cosmopolitan values we have to define international structures of governance and decision-making that are appropriate from a cosmopolitan point of view (Held 1995; Sørensen and Thorup 2004: 15). The fundamental questions of cosmopolitanism that we are facing can be formulated in this way: What kind of governance do we need in the international community? How do we formulate an alternative to the neoliberalist idea of total pluralism and freedom? How can we define an integrated and more just international world order? What is world governance – federation or international civil cooperation? What is the role of civil society in this new community of international world governance? Does it really give meaning to talk about a cosmopolitan democracy? And what does such a democracy contain?

So with this move toward a political interpretation of cosmopolitanism going beyond the ethical idea of hospitality, we see that civil society is considered very important for the development of the global cosmopolitan order. We should mention here the importance of international civil society, where many forms of non-state actors like businesses and corporations contribute to create the cosmopolitan sphere between the states. Although corporations have a bad reputation, they are becoming important actors for forming such an international civil society. We can also mention international NGOs, e.g. Amnesty International or Human Rights Watch. They are all contributing to the formation of such a global civil society (Brown and Held 2010; Taraborrelli 2011). So we can say that non-state actors are constructing an international community of civil society that is essential for the formation and development of the cosmopolitan agenda of an international political community beyond nation states.

From historical cosmopolitanism to Kantian cosmopolitanism

How can we demonstrate the tensions and double edges of cosmopolitanism in the historical origins of the concept? And what really are the historical origins of the modern cosmopolitan project? Looking at Ancient Greece, we are already faced with dimensions of cosmopolitanism: Ulysses can be said to be cosmopolitan, with his travel all around the known world of the time. And Diogenes said: "I am a world citizen. I do not belong to a particular community in order to show the consequences of cosmopolitanism" (C. V. Sørensen 2004: 39; Rendtorff 2012).

In Ancient Greek society, cosmos is the order of the world as we know it. And polis is the concept of the city and the state. From the Greek perspective, the cosmo-polis is the global state or city. With this point of view we can argue that human beings belong to the polis. They are political animals – sociable human beings, members of the political community – but the Greek city state was also local, so there is already in the beginning a tension between local and international community in the concept of Greek cosmopolitanism. On the other hand, if we look deeper into the ideas of Socrates, according to later Stoic interpretations, we can see that Socrates conceived himself as a world citizen, a member of the world community. For example, the search for wisdom and the intellectual virtues of the educated philosopher go beyond the participation in the city state. Accordingly, Socrates argued from the perspective of cosmo-polis, that is, from the point of view of universality and of universal reason. When we speak about cosmopolitan business ethics as a global philosophy of management, the idea is to adopt this kind of universality of reason as the basis for business philosophy in the international community. Cosmopolitan business ethics implies the capacity of the business corporation to think and argue for cosmopolitan reason and engagement in society.

Stoic philosophy and the origins of cosmopolitanism

We can argue that the Stoic vision of cosmo-polis was fundamentally inspired by the philosophy of Socrates, who conceived the philosopher as in tension and beyond the nation state (Nussbaum 1997; Rendtorff 2012). The Stoic conception of cosmo-polis was present all through the development of this philosophy, culminating with the works of Seneca and Cicero. Fundamentally, the Stoic argument for cosmopolitanism was a moral argument based on reason. In particular, rationality and nature expressed universal dimensions of human dignity, which in Stoic philosophy were given a foundation in the cosmological participation of human beings in the totality of the world. The Stoics argued that there is a fundamental order of humanity that goes beyond the participation in the political community of the state. According to Stoic natural law theory, humanity is searching to conform to cosmic order of reason and we are striving toward cosmic unity where humanity is defined by the fact that human beings are intersubjectively related to the logos of cosmos and of the world. We can say that human beings belong to the common universal cosmos of reason and dignity. So the Stoic philosophy of cosmopolitanism represented a natural law which was going beyond the Aristotelian concept of the city state, where morality and politics was based on ethics and practical reason within that particular society. As a correction to Aristotelian philosophy of practical wisdom and judgment in the particular, the Stoic heritage is the heritage of universal natural law. It is a fundamental natural law related to the cosmos of humanity. The cosmic dimension of the law is the basis of the universality of natural law and this natural law includes the particular in the universal. In this sense, the Stoics wanted to solve the double edge and tension between the particular and the universal by arguing for a convergence between the laws of the polis and of the political community, and the universal law of cosmos.

In order to solve the double edge of the universal and the particular the Stoics argued that the universal natural law is incarnated in the customs and ethics of each human culture as an expression of common humanity (Nussbaum 1997). As both citizen and individual, human beings have a universal significance that points to their position in the cosmo-political order that goes beyond the particular state. It is a basic moral principle (according to the Stoics) that particular human beings in all their actions should see themselves as inscribed in a larger social order of society, and the idea of world citizenship expresses this moral responsibility of individuals to transcend their particular point of view and see the world from the point of view of common humanity. In the Roman Empire the political consequence of this doctrine was conceived as the idea of common institutions for the whole world. Emperor Marcus Aurelius wanted to create such a Stoic world community. Here, we have early manifestations of the idea of a global community of a common world state and world governance. Marcus Aurelius says that human beings belong to two cities. He calls them the community within the state community and the community within the world community. Seneca sees cosmopolitanism as the unity as the duties as a citizen and of the duties as a member of the world community – if you have no duties as a citizen nevertheless you have duties as a human being. The Stoics were also aware of the potential solitude of cosmopolitan human beings. This is perhaps an existentialist double edge of cosmopolitanism. There is the danger of a rootless loneliness where there are no local limits left. There is the danger of the nostalgic search for a group or a state that an individual starts in order to escape the anguish of solitude of having nowhere to belong (Nussbaum 1997).

With Christian religion we see a continuation of this connection between humanity, society, and the fraternity of community. The Christians emphasized the universality of human dignity beyond the participation in and belonging to a particular community. The potential tension between universal and particular which was present in Stoic philosophy is repeated in the Kantian concept of cosmopolitanism (Lettevall 2004: 55; Rendtorff 2012). We can say that Kant, as a child of the philosophy of the enlightenment, went beyond a somewhat superficial cosmopolitanism of popular culture but also in the reception of earlier philosophy toward a fully developed theory of world citizenship.

Kant's position should in this way be seen in contrast to some of the ideas of his time. He was critical toward cultural cosmopolitanism (which was popular in his time) because it did not go deep enough to understand the moral and political consequences of cosmopolitanism. Kant wanted to go deeper than cultural cosmopolitanism. Cultural cosmopolitans see cosmopolitanism as a way of life. They travel, they read, and they are interested in other cultures. That was the European cosmopolitanism. This concept of cosmopolitanism was linked to tolerance and humanism in French enlightenment tradition from the 17th century. To travel around the world was seen as an aristocratic ideal. This cosmopolitanism indeed expresses the double edge of the concept: there was a potential tension between cosmopolitanism and patriotism in cultural cosmopolitanism, because many people were worried that cosmopolitanism would destroy patriotism. Many people also argued that cosmopolitism destroyed the sense of belonging to a community so that the cultural cosmopolitanism makes the human being become a detached individual who has lost his relation to history and culture (Lettevall 2004: 55; Rendtorff 2012).

Kant's moral and political cosmopolitanism is a fundamental argument against this double edge of cosmopolitanism. He wants to go beyond cultural cosmopolitanism. In defense of eternal peace, Kant argues for a cosmopolitan political and legal order, and for cosmopolitan citizenship. The basis for this law of world citizenship is universal human rights, and the rights of individuals in the international community should be protected because of the universal values and dignity of human beings. According to Kant, it is very important to recognize respect for public human rights as a fundamental step toward perpetual peace in the world community.

In his formulation of such universal human rights, Kant argues for the right of world citizenship but he also restricts this right to the right of hospitality. In this sense, due to his submission to state sovereignty, he is still marked by the double edge of cosmopolitanism. The right to visit and to be recognized as a visitor and respected as a stranger is a central dimension to the cosmopolitan vision of citizenship. Accordingly, Kantian cosmopolitanism is formulated as the right to hospitality with the position that he argues, that the law of peoples must be based on hospitality and the right to visit a foreign country. From the Kantian perspective, international law and world citizen law are not the same. State citizenship is not a condition for world citizenship, but we have to recognize fundamental moral rights of human beings that go beyond the citizen rights as a member of the nation state. So the Kantian concept of cosmopolitan rights is potentially very weak. It seems like it is nothing more than some version of respect for international humanitarian rights. It is characteristic of the Kantian notion of the law of peoples that it is limited to the right to moral humanitarian rights rather than being a vision of legal and political rights in the international community. Maybe Kant proposes this limitation as a critique of the Western concept of colonialism (Lettevall 2004).

However, there must be something more to the Kantian concept of cosmopolitan rights. It cannot be restricted to the legal right of hospitality. We must argue that from the point of view of cosmopolitanism every human being belongs to the realm of freedom which goes beyond the limitations by the state. If we compare Kantian and Stoic cosmopolitanism, Kant also wanted to justify human dignity and rationality beyond the limits of the nation state. Stoic cosmopolitism understood the separation of human beings in particular communities. It was aware of the importance of uniting human beings in a common vision, and this is also the project of Kant. We can say, with Martha Nussbaum (1997), that Stoic cosmopolitanism requires adults with a strong capacity to be themselves, and this idea is also present in Kantian cosmopolitanism. So the Kantian search for eternal peace is inspired by the Stoic conception of cosmopolitanism (Brown and Held 2010; Taraborrelli 2011). In both philosophies, dignity and freedom are universal ideas for the development of humanity that go beyond the politics of identity and culture of a particular community. And this is the foundation of cosmopolitan business ethics.

7 The citizen of the world and education of humanity for world citizenship

The Danish philosopher Peter Kemp, who is the president of the international study group Eco-Ethica, uniting philosophers from the East and the West, provides a modern interpretation of the concept of cosmopolitanism with his interpretation of Immanuel Kant's concept of the citizen of the world from a modern perspective (Kemp 2011; Rendtorff 2012). This view of the world situation constitutes an excellent basis for the concept of the world citizen in cosmopolitan business ethics. This perspective combines pedagogic and political philosophy, relating them to globalization and cosmopolitanism with a conceptual and historical perspective. The idea of cultivating humanity for world citizenship is based on the vision of the need to educate young children to be citizens of the world who can deal with the great problems of humanity for our civilization, i.e. the problem of the financial crisis, the clash of civilizations, and the need for sustainable development of humanity in order to survive. The central theme of the book is how to educate humanity to be able to deal with its common problems. This social and political ideal goes back to ancient philosophy and it has been an ideal for philosophers like Diogenes, Cicero, and Seneca. The Stoic philosophy talked about world citizenship in the world today. In particular, Immanuel Kant was also someone who advocated the idea of world citizenship (Kemp 2011).

The concept of the citizen of the world

If we try to interpret this concept of world citizenship for the present world we can argue that the citizen of the world today should be able to deal with its current problems: "international criminality, genocide, terrorism, state terrorism, struggle for domination" (Kemp 2011: 25). In the present world, we are confronted with the danger of total domination as described in *Empire* by Hardt and Negri (2001). But we have also descriptions of the need for cosmopolitan governance, as it is described by David Held in *Democracy and the Global Order* (1995). On this line of thought we can define the task of world citizenship as confronting the "eco-typical key problems" of today. When we talk about sustainable development we try to focus on the key problems in the world and we are also facing the ambiguities of globalization between casino capitalism and world financial markets, with the danger of global economic crisis on the one hand, confronted with the possibilities of the global village and knowledge society on the other. Financial globalization may in some cases lead to the "parade of the horrible" (Kemp 2011) which has led to the proposal of another globalization (altermondialization) by social movements like Attack. It shows how globalization is a process with both negative and positive consequences with the market and its contradictions (Kemp 2011).

There is also a paradox of the nation state as it is described by Montesquieu in the spirit of the laws. The nation state is a cultural experience, and the problem is whether there can be a revolution of the nation state in direction of cosmopolitanism without a reformation. Another issue is whether we can go from the state to cosmopolitanism or whether cosmopolitanism means that we have to declare that it is over with the nation state. In some sense the European Union can be seen as an image of the cosmopolitan nation state where the states are left to the universal. The European Union is the universal in the small. In fact in Nussbaum we have the idea of cultivating humanity where we should be educated in a multicultural cosmopolitanism in order to deal with world culture clash. The capacity to deal with cosmopolitanism is based on the ability to participate in a multicultural dialogue including: (1) everyday conversation; (2) intellectual conversation; (3) the listening conversation; (4) intense conversation (Kemp 2011).

The education for cosmopolitanism is an education to go beyond the clash of civilizations toward a global conversation of understanding. Peter Kemp presents a hermeneutic philosophy to overcome the clash of civilizations. From the perspective of this hermeneutic philosophy we would have to learn more about the other instead of fighting the other. To learn more about the other is based on training in cosmopolitanism and it is a hope for cosmopolitanism, says Peter Kemp (2011), inspired by Martha Nussbaum.

It is the vision or utopia of sustainability that would have to function as this realization of the hope for cosmopolitanism. The hope for sustainability is based on the "long term vision of the good life in the context of nature" (Kemp 2011: 74). Peter Kemp takes as his starting point the Brundtland Report of the United Nations World Commission on Environment and Development (1987), when he defines the concept of sustainability. Sustainability includes ethical, social, scientific, economic, and legal dimensions of sustainable development. Sustainability also contains an element of justice related to fair distribution of resources, capabilities, and possibilities all over the globe. Sustainable development relates to our responsible behavior toward the environment. The ethical dimension is primarily the effort to give future generations the right to life and the justice of sustainable development is also justice toward future generations. The scientific dimension implies the respect for vulnerable nature and that we should work the existence of genuine human life in the future. The economic dimension implies economic and social equity and respect for the fact that every human being has the right to genuine "environmental space." The legal dimension implies the realization of laws that realize this economic dimension.

In general, law and ethics should be based on the consideration of the other, from what Peter Kemp calls the "anthropocentrifugal perspective," which can be considered as an ethics of the Anthropocene, where the human respect for ethics and morality is extended to the other, i.e. the rights of animals, plants and the whole living biosphere. Thus, the fundamental question is how a human world can exist in the future (Kemp 2011). Kemp argues that we should at least adopt a weak concept of sustainable development as a self-evident ethical ideal for the future. He defends a close relation between utopia and responsibility. According to Kant, utopia is a political creation, a world that one can hope for and realize through reformation, not revolution. For Kemp, the vision of citizen of the world as an ideal of education closely linked to sustainability belongs to a future-oriented concept of utopia that is a guiding star for the global development of the world. This concept of utopia is linked to responsibility in the sense that human beings have responsibility for educating children and for the future of mankind so that there will be sustainable life on Earth in the future. Kemp is here inspired by Kant, Ernst Bloch, and Hans Jonas's ethics of responsibility. So with Jonas we can demand a cultivation of education for concrete responsibility for sustainable development. Kemp says that "the citizen of the world in us all" is an integrated utopia or ideal in the consciousness of those who have responsibility.

It is essential that Peter Kemp develops the concept of cosmopolitanism related to the individual. But we may ask, what is the relation to world government? It seems that this question remains unanswered. We can ask a question about sustainability: Is sustainability enough as an ideal for world development? It is important that Kemp goes beyond the utilitarian definition of sustainability, but is this really possible? Yes, we would answer. This is exactly the idea of a responsible cosmopolitan ethics for the future of humanity that can provide this concern.

The history of the world citizen in the framework of the history of cosmopolitanism

From the perspective of his hermeneutic approach, Peter Kemp analyzes the history of the concept of the world citizen on the foundations of the history of cosmopolitanism. He argues that we can trace the concept back as part of a world history of ideas both in European thought and in other cultures, for example in Confucianism. The concept of the citizen of the world depends on universalist thinking, which is developed in travel and in the encounter with others. Travel is dangerous and therefore hospitality to strangers (*proxenos*) becomes a virtue of cosmopolitanism (Kemp 2011). Indeed, travel was important for development of history and philosophy in the Greek world, e.g. with the writings of Homer about Odysseus. It is important to analyze the concept of world in order to define the world citizen. World refers to *kosmos*, world system, or world as a "whole." With world citizenship we refer to the world as a unity. The citizen (*polítes*) is someone who is free to deliberate about the future of the state, so the cosmopolitan (*kosmopolítes*) is a world citizen who freely deliberates about the future of the world, for whom the world is his homeland. He sees himself like Anaxagoras in the 5th century before Christ as belonging to a cosmos or an order. Later the emperor Alexander the Great became a true cosmopolitan. Like the Stoic philosopher Cicero he regarded world citizenship as a condition for good world citizenship.

In this sense, it was indeed in Stoicism that the concept of cosmopolitanism was developed. In order to speak as a *kosmopolites* it was necessary for the Stoic to understand him or herself as a citizen of the world as a cosmos. The living creature chooses in accord with nature in the cosmos. The life-force becomes reason (*logos*) and by choosing the correct action the individual chooses to live in accordance with nature. Cicero continued Stoic thinking and he saw the presentation of *humanitas* (humanity, humanness) as an ideal. According to Kemp, *humanitas* involves aspects of cultivation, liberal education, formation of character, generosity and magnanimity, piety, considerateness, and the natural unfolding of innate abilities. Care and justice and honesty are related to those concepts. The idea of the citizen of the world is that individual takes part of a "community of mankind" that is integrated through the law of peoples with world society. In this sense Cicero and the Stoics were predecessors of the law of peoples, along with Hugo Grotius and the UN Charter.

Later Stoicists united world and heaven and Epictetus said "I am of the world, I am God's son." Markus Aurelius saw himself as a citizen of the universe and he argued for a common universe where everything was interwoven. In Christianity, cosmopolitanism was further developed. The Christians made a connection between world reason and world citizenship, and the Christian universalism became prophetic and eschatological cosmopolitanism directed toward the hope for a better world. For example the cosmopolitanism in Aurelius Augustine's *The City of God* represents this Stoicism where we face a universal Catholic community founded on world citizenship and peace. This idea of the law of peoples was further developed by Thomas Aquinas in his theory of natural law with the different concepts of *lex humana* (human law) and *lex naturalis* (which holds for every living creature, where human beings had inclination toward life with other human beings and search for the divine. We can on this basis ask, why we should educate people to be world citizens? Why is it so important to be cultivated as a citizen of the world? Is there the danger of detachment of the local culture? And are we not in danger of being cynical if we live as detached? Indeed we may ask how we help to educate for world citizenship so that world citizenship becomes engaged and responsible world citizenship!

Modern cosmopolitanism

Modern cosmopolitanism may be said to start with Dante who declared "My country is my whole world" and added "Can I not everywhere behold the light of the sun and stars" (Kemp 2011: 123). With Hugo Grotius, international law later developed as the law of states, but still the ancient concept of world citizenship was behind this law of states. For example, with the ideal of the League of Nations that later became the United Nations we can say that the UN Charter contains the oppositions between the law of states and the law of the international community – international law.

It is, however, with Immanuel Kant that we find the real development of the movement from the international law of states to cosmopolitan law (Kleingeld 2012). Kant's concept of citizen of the world was conceived as a key concept. Kant argued that the function of law is to make the kingdom of ends possible in the metaphysics of morals. The kingdom of ends is a function of the categorical imperative according to which man should act according to a universal law. Therefore jurisprudence is also subject to the categorical imperative. Essentially also the function of law is to protect the right to freedom in the light of the categorical imperative. According to Kant, public law relates to a group of people who are citizens in a society and who relate to each other, but when we deal with the relations between these groups we have the law of states.

Beyond that, Kant also defined cosmopolitan law which, according to Kemp, should be understood as an internal relation between peoples and individuals that occurs in international law, and Kant would call this cosmopolitan law. The problem with state law is that the states close themselves in relation to one another. International law is, for example, primarily a law of the rules of warfare and the right to peace. International law concerns the relation between just and unjust wars. However, to move to a permanent congress of states in an international state seems to Kant to be unrealistic.

According to Kant, the idea of cosmopolitan law becomes a supplementary notion. Cosmopolitan law seeks peace based on the fact that we live on the same globe. Cosmopolitan law implies a peaceful relation between peoples and includes the right to hospitality. Cosmopolitan law aims at creating a society of freedom enforced by the law of just civil constitutions. The cosmopolitan society is the highest goal of mankind and the hidden plan of nature. In order to realize this ideal, Kant laid great emphasis on the concept of the citizen of the world.

We can see John Rawls' theory of the law of peoples as a development of Kant's concept of international law, even though Rawls does not agree with Kant's cosmopolitanism. Rawls wants to be realistic and therefore he does not regard cosmopolitanism as the most important principle. But, he defends a kind of liberal citizen working for justice as fairness in the international community. However, Peter Kemp thinks that we have to move beyond both Kant's concept of world citizen and Rawls' liberal citizen because in our times the required responsibilities and hopes for the world citizen must be much greater.

We may ask, how it is possible to move from liberal citizenship to the concept of world citizenship? How can I be responsible for everything in the world and how can I act as a citizen in relation to states and communities where I have to direct political citizenship? Moreover, we may ask what the ideal of the world citizen really implies for world government. It seems that it is possible to be a world citizen without being part of a society of a world government, but large institutional questions remain, or may we say that world citizenship is the condition for dealing with international problems?

Educational philosophy as philosophical hermeneutics

On the foundation of the discussions of international law we can develop the concept of the citizen of the world as an ideal for education in the 21st century (Kemp 2011). So therefore Peter Kemp argues that reflection on the citizen of the world is one of the most important tasks for a future philosophy of education. This idea of philosophy of education goes back to Plato and Aristotle in classical Greece. In Plato's academy the idea of virtue, principle and reason, and education of a wise man was a central preoccupation. Plato and Aristotle ask for rational cultivation of reason according to the principal of *paideia*, to teach wisdom to the student. *Paideia* was translated by Cicero into the concept of *humanitas*, humanity, human culture, or today, "cultivation." For Hegel, the philosopher of German idealism, there was a close connection between cultivation and the development of spirit in the phenomenology of spirit in the course of history.

This idea of cultivation is central to Peter Kemp's vision of education for the world citizen. Education means to provide people with a cultural upbringing to give them an ethical goal. In modern society, due to complexity of knowledge, cultivation is closely related to knowledge. Cultivation means "elevation to humanity." Accordingly, today we cannot have a sharp distinction between cultivation and instruction in the concept of education. On this basis, Peter Kemp argues that the goal of cultivation and instruction is to promote: (1) insight and maturation in young people individually and generally, that is, both personally and as citizens of society; (2) adult learning throughout a lifetime, not as an ever-increasing burden but as a continual openness to new experience; (3) cultivation and instruction for "the good life with and for others in just institutions" which is based on Ricoeur's definition of ethics.

Peter Kemp refers to Hans Jonas, who says in *The Imperative of Responsibility* (1979), "The Parent-Child relation is the archetype of responsibility" to understand the concept of responsibility in education. So the teacher must learn how to take responsibility in learning for the child and transfer to this responsibility for the child so that the child also has responsibility for learning.

When referring to Ricoeur, Peter Kemp argues that "cultivation and instruction are not and cannot be value-neutral, cannot be without a vision of the good life, a relationship to others and a desire for a just social order to realize this vision" (2011: 158). He relies on Ricoeur's ethics to understand vision of the good life implied in the practical wisdom of education. Education is a function of the existential life-plan of the individual and this is also integrated in the common life-plan of living together in a community. So education is a part of our proposal of living together in just institutions and we are also responsible for this process of learning.

So Peter Kemp emphasizes that philosophy of education is a humanistic ideal focusing on the development of a historical, empirical, and logical consciousness and directed toward axiological consciousness where the philosophy of education becomes a kind of educational enterprise of reflective thinking. Cultivation becomes moral training and there is a close connection between cultivation and instruction, like in the relation between explanation and understanding.

For philosophers like Hegel and Marx, cultivation was an important element of historical development. But this was what the existentialist philosophers like Nietzsche and Kierkegaard were against. The debate is repeated in modern times between structure and actor and between existentialism and structuralism, where Sartre says: "The essential thing is not what one has done with man but what he does with what one has done with him" (cited by Kemp 2011: 167). So cosmopolitan education is against reductionism, although it is not against understanding human beings in their historical and scientific context between explanation and understanding – maybe a little bit as it is explained by Sartre with his progressive–regressive method.

Peter Kemp proposes philosophy of education as hermeneutics. In particular he refers to the concept of mimesis as central for understanding the transmission of knowledge. Inspired by Rousseau he can talk about enlightenment for life seeing education as "ethical-aesthetic affair." Kant also talks about the art of education that is dependent on a person's judgment and the search for perfection. Important in this art is, from the hermeneutic perspective, the art of understanding. As hermeneutics, philosophy of education also deals with a vision of the good life. Philosophy of education is a hermeneutic art that deals with the science of understanding as hermeneutics.

Accordingly, Kemp proposes a history of hermeneutics as essential to pedagogical philosophy. Hermeneutics is a theory and phenomenology of understanding that is also defined as critical hermeneutics. Kemp discusses the history of hermeneutics back to Kant, Schleiermacher, Schopenhauer, Marx, Nietzsche, and Dilthey. Kant proposed interpretation of beautiful for forms in his critique of judgment. Marx referred to the concept of interpretation when he says that it has to be put into practice and for Nietzsche the world is a world of interpretation. Dilthey can be said to try to collect the different approaches in a general theory of historical interpretation as an expression of life. This was further developed in Heidegger's concept of the hermeneutics, where the concept of *Dasein* is. an expression of Dilthey's concept of life (*Leben*) (Kemp 2011).

In modern times the hermeneutic approach was in particular developed by Gadamer, who in his work on truth and method makes cultivation of the individual for the human sciences an essential element of the hermeneutic approach. With his concept of experience of a work of art and *Wirkungsgeschichte*, a history of effects and his concept of legitimate prejudges as essential for understanding, Gadamer makes a foundation in his concept of the "fusion of horizons" (Kemp 2011).

We may ask, why is it really the hermeneutic approach that is essential for philosophy of education? It could be argued that with the complexity of the modern world with all its technology and scientific developments the hermeneutic approach cannot stand alone but must be accomplished with a multitude of disciplines in order to understand the complexity of the human phenomenon. Here we can ask, is the hermeneutic approach nothing more than a foundation that needs critical accomplishment by the sciences?

Educational philosophy as based on mimesis

The French philosopher Paul Ricoeur is for Peter Kemp (2011) the most important hermeneutical philosopher. He has developed the triple mimesis based on prefiguration, configuration, and refiguration understood as "emplotment" or enactment as the most important concept in hermeneutic philosophy. Kemp translates Ricoeur's theory of mimesis into a theory of hermeneutic figuration. This model can be used for understanding the moment of cultivation. It is a circle of understanding from the lived world of acts and events over text to the process of understanding in the mind of the individual.

Peter Kemp also uses mimesis to understand the pedagogical moment of understanding as such. He says that the pupil imitates the master and he wants to do what the master does just a little bit better. Kemp (2011) refers to his own experience as a reader and writer to understand the mimesis saying that when he read Sartre, Merleau-Ponty, and others, he just wanted to do it a little bit better. The idea is that the student should imitate the master, not just cultivate him or herself on their own terms. However, strangely enough, the idea of mimesis has been repressed in most educational theory, for example, with regard to copyright today where one is no longer allowed to mimic others and where it is considered wrong to mimic others.

Mimesis and imitation has been strongly criticized, for example by Luther, who says creative productive life is a part of imitation. However, for example, Rene Girard rediscovers the need for imitation in the teacher–student relation. Students are today in the dilemma between imitate me – do not imitate me. This dilemma can end in violence, so we need another way out of the dilemma. Therefore we need to find a new relation of imitation. In fact, there is new research on apprenticeship going on today. Peter Kemp (2011) mentions that we need creative mimesis in the master–pupil relation and we need to redefine the master–student relationship beyond a strict conception of authority. Initially we seek to be like the master but then we also strive to move beyond the master.

So mimesis should be considered as productive imitation in cultivation and instruction. Mimesis is considered as creative mimesis. It is through this creative mimesis that the student is made autonomous and although the teacher forms the student the student also forms him or herself. And after a while the teacher also becomes a student of the student – so there is a mutual relation beyond authority.

Here we may ask the question, is it legitimate to make educational philosophy into mimesis? What about creativity and innovation? Can the concept of mimesis really include the dimensions of creativity and innovation? What is missing from these aspects when we define education with mimesis? Are we back in a kind of Platonian idealism? Moreover, we can ask, how does mimesis relate to ideals of originality and anti-plagiarism that are so dominant in today's discussions of university education?

Cosmopolitanism as political philosophy

On this basis, Peter Kemp (2011) discusses the need for a philosophy of education in the framework of a cosmopolitan theory of cultivation. He argues that we need an educational-philosophical hermeneutics and a normative-cosmopolitan theory of cultivation in modern society. This philosophy of education is also a philosophy of emancipation conceived as critical hermeneutics in the tension between explanation and understanding, where Kemp, with Ricoeur, emphasizes that to "Explain more is to understand better" (Kemp 2011). But hermeneutics is also critical hermeneutics as it was the result of a confrontation between Habermas and Gadamer with regard to the debate about critique of ideology, where Habermas mentions the technical, practical, and liberating knowledge interests. With Ricoeur, Kemp unites explanation and understanding with a critique of ideology in the concept of critical hermeneutics.

Important for philosophy of education is the development of the self and transmission of knowledge to the self. The philosophy of hermeneutics is about interpreting self and others in the community. Education is also about discipline and socialization and relates to the development of the self in its different contexts. Here Kemp (2011) refers to Paul Ricoeur's concept of oneself as another where the concept of the good life is tested according to the moral norm. Practical wisdom and critical social thinking relates to development of the self in its different contexts. Here, we can refer to the development of pedagogical hermeneutics where hermeneutics is closely defined in relation to the science of education. It is about cultivation of the implied people. Kemp emphasizes the importance of cultivation: "Cultivation then is what becomes a category of the student's own intellectual life" (2011: 212). But this does exclude the educational critique of ideology and the need for emancipation. Critical hermeneutics is also critical pedagogy. But true politization is, like cultivation, a well-considered theory of cultivation in relation to "epoch-typical key problems" (2011: 217).

The problem then is how to educate children in relation to being able to deal with epoch-typical key problems of the modern world: financial globalization, relationship between nations and cultures, and the globe's sustainability for future generations. Here we can say that the ideal of the citizen of the world is essential for the development of pedagogical treatment of children. Indeed, the problem of education is a problem of political construction. The ideal of the global cosmopolitan is that it deals with education in relation to the state and it also deals with how the state is responsible for the construction of individuality. Indeed, the problem also is how institutions are contributing to the cultivation of individuals. We may emphasize that not only individuals but the relation to society is important for "cosmopolitan cultivation of human beings." So what is needed is education toward the cosmopolitan world order where the individuals have the power to shape the moral. It was indeed the dream of Durkheim to see the state as educator. Kemp mentions, for example, that in the debate about the Iraq war it could be seen as the educational responsibility of politicians to contribute to the education of the citizens. As Kemp states, the true citizen of the world is able to detect lies in politics and the citizen of the world is also able to evaluate world problems, i.e. war problems, critically. Bergson referred, for example, to "what can open the closed society" as the task of this kind of society.

We can say that it is the task of citizenship education to respect every human being as a rational creature. The formation of the self as a world citizen is central to education. Human self-actualization is central to this realization both in relation to the individual and collectively. But as Habermas says, "No emancipation without ethics." It is a project of the education of the child to be a good citizen and to live in a cosmopolitan community, but not without respecting the irreplaceability of the multiplicity of culture. We need to see the culture as a part of the individual and protect the individual as a part of the culture (Kemp 2011). This is an essential dimension of the cosmopolitan self in the 21st century. The good student and pupil is someone who learns this concern for cosmopolitanism by learning through imitation and transforming experience into useful knowledge of the real world as suggested by pragmatic ideals of learning as a reconstructing and reorganizing experience. The global cosmopolitan ideal is to teach individuals to take an active part in a global political community (Kemp 2011).

Peter Kemp's theory of the world citizen has accordingly provided the philosophical foundation for cosmopolitan business ethics. This is a framework of critical hermeneutics that suggests historical and political cosmopolitanism as the basis for cosmopolitanism in economic ethics. We can say that the framework of world citizenship is the basis for cosmopolitan business ethics. Indeed, the idea of educating humanity is important for developing a cosmopolitan spirit of management and leadership in corporations.

8 Responsibility, ethical economy, and order ethics in globalization

What is the state of cosmopolitan business ethics in the context of contemporary philosophy of management? Now, we will present the major paradigms of cosmopolitan business ethics from the perspective of continental European and German business ethics (*Wirtschaftsethik*). With the examination of these traditional paradigms and schools of business ethics we can analyze their potential for developing cosmopolitan business ethics as a global philosophy of management. In Germany, as a relatively large academic community with many scholars and professors, a school formation of business ethics has developed since the beginning of the discipline in the 1970s. These schools have had importance nationally in Germany, although they have not been very important internationally and they are nearly unknown in the context of Anglo-Saxon business ethics. In the following, it is my aim to present these different schools of German business ethics in order to contribute to the international debate on cosmopolitan business ethics.

European schools of business ethics and philosophy of management

In this presentation of the schools of business the concept of the relation between economics and philosophy and politics is important. How can we apply this to the future of the business corporation? What is the legitimacy of the school in relation to this? What is the criticism of the idea of the school in this context? We could apply the concept of philosophy, management, and politics in relation to the schools of business ethics. What is the grand theory in this context? What is the international context of cosmopolitanism and the future for the business of the international society? This chapter addresses both issues of the international importance of the business ethics theories and it also addresses the concept of cosmopolitanism addressed in the different concepts of business ethics of the theories. In this context the chapter also addresses the concept of business ethics at the micro-, macro-, and meso-levels of society in order to look at the particularities of each school of business ethics. The concept of *Wirtschaftsethik* includes ontology, epistemology, and normativity, as well as the micro-, meso-, and macro-levels.

The deeper question therefore is: How can the whole debate of *Wirtschaftsethik* be translated to the global society? In fact, each school seems to work with a particular ontology and epistemology that have an influence on their definition of their fundamental concepts of business ethics and ethical economy. The concept of business ethics in each school involves a vision of the thought process relating to fundamental conceptions of the aim and meaning of philosophy. Maybe the concept of business ethics in Germany is restricted to a certain space and cannot be translated. But the vision is that

Wirtschaftsethik in the German sense may be applied all over the world. This is the vision for a global society. How can we assure this? With this presentation of the schools of business ethics in German society I hope to respond to these questions.

The ethics of responsibility

The ethics of responsibility was, as already mentioned, developed by the German-Jewish philosopher Hans Jonas with his book *The Imperative of Responsibility* (1979), written in the United States, to which Jonas had emigrated during the Second World War. The ethics of responsibility has been developed by the philosopher of technology Hans Lenk and his colleague Matthias Maring from Karlsrue. Although their position is not really defined as a school of business ethics in the strict sense, this approach can be said to propose an important framework for business ethics.

This approach to the ethics of responsibility begins with a general approach to ethics and integrates the particular debates about business ethics in this framework. The ethics of responsibility is critical toward a position that bases ethics only on economics. It is also critical toward a discourse ethical program of foundations, although it shares many points of view of integrative business ethics, searching to integrate ethics and economics rather than keeping them apart. Moreover, the ethics of responsibility is critical toward a religious foundation of ethics as suggested by different theological approaches. Instead the ethics of responsibility proposes a concrete framework for ethical reflection. This is a framework of what Hans Lenk calls "*Konkrete Humanitätsethik,*" i.e. concrete ethics of humanity. This ethics of humanity addresses the problem of responsibility in relation to different areas of applied ethics, i.e. ethics of the sciences, bioethics, business ethics, and other fields of applied ethics (Maring 2014). However, it is argued that the fields of ethics should not be considered as fundamentally different from the general approach to ethics based on the ethics of responsibility and of concrete humanity.

An often-stated criticism of the ethics of responsibility is that it is future-oriented and therefore seems to forget the present. It is therefore important to remember that the imperative of responsibility is not only oriented toward the future or the past but indeed also directed toward the past and the present. The scope of responsibility depends on power and position. Responsibility should not necessarily be defined as absolute but it is also a question of co-responsibility and common concern. One is responsible when one has to decide between a number of possible choices of action.

In the work of Matthias Maring, responsibility is extended from individuals to corporations. It is accordingly possible to work with responsibility at the collective and systemic level of organizations. We can argue for a secondary moral responsibility at the level of action systems in organizations. It is possible to talk about action in systems and systemic actions. Systems can be ascribed responsibility as organizational systems of actions. This is the basis for an economic ethic based on responsibility in the business sciences.

The ethics of responsibility in cosmopolitan business ethics proceeds otherwise than is the case in a discourse ethical approach to foundations of business ethics. Also in contrast to the program of foundation of critical rationalism, the ethics of responsibility proposes some moral rules and principles as a basis for action without beginning with the efforts of moral foundations. This approach is based on a hierarchical three-step construction of the moral rules of rights and negative and positive utilitarianism. First, we can mention the principle of responsibility. After this, principles of respect for basic rights are important, and finally the calculations concerning utility. This is an attempt to give the ethics of responsibility a concrete content for decision-making.

Ludger Heidbrink, a professor from Kiel, is inspired by the philosophy of responsibility. He develops a philosophy of responsibility which can be said to integrate responsibility and cosmopolitan business ethics. This approach tries to define the ontological foundations of global corporate responsibility (Heidbrink 2008). In this context it is important to perform concrete analysis of relations of responsibility in specific cases of business ethics.

This ethics of responsibility can be combined with the study of responsibility in particular cases of business ethics or other fields of ethics, for example, whistle-blowing in information ethics. The case-oriented ethics approach is inspired by US business ethics, which has been focusing on the study of cases as the basis for decision-making. By looking at responsibility relations in concrete cases it is possible to understand the scope and basis of responsibility, for example when it is discussed whether the German government is responsible for the underpayment of employees in the sweat-shop factories in developing countries.

This ethics of responsibility could also be considered as the basis for understanding the impact of corporate social responsibility. The concept of CSR can be related to the fundamental ethical and political responsibility for concrete humanity that is suggested by the ethics of responsibility. This concrete responsibility for humanity is a realization of the concept of universal responsibility at the level of particular individuals in society. Responsibility expresses concrete concern for human beings in socio-technical organizational systems.

Ethics and economics or ethical economy: A framework for business ethics

The discussion about ethics and economics and the focus on the idea of economic ethics or ethical economy as an important concept of cosmopolitanism was initiated by the philosopher and economist Peter Koslowski, who for many years worked on the relation between ethics and economics. He was particularly interested in the principles of ethical economy, and later he also applied this discussion to the foundations of philosophy of management and corporations. Koslowski wanted to develop a philosophy of ethics and economics or ethical economy. In his book *Principles of Ethical Economy* (2008) we find the basis for such an approach to philosophy of management. The book argues that ethics and economics must accept one another and unite themselves in a comprehensive theory of rational action (Koslowski 2008: 1). With the idea of ethical economy we find a contribution to defining the outline of the discussion of the relation between ethics and economy in cosmopolitan business ethics.

According to Koslowski's ethical economy, which combined hermeneutics with catholic social theory in relation to the conceptualization of market and society, there is a close interaction between culture, ethics, and economics in the definition of the basis for economic markets. According to this definition, economic ethics or ethical economy is a theory of the economy and of ethics. As an ethical economy it unites ethical and economic judgments and constitutes the complement of political economy. Ethical economy and political economy are linked to macro-economic and economic theory of rational action. But we can also make a connection between ethical economy and business ethics and philosophy of management. In this sense the relation between ethical economy and the philosophy of management and corporation is that ethical economy proposes the analysis of the institutional and economic frame of the reflections about philosophy of management and corporations.

Following this approach to ethics and economics we can propose a general definition of the general approach to philosophy of management and corporations (Koslowski 1988a, 1988b). This approach focuses on issues like the ontology and epistemology of organizations, including issues of business ethics and practical philosophy of management. But we can also say that it opens reflections on business ethics in the framework of hermeneutics and reflective judgment. This approach to ethics and economics is not only hermeneutic and Aristotelian, as well as inspired by Thomas Aquinas' view of economics, but it also implies a Kantian view of the legitimacy of business ethics. We can say that Immanuel Kant's distinction between theoretical, practical, and aesthetic reason and judgment helps to define the basis for economics and ethics applied to corporations, firms, and organizations.

From this philosophical viewpoint the ontology of organizations includes questions like: What is an organization? How do we define organizational identity and personhood? What are the foundations of different organizational systems? Likewise the problem of the epistemology of organizations includes questions like: What frames our knowledge and what are the categories of our understanding and reason and the limits of our conceptions of the world? Accordingly, from the framework of ethical economy we can argue that philosophy of management and economics deals with issues of the role of ethical responsibility in economics, individualism, and altruism in economic ethics, the role of ethics in economic rationality, and the interactions and tensions between ethics and economics.

Definition of the ethical economy

This framework for the work on business ethics and philosophy of economics is summarized by Koslowski with the following definition of the ethical economy:

> Economic ethics or ethical economy is, accordingly, on the one hand, an economic theory of the ethical and of economics and of ethical institutions and rules, and, on the other hand, the ethics of the economy. Like political economy, it has a double meaning. It is the theory of ethics that uses economic instruments of analysis, a theory of ethics oriented towards economics, just as political economy is a political theory that uses economic instruments of analysis. But ethical economy or economic ethics is also a theory of the ethical presuppositions of the cultural system of the economy, a theory of the ethical rules and attitudes that presuppose market coordination and the price system in order to function. The component of the ethical economy, which is more strongly oriented toward application, is called here "economic ethics" (*Wirtschaftsethik*), although the terms "ethical economy" and "economic ethics" merge and the present work also attempts to deal with fundamental and applied questions of ethical economy and economic ethics. The term "ethical economy" (*Ethische Ökonomie*) goes beyond the research objectives of economic ethics, understood as the ethics of the economy, to achieve an integration of ethical theory and economic theory. Ethical economy must be more than simply "economics and ethics."
>
> (Koslowski 2008: 3)

So with this definition we can say that Peter Koslowski argues for the analysis of business ethics as a practical philosophy of management. This includes the investigation of themes like corporate social responsibility, values-driven management, and corporate citizenship in the framework of an ethical economy. From the perspective of this approach we can argue for a cultural and historical approach to the economy that includes an approach to ethical judgment between law, economics, and politics (Rendtorff 2016c).

Jörg Althammer, a professor in Ingolstadt, follows Peter Koslowski in his development of an ethical economy, which is applied to social issues and family policies. Althammer criticizes the instrumental character of the framework conditions as it is proposed in the theory of order ethics (Althammer 2000). Instead we can say that the ethical economy searches to define the ethical basis for the economy as suggested by Koslowski. Ethics cannot be reduced to economics. Rather it is necessary to define the correct ethical conditions for economic action with regard to definition of the good in relation to ethical decision-making in the economy. The instrumental economic approach is criticized by the ethical approach as not being sufficient for dealing with the ethical conditions of a good society.

In contrast to the ethics of the market with its criticism of the social state and of the welfare state, the approach of the Koslowski and Althammer school suggests ethical limits to the economic system based on social and political regulation of the market. The capability approach following Sen and Nussbaum represents such a normative approach to the ethical economy within the welfare state. Concepts of corporate social responsibility, corporate citizenship, and social entrepreneurship find their meaning within in the framework concept of the social welfare state. Ethical economy is not only business ethics or managerial ethics but it is rather the strong effort of the ethical economy approach to develop a general normative political economy to regulate the economic market. This economy focuses on the concept of the social welfare state in relation to the regulation of the economic market. The position of the ethical economy integrates philosophical reflections about the justice and constitutional foundations of the market in the reflections about the ethics of economy. The aim of ethical economy is not only to study the ethics of the market, but also to look at the societal institutions of the welfare state and find the right relations between market and state. According to Althammer this has to be based on a humanism of solidarity in contrast to an economic egoism of the market based on "*homo economicus*." One way to discuss this is through reflections about the minimum conditions of the social welfare state based on social support to individuals, for example in the form of minimum basic income.

Order ethics and framework conditions

The order ethics position is considered to be the classical European theory of business ethics (*Ordnungsethik*). This theory was developed by Munich professor of philosophy Karl Homann. Homann was inspired by the classical German theory of Ordo-liberalism that argued for legal and institutional regulation of a free market society as essential for a good political and social order. The concept of order as it is suggested by order ethics is inspired by the economic theory of order (Homann 2002, 2003). Ordo refers to the concept of economic order. According to Homann, ethical reflection needs to move beyond morality and look at economic and legal regulation in order to find the basis for ethics in society. Order ethics searches for the institutional conditions of ethics in order to regulate individual behavior, knowing that individuals who are always egoistic can only act morally when they are constrained by institutional limitations.

Ingo Pies from Wittenberg has in particular tried to work out the concept of limit conditions of economic action, which is defined by the concept of order (Homann and Pies 1994, 2000). Today, Pies works on the problem of defining international institutions as the general framework for economic action. Christoph Lütge, a professor at the Technical University of Munich, has a broad conception of order ethics, and he has recently tried to show the importance of competition for creating the best solutions at the economic markets (Lütge 2014). With a broader concept of virtues and bourgeois ethics, Christoph Lütge is inspired by the US economist Deirdre N. McCloskey, who has developed a business ethics moving from liberal economics to bourgeois virtues staying in dialogue with neoclassical economic theory (McCloskey 2006, 2010).

In many ways, order ethics can be defined as a Hegelian system-oriented approach to business ethics. Homann wanted to combine economics, ethics, and philosophy within the system of order ethics. He argued that the ethics cannot really solve the problems of modern business. Therefore, we need to look at economic rationality in order to provide a possible solution at the system level for modern economics. Accordingly, it is not the task of particular businesses to act morally. Rather it is the task of the state to provide general framework conditions to ensure the ethical regulation of business with laws and economic regulation. Ethics is not a matter of personal convictions but of a systemic relation of business.

According to the position of order ethics, morality is determined by economics, so business ethics must be a part of economic action in order to function (Homann 1993). There must be incentives to ethics and the fundamental aim of business is profit maximization. This competition in the economic market is shaped by order, which functions as rules that market actors are obliged to follow. The rules function as security for the market. Within the rules, market actors are determined by prisoners' dilemma situations of cooperation and competition (Homann 2001). The rules governing the market as order are based on universality in the sense as they should be the same for all actors. They should also be recognized by all actors and they include sanctions if they are not respected. Moreover, these rules should endorse the ethics of the competition and have some institutional temporal stability so that actors can recognize them as legitimate conditions of market interaction (Assländer 2011: 116).

With the position of order ethics Homann is very inspired by the US economists from the Chicago School Milton Friedman and Gary Becker. In particular, Homann proposed an interpretation of Friedman, somewhat different from the traditional US scapegoat criticism of Friedman. Rather, Homann looks at the other side of Friedman's famous dictum "The social responsibility of business is to increase its profits" (1970), which was Friedman's condition of "within the rules and customs of society." This other side goes beyond the responsibility of business to increase profits to point to the legal regulations of economic actions in society, i.e. the social conditions for regulations (Homann and Lütge 2004).

The concept of order liberalism refers to the theory of economic markets that argues for a regulation of the market through the state in order to create an order to the competition at the market. Regulation of the market through legal rules was in this context institutionalized by the state limits of competition within a relevant context. Egoism and freedom of action is central to the concept of the market in the order ethics position. This is basically a liberalist approach to business ethics. The order ethics position implies some basic presuppositions about philosophical anthropology and the constitution of society. We can say that the order ethics position as a theory needs to address the normative foundations of modern society in an era of globalization. The defenders of order ethics need to show the potentiality of order ethics as the foundation of stability in present society. The basic question is whether it is necessary to have strong moral foundations (moral surplus) for the compliance of individuals with institutions and rules of society. The approach of order ethics argues that the "order ethics position" taking the basis for this in the individual's self-interest can provide the foundation of understanding such compliance with rules and institutions in globalization and that no stronger moral theory is needed.

In order to characterize this position we can confront order ethics with a number of important contemporary positions in political theory and philosophy, as well as economic theory and ethics. The project of order ethics considers the positions of philosophers like Otfried Höffe and John Rawls as positions that despite their differences and disagreements argue for strong anthropological foundations of political philosophy in globalization. Such cosmopolitan positions seem, according to the criticism of order ethics, to share the arguments that some sense of global rights, global justice, global citizenship, and global public spirit is necessary in order to think globalization. While Höffe argues for a world state, Rawls is less ambitious even though he shares the concern for the need of global civic virtues and a sense of justice.

Order ethics and the problem of globalization

In contrast to these approaches to globalization and cosmopolitanism, order ethics understands itself as a position that is based on the reference to self-interest and a logic of advantages and incentives that does not presuppose the strong anthropological foundations as it is the case of the positions of Höffe and Rawls. The order ethics position draws a lot on the theory of the prisoner's dilemma and economic theory based on the examination of the concept of self-interest as the basis for social action. The order ethics does not want to argue for big ideas of shared sense of justice. Instead it focuses on self-interest, incentives, and constraints on situations. It is a position that is inspired by Hobbes, Hume, and Spinoza, who all argued that self-interest may be important for establishing social order. Order ethics also refers to game theory as the basis for social contract and it shows how behavioral ethics may indicate the importance for incentives and self-interest for ethical behavior. In this context ethics is, for example, an important instrument for reducing uncertainty.

Moreover, order ethics has a strong pragmatic element because it is about pragmatic incentives rather than deep moral motivation. On the basis of this concept of order ethics it is possible to have a critical view at different contemporary theories that seem to propose moral surplus value in contrast to the idea of order ethics. The approach of order ethics to the problem of institutionalization of moral norms in the international community in times of globalization is a search for an ethics that combines self-interest with regulative frameworks. The position of order ethics argues that an ethics that is not based on anthropology and conceptions of positive human morality, but rather on conditions of action is needed. The order ethics position refers to sufficient conditions of stability based on self-interest and incentives. These are sociality, an ability to communicate, and an ability to invest. These conditions are essential conditions of order ethics in contrast to the "moral surplus value anthropology."

The argument is mainly presented as a critical analysis of contemporary positions based on the idea of "moral surplus value" and philosophical anthropology as the basis of ethics.

So the major contribution of order ethics is an argument based on self-interest as an alternative to all kinds of idealistic concepts of the foundations of international norms. Order ethics provides a good argument for a more realist, pragmatic, and institutionalist approach that does not have to presuppose good people to reform international institutions and give us hope for solving international problems. Some people may feel offended by the order ethics position. Those are the people who believe in the moral surplus position. They may feel offended by the polemical edge of the order ethics position that defends self-interest against good moral sense. Some may argue that the reduction of those positions under the label "anthropology" may be too restrictive.

An important criticism of the concept of order ethics points to the relation between rules and virtues. It is difficult to see what the back-up of institutions should be when it is not the virtues. Is it a circular argument to argue that self-interest would generate empathy? It seems like order ethics argues that anthropology of virtues is impossible and that they introduce anthropology of institutions and rules, but then would need virtues and ethics to make people follow the rules. The same kind of argument may be put forward in relation to the tension between values and rules, saying that rules really are not possible without values.

A further argument that is often put forward against order ethics is that this kind of ethics only works within the national borders of a society based on a constitution that defines the rules and regulations that self-interested individuals follow because they need to follow them out of self-interest. But such a constitutional power does not exist in the international community. Accordingly, it is not possible to have order ethics at the global scale because there is no order. This is a problem that order ethics is required to address in relation to the difference of the international community and to the problems of order ethics in the international context. Moreover, some explanation of the kind of institutions following from order ethics (cosmopolitanism or world state) is also something that the order ethics position is required to promote.

However, as we have seen, there is a cosmopolitan potential of order ethics. In fact the three positions of global ethical responsibility, ethical economy, and order ethics should be considered from the cosmopolitan perspective. Here, we see that ethical responsibility of corporations is not limited to the territory of the nation state and that the ethical economy moves beyond borders which should also be the bases for the order or framework of the market economy with a global reach.

9 Republicanism, integrative economic ethics, and global governance

In this chapter we continue with the presentation of the schools and of the theories of German and European business ethics that can be considered as cosmopolitan accomplishments of the concepts of ethical responsibility, ethical economy, and order ethics in the international community. Republican business ethics can be interpreted from a cosmopolitan perspective as a vision of social peace in the international community. Integrative economic ethics focuses on the importance of political deliberations and democratic regulations of business. Governance ethics extends values-driven management to institutional dimensions of business, and finally, with the idea of business ethics and world ethos, we find the extension of economics ethics toward global business ethics.

Republican business ethics and corporate citizenship

Even though it has not been the case with the dominant position of order ethics, it is possible to integrate this conception in what could be defined as a republican approach, which has been put forward by professor Horst Steinmann from Nuremberg and his followers (Steinmann and Löhr 1994; Steinmann and Löhr 1996; Kumar, Osterloh, and Schreyögg 1999). But here we move beyond Karl Homann and his most important pupils. They don't think about the market in republican terms because they are most likely to defend a liberal concept of political theory and legal regulation. According to the order school the most important is economic order and only afterwards we have political order. It is the opposite with the republican school of business ethics. It prioritizes the political regulation of economic order in contrast to the priority of the political regulation of economic activities. With this approach the ethical and legal regulation functions as the foundation of social order and coherence in society. However, it is considered as an empirical and historical fact that there is no alternative to the social market society, so ethics is always with the recognition of the reality of the market, including the rule of profit maximization. In this sense it is possible to define a connection between republican political philosophy and market thinking in relation to the freedom of the market. We can say that republican business ethics integrates the concern for the common good in the concept of social order of society.

The republican position considers the role of law as very important for the institutionalization of business ethics norms in society (Steinmann and Löhr 1996). Society is considered as a "republica" where each individual is supposed to act as a good-willing legal subject and republican citizen oriented toward the common good. Horst Steinmann and his colleague Albert Löhr (1994) emphasize that business ethics is about peaceful conflict solutions in post-traditional societies. Republican business ethics is a dialogical philosophy that through dialogue searches the best solution to conflicts in the business market (Assländer 2011: 108). This dialogical ethics considers institutional peace and social cooperation as an important outcome of business ethics. Business corporations are considered as organization citizens with important duties toward the common good in society. This should be reflected as well in the external interaction with society but also in the organizational culture and structure of the business corporation.

In the republican position the concept of corporate citizenship becomes important in order to define the republican duties of the business corporation. The essential problem in this context is how to justify the ethical and legal responsibility of corporations in the republican context. The problem of the legal and ethical personality is closely linked to this question. The republican position provides an argument for business ethics and legal responsibility. As a moral and legal entity the corporation has a wide range of citizenship responsibilities and should be submitted to sanctions and fines if it does not follow these responsibilities. Therefore, it is important to find a place for the concept of legal and ethical personality of the corporation in law and in particular in criminal law (Crane, Matten, and Moon 2008; Hettinger 2002; Steinmann 2011).

Recently, this approach to republicanism has developed toward a world citizenship ethics where politics comes before markets. Here it is argued that national business ethics is not sufficient. Rather it is necessary to teach citizens and also corporate citizens about world citizen ethics so that they have not only a sense of national republican business ethics but are also committed to a cosmopolitan concept of business ethics. Following Horst Steinman, George Scherer (2002) has developed the position of corporate citizenship into a philosophy of global citizenship responsibilities. Steinmann follows this approach when he argues that we need determination of international responsibilities of business corporations and international regulation of the role of businesses within the normative plurality of different legal orders. Regulation of transnational corporations should develop norms of responsibility in order to ensure concern for the common good at the international level. Such shared norms of responsibility in the European and international markets would contribute to institutionalization of corporate citizenship in an international context contribution to the development of a world business law (Emmerich-Fritsche 2007). This is the basis for formulating a cosmopolitan approach to corporate citizenship within the position of republican business ethics.

In the republican position, law and politics are closely connected and it is necessary to give the market a social and political legitimation (Steinmann 1997). This is constituted through the political legitimation of the market through democratic processes. In this sense, legitimation of the market is fostered through the democratic processes and the foundations of the market are the legitimation through public processes. Political decision-making is justified through public processes of deliberation based on inclusive public participation and decisions are framed through piecemeal social engineering (Popper 1957). In the republican approach, corporations act politically as good corporate citizens. This means that business corporations act responsibly in the social context. In the republican context, cosmopolitan business ethics implies a legal order based on good will in relation to the community of its participants and openness for new participants in the legal order. What is important here is the freedom of businesses and individuals in relation to the republican community (Steinmann and Oppenrieder 1985; Steinmann and Schreyögg 2005).

The republican position emphasizes the importance of a republican community-oriented business culture. Culture is important in order to create unity in the business system (Steinmann and Scherer 1998). This implies a criticism of the individualism of the order ethics position. Business ethics culture should be based on a concern for cooperation rather than on individual utility maximization. Horst Steinmann has developed this point in collaboration with Andreas Scherer (Scherer and Palazzo 2008). When the culture of business is evaluated from the republican perspective, emphasis is put on the discursive opening of the world in the practice of common understanding.

Philosophical foundations: Constructivism and republican business ethics

In his development of the republican position of business ethics, Horst Steinmann was in particular inspired by the philosophical theory of constructivism, as proposed by the Erlanger school and one of its most important members, Paul Lorenzen. In his methodological approach, Steinmann refers in particular to the works of the philosopher Peter Janich (2002). This use of the constructivist theory of science as the foundation of business ethics is put forward to solve the problem of beginning (*Das Problem der Anfang*) when one wants to develop a theory of business ethics. This reference to the Erlanger school suggests a methodological foundation of business ethics in the critical rationality of constructivism. The method of the Erlanger school was defined as the requirement to proceed without absolute foundations, step by step and without circular deductions in the argumentation. Also it is required to separate the question of truth from the question of validity. This constructivist approach is based on the critical use of reason in deliberation. In business ethics it is important to have a culture of reason. Rationality must be based on reason and reasoning, as is the case in the rational and deliberative constructions of foundations by philosophers as John Rawls (justice as fairness) and Jürgen Habermas (communicative rationality). According to the constructivist position a culture of reason is essential to rational reasoning in business ethics, as suggested by Steinmann and Löhr. Such rational and constructive deliberation recognizes the contingency of the beginning and the impossibility of absolute foundations of thought. It is a new pragmatic thinking (Wohlrapp 2012) which is combined with Mittelstrass criticism of absolute foundations in Habermas' and Apel's discursive turn of philosophy.

From this perspective we can address the problem of leadership ethics. The republican view stresses the importance of implementing basic ethical models in order to ensure ethical and strategic control of management decisions. From this point of view it is necessary to determine the decision-making model in management from the point of view of discourse theory. Often ethics dilemmas and problems in business corporations, for example in the case of the US Challenger catastrophe, are due to the lack of possibility of free speech and deliberation. With regard to the problem of ethics in organizations the problem of discourse ability is essential. Moreover, rational deliberation about business ethics choices helps to define rational foundations of decision-making, taking into account the issues of foundation and cultural basis of business values. In rational deliberation about decision-making the republican and discursive transformation of philosophy expresses a discursive turn of pragmatic philosophy that contributes to reasonable foundations of legislation.

Concerning the relation between private and public administration we can also emphasize the importance of the discourse and constructive view of ethical rationality. The republican position emphasizes the importance of the respect for the position as a public servant. In the public organization and institutions the management should be understood as a public servant carrying the vocation of the office as an expression of the public interest with regard to the common good. Efficiency is not a basic element in this public space and the public employee must be respected as the carrier of the vocation and position as a public responsible official. From the republican point of view it is important to integrate ethics into the management functions of the business corporations. Personal and organizational integrity emerge out of the rational and reconstructive, discursive dialogue. Here, Steinmann and Löhr have contributed with an important typology of the morality of managers. They distinguish between: (1) the Eichmann type, the manager who has no moral thought; (2) the Richard III type, a manager who acts immorally, but knows about morality; (3) the Faust type, a manager who is so committed to a task that he disregards the moral consequences; (4) the organizational citizen type, a manager who assumes his moral and political responsibility as a good corporate citizen (Assländer 2011: 114). Ethics must be part of the planning of management. Here, strategic control is important. Compliance programs can contribute to ensure this integration of ethics and organization in the management of the organization. Here, the responsible employee is open to whistle-blowing and understands his or her responsibility toward the community. In contrast to Taylor's scientific management, we can refer here to the concept of the responsible attentive corporate citizen.

Integrative economic ethics

The position of integrative economic ethics was developed by Professor Peter Ulrich from St. Galen, Switzerland. This position takes elements of order ethics and integrates them into a general ethics of the republican citizenship responsibilities of business, but at the same time it is fundamentally the opposite of the order ethics of Karl Homann and it could be argued that in reality there only exist two schools of business ethics, namely the economic order ethics of Karl Homann versus the integrative economics of Peter Ulrich. And this implies a break with order ethics that traditionally proposes a liberal minimalist conception of the state. However, the proposal of integrative business ethics agrees that it is important to create an ordo-liberal or order ethical framework for economic action, even though this concept of integrative economic ethics does not accept the philosophical anthropology of order ethics. Peter Ulrich was, in contrast to order ethics, very critical toward capitalism and in general his position developed into a critical position, laying the emphasis on political regulation of business activities through stakeholder engagement and civil society activities, even though it was not conceived as such in the beginning. The political regulation of the market was in fact what Ulrich suggested as the solution to the problem of the lack of business ethics in economic action. This political regulation should be based on citizens' engagement and inclusion of citizens in decision-making.

Accordingly, Peter Ulrich proposes that business and the economy should be seen from the perspective of social and human life in general. He proposes a political theory of business and the economy where business should be considered as a productive social system in service of society (Ulrich 1993, 1994, 1998, 2002). This implies a criticism of an inefficient capitalist system, arguing that economic reason should be transformed into economic integration of life and market where the market serves human culture and society. Communicative ethics and deliberative political rationality should service this transformation of business into the good virtues of republicanism.

Peter Ulrich, together with his colleague Thomas Maak (1997), proposed the definition of business ethics as "integrative business ethics." Here integrative business ethics can be said to propose mediation between economic and political rationality and ethical reasoning within the field of ethical reflection. The integrative approach to business ethics argues for critical reflection of economics and considers that we should discuss the foundations of economics as a truly value-creating science (Ulrich and Maak 1997: 28). We can maintain that this task of covering human needs and wants always has been a moral project as a part of the search of human beings for the good life and just institutions. Business ethics is about finding the right principles for human social life and our relations with the natural environment. Therefore we should not separate economics, politics, and law from ethics, but rather consider them as serving the common purpose of the good life of humanity.

Integrative business ethics starts with the philosopher Jürgen Habermas' analysis of the division of system and life-world in modernity. Instead of operating with a sharp divide between different kinds of rationalities, critical ethical reflection is about the foundations of business economics and overcoming the strict separations between economics and ethics. Business ethics should generate knowledge about values and norms in corporations and their social environments, but it should also discuss foundations and preconditions for business and economic systems. Ulrich and Maak (1997: 31) think that rational business practice would relate practical reason to instrumental and strategic rationality. Ethical reflection in business should be concerned with foundational normative issues and then apply these insights to the institutional context of business organizations.

Thus, integrative business ethics argues against the opposition between an "applied ethics of business" and economics. If we only understand ethics as the task of formulating outer limitations of economics, we might be able to impose some restrictions on business, but business ethics will remain external to economic rationality and therefore we would probably enlarge the divide between ethics and business. However, it would not be a better solution to argue for an "economic theory of morals" in which ethics is reduced to morals and only taken into account in so far that it would contribute to economic efficiency. This endorsement of the morality of the market would make ethics dependent on economics and ignore the search for just institutions and rights beyond the free market (Ulrich and Maak 1997: 32).

Instead the integrative approach considers the aim of business ethics to formulate a global concept of practical reason and rationality in business, which combines economic rationality with a concern for social and political legitimacy (Ulrich and Maak 1997: 33). This concern for legitimacy situates value creation with economics and business within a larger horizon of the political and social aims of democratic society. Integrative business ethics here concerns the institutional limitations of markets based on political and legal regulations of business activities in national economies, but also in the global market with creation of international regimes. At the level of values-driven management in corporations, integrative business concerns the obligations of corporations as members of the community, their responsibilities toward employees and consumers and concern for stable and just business systems.

The normative foundations of business ethics proposed by integrative economic ethics can be said to combine the integrative view on business ethics with elements from the republican theory of business ethics and liberal democracy. According to this view it is the aim of economic markets to contribute to the good life in the political community among free and responsible citizens. From this perspective, we may find external limitations and justice by seeing business in the light of social development toward a free and just society. Business should contribute to the promotion of the rights of individuals and "economic citizenship" in the political community (Ulrich 1998: 235).

Contracts and agreements within a business community are only really legitimate in so far as they contribute to development of political and social structures of society. Business should respond to the quest for legitimacy in a public political debate among members of a deliberative democracy of society. We may even attribute to business ethics and values-driven management an emancipatory ideal of contributing to more liberty in society (Ulrich 1998: 283). Business corporations should act in a continuing dialogue with community. Concrete development of rights of economic citizenship goes on in the framework of political structures of deliberative democracy.

This may be determined as an open community of argumentation and communication. In the integrative conception, in order to acquire legitimacy, economic action should be based on recognition of critical public reason as the basis for definitions of responsibilities and inclusion of stakeholders of the firm. Economic actors should strive at behaving according to republican virtues in order to constitute a just economic market. The social ideal of democratic business ethics is integrative liberalism with a critical democratic public sphere as the basis for decision-making (Ulrich 1998: 304). In order to be acceptable with regard to the rule of law, private economic actions on economic markets may be in accordance with public reason on the basis of deliberate reflection among rational participants in a community of communication and argumentation.

From this perspective it is the task of public debates in the political community to contribute to the formation of the normative structures of legitimate business activity. In such a "civilizing" of civil society, the legitimacy of the economic system depends on the critical public sphere of society. The logic of the market is not independent, but depends on public opinion about how to structure the norms of the economic system. This view might be called "New Constitutional Economics" (Ulrich 1998: 346). This view goes further than the liberal tradition which bases economics on negative rights of freedom and ownership. The economic system is viewed as an aspect of the political structure of society.

The economic market is integrated into the political community. Economics is used as an active instrument for achieving collective social and political goals aiming at the common good of society. This constitutional conception of economics views business ethics as a part of the deliberative politics of liberal democracy. Within this framework, rights of citizens are formulated in accordance with critical public reason. Indeed, stakeholder dialogue based on integrated social contract theory is an important way of ensuring integration of economic behavior into the political community. In particular, the privileges of ownership and power within free economic markets are subject to critical debates. If economic inequality is permitted in liberal quests for freedom and on economic grounds of efficiency, democratic structures of governance may neutralize such social differences by facilitating public debates and access of individuals to common goods.

Moreover, stakeholder dialogue based on public reason may help to identify relevant stakeholders in a deliberative public communication (Ulrich 1998: 443). Public relations dialogue is a very important way in which the firm in a deliberative political democracy can help to be aware of stakeholder concerns and stakeholder rights in order to make them an internal part of the values of the firm. In this way, republican business ethics aims at making democratic values the core of values-driven management of responsible corporations.

It is often debated whether the integrative concept of business ethics really can endorse capitalism. Peter Ulrich has been very critical toward the concept of profit-maximization and the philosophical anthropology of self-interest as suggested by order-ethics. While the republican concept of business ethics as suggested by Steinmann still defends the principle of profit-maximization, this is not the case with the integrative economic ethics that has been directly critical of the foundations of capitalist economy.

Thomas Beschorner from St. Galen and Thomas Maak have developed Peter Ulrich's positions in relation to the concept of corporate social responsibility, defining the basis of responsibility in terms of an integrative ethical economy. Beschorner proposes to define responsibility in relation to the concept of creating shared value in order to understand the function of the ethical economy (Beschorner and Hajduk 2014).

Another follower of Peter Ulrich has been Ulrich Thielemann. He has radicalized Ulrich's position in order to propose a fundamentalist criticism of the capitalist system (Ulrich and Thielemann 2009). He proposes a critical approach to capitalism and neo-liberal society on a basis of a critical concept of integrative economic ethics. He can be said to develop the fundamentally critical perspective in Peter Ulrich's philosophy (Thielemann 2010). Ulrich searches the foundations of ethics in the practices of the life-world, like Habermas. Therefore, he is fundamentally critical toward the capitalist system of economics. An example of this critical approach is Ulrich's critical study of the banking system in Liechtenstein.

Basic income for all and integrative business ethics

One element of this concern of equality has been Peter Ulrich's endorsement of the ideas of economic justice by the Belgian philosopher Philippe Van Parijs, who defends the concept of universal basic income for everybody. Van Parijs argues in *Real Freedom for All: What (if Anything) Can Justify Capitalism?* (1995) that the idea of basic income is the only way to ensure freedom of choice of citizens. Maybe we should take his work seriously if we want to combine freedom and equality. Van Parijs introduces the ideas of "basic income" for all and "negative income taxes" as a possible solution. Perhaps that is an additional way to overcome the present increasing inequality in our economic system and ensure "equality of resources."

Van Parijs started the Basic Income Earth Network (BIEN; until 2004 Basic Income European Network), which is a network of social activists and academics who want to ensure a guaranteed minimum income everywhere on Earth based only on citizenship and not on work or charity. The network defines basic income as "an income unconditionally granted to all on an individual basis, without means test or work requirement." Basic income for all can be interpreted as a proposal for concrete realization of distributive equality as the basis for freedom. If one cannot afford things like taking care of children at home or realizing dreams of doing artistic painting then one really does not have freedom of choice (Rendtorff 2015a).

Van Parijs argues that basic income for all can be financed by taxing of work and jobs, but with the insights of Piketty we might add that basic income can be financed with a tax on capital income so we experience an economic redistribution from the rich to the poor in order to ensure distributive equality. However, basic income does not imply a break with capitalism since it is possible to have a capitalist economic system together with the idea of basic income for all based on redistribution of money made on economic markets.

In "The need for basic income: An interview with Philippe Van Parijs" conducted by Christopher Bertram (1997) the position of basic income is explained. Van Parijs tells us that basic income follows the tradition of guaranteeing basic income in some European social welfare states while being at the same time a distinct new idea:

> First, basic income is strictly individual, given to all people on an individual basis irrespective of their household situation; second, it is given to all irrespective of income from other sources (labor income or capital income); third, basic income is not subject to whether people are willing to work. It is not restricted to the involuntarily unemployed, but it would be paid to people who choose to not to engage in paid work (for example, housewives, househusbands, students, and tramps).
>
> (Bertram 1997)

In the long term, basic income might be quite solid but in the short term it corresponds to minimum income in some European countries.

Governance ethics and values-driven management

Joseph Wieland, a professor in Friedrichshafen, has developed the concept of governance ethics that is an approach to practical governance and values-driven management with the system conception of business ethics. Wieland (1989, 1993, 1996, 1999) distinguishes his approach from order ethics by proposing a critical view on main-stream economic theory. In relation to the schools of good corporate citizenship he argues that these schools are too abstract, focusing on foundations rather than looking on concrete issues of practical management. Wieland discovered business ethics as a visiting professor in Berkeley and New York in the 1980s. He wanted to criticize the economy from the outside. In contrast to the endorsement of rational choice by the order ethics school, Wieland began his economics of governance with the analysis of the dogmatism of the history of economics. He wanted to make a critique of rationality within the economy. Governance ethics implies an approach to sociological economics based of a system theory of integration and differentiation of systems of action at the micro-, meso-, and macro-levels of society. In this sense, Wieland uses elements of Luhmann's system sociology, considering morality as a functional system of coordination in a multireferential reality of modern functional systems (Assländer 2011: 126).

Moreover, with the concepts of governance ethics and economics of governance, Wieland wanted to develop a practical philosophy of governance of business corporations. This economics of governance is not only a descriptive ethics of governance structures, but it is also an effort to define a normative theory of economic virtues and of the virtues of the business people. The starting point of Wieland's position is the new institutional economics of Williamson based on transaction costs economics. Transaction governance is not only based on legal contracts but also on psychological contracts involving ethical dimensions of fairness, loyalty, and integrity (Assländer 2011: 126). Moral coordination becomes an important element of governance of the firm. Without being instrumentalized, ethics and ethical virtues contribute to social integration of the firm (Wieland 2014).

Wieland combines institutional economics with stakeholder theory. This was an important part of his habilitation work where he argues that there is room for stakeholder respect through the concept of atmosphere that is evoked a few times in Williamson's institutional economics. It is in this idea of the atmosphere of the firm that Wieland finds an openness toward stakeholders of the firm. Wieland defines values-driven management as the normative dimension of the firm. It combines individual and systemic virtues of the business corporation (Wieland 2014). Values-driven management is defined by the use of different programs of compliance, CSR, and integrity.

Wieland is inspired by the economics of governance and transaction cost economics as proposed by Williamson as the foundation of this approach to the institutions of business in modern economics (Wieland 2014).

While the schools of republican and integrative business ethics of Steinman and Ulrich seem to begin with Habermas and philosophical foundations and the order ethics begins with a search for efficient markets and rational economic regulation, the values-driven management approach combines Williamson's theory of institutional economics with an Aristotelian search for good governance and practical reason. Wieland wrote his habilitation on the application of classical Greek philosophy to modern business ethics (Wieland 1996, 1999). We can refer to political philosophy in order to understand the governance structures of the business corporation. Wieland considers the business corporation as the site of a political space of governance. This is the basis for personal virtue and character of the individual, but it is also the basis for different technologies of organization that Aristotle defined as the basis for economic action. In this sense there is a philosophy of organization present in classical Greek philosophy.

While neoclassical economics looks at the different markets and the basis for economic markets, the approach of values-driven management takes as its starting point the application of different concepts of organization in order to develop a practical philosophy of governance (Wieland 2005, 2013). This approach focuses on the practical applicability of values-driven management to contribute to good governance of organizations. Wieland refers in his approach to the school of values-driven management developed in Berkeley, California, and he is also inspired by Michael Hoffman, who in particular has developed the concept of values-driven management as a practical approach to management in the US context (Hoffman and Schwartz 2001). In the US, values-driven management was developed according to the Federal Sentencing Guidelines for Organizations, according to which an ethics and compliance program is a mitigating factor in court when corporations are charged with wrongdoing. In the Federal Sentencing Guidelines, corporations are encouraged to develop ethics and compliance programs in order to promote ethical behavior. This approach has also had an impact on German companies, which are also required to follow ethics guidelines when they cooperate with US corporations. The integrity approach moving beyond compliance toward values, as suggested by Michael Hoffman, is in particular important for Wieland, who also considers it essential to propose practical advice to corporations when they are working with ethics programs. In Germany, the scandal of corruption in the Siemens Corporation was particularly important for developing a concern for business ethics with a focus on ethics and compliance programs. In this sense, ethics and compliance programs represent a system response to the problem of ensuring ethics in corporations.

Governance ethics in practical business life

Alexander Brink, a professor in Bayreuth, can be said to follow the ideas of Wieland, and at the same time Brink develops his own position on business ethics. Brink disagrees a lot with Wieland's governance ethics, but he has also been very practical in his approach in taking part of a business consultancy with the name *Konzern*. Alexander Brink belongs to the new generation who are critical toward the traditional schools of business in Germany (Brink 2007). In fact, we can say that these schools debated the relation between ethics and economics, while the younger generation now has moved beyond the philosophical schools toward formulating positions with a closer relation between ethics and economics. Brink has contributed to the study program of economics and philosophy. In this praxis of philosophy there is a closer relation between economics and ethics. Here we conceive ethics and economics as a practical and applied approach to the study of business rather than the development of big theoretical systems of thought. Such a practical governance approach contributes to solving practical problems of business and looks at concrete problems of ethics in the practice of business corporations. Here practice-oriented solution of problems in business is essential to the governance approach. It is important to create structures of integrity in business and this is implemented practically with the concepts of structures of governance.

Global business ethics

The position of global ethics follows the work of the world-famous professor of theology Hans Küng from University of Tübingen. For many years he has worked on a project of formulating a world ethics, and this has also been applied to business ethics (Küng 1990, 2010). This project proceeds hermeneutically and ecumenically in trying to find common ethical principles among world religions and world ethical systems (Küng 1990). In his world ethos, Küng found that the golden rule of not doing to others what you do not want to be done to yourself was a basic principle in most cultures and religions. He applied this principle deductively in relation to business ethics (Küng 2010). The concept of world ethics is therefore a mediating concept that finds the common denominator of different positions in different cultural and ethical systems. The world ethics project is a mediating project that tries to find common agreements between different ethical positions in different parts of the world.

Claus Dierksmeier, who is the director of the center for global ethics at the University of Tübingen, follows Küng's approach with the perspective of Kantian and Universalist and global approaches to business ethics, inspired by the German economist Karl Christian Friedrich Krause (1781–1832) who was inspired by German idealism and developed a theory of the right of perfect law. Through Spanish economists, Krause's philosophy was mobilized to deal with the methodology of economics (Dierksmeier 2003). According to Dierksmeier, Krause contributes with an important combination of induction and deduction which develops an inclusive and integrative application of economics. Dierksmeier (2003) develops a methodology for global ethical economy based on the combination of idealism and pragmatism in the economic philosophy of Krause.

Dierksmeier works on a theory of relational freedom that is supposed to function as the foundation of a concept of an institutional connection between individuals in business corporations (Dierksmeier 2010, 2011a, 2011b). This theory of relational freedom is applied at the meso level of analysis. The meso-level is the level where the institutional relations in businesses are analyzed. This does not only imply the macro-level of the analysis of the relation between ethics and economics, but also the meso- and micro-level of normative institutionalization of freedom in organizations. In contrast to the order ethics theory, it is not only rational decision-making that is at stake but there is a lot of possibility for a space of freedom and moral actions in business corporations. We need to overcome the principal–agent theory in our conceptions of institutional actions in business corporations. The concept of the freedom of corporations should be developed in relation to these institutional contexts of decision-making.

Claus Dierksmeier makes an effort to combine humanistic management with the project of world ethos in relation to business ethics. His focus is Kantian and universal business ethics. In his article about the concept of freedom (Dierksmeier 2011b) this position with an analysis of the concept of freedom is put in dialogue with the German philosophical tradition, including Kant, Fichte, and Hegel. There is a close relation between freedom, responsibility, and ethics.

It is important to emphasize that concepts of dignity and liberty are essential for understanding the unity of Europe (Dierksmeier 2011a, 2011b). Dierksmeier applied his concepts of quantitative and qualitative freedom to the understanding of the European tradition of business ethics. However, this soon becomes a question of world ethics since we live in a context of rapid transformations of the life-world with its social networks and civil society movements. In the world of globalization, businesses are facing many global stakeholders, and management is required to act globally. In this sense, history has made us all cosmopolitans, and Dierksmeier argues that managers need to become philosophers about globalization in order to understand the complexity of the processes of globalization in relation to individuals and community. Accordingly, the paradigm of the world ethos including its responsibility for future generations implies that we need to formulate a cosmopolitan and intergenerational concept of responsibility in order to deal with global problems. We can say that the defense of European values has shifted from local to global and Europe has transformed from a continental soft power into a world power with global influence.

Dierksmeier proposes the values of liberty and dignity as European core values. The future of Europe is a cosmopolitan Europe. The normative unity of this future Europe is the respect for the diversity of freedom and the concern for dignity. Dierksmeier argues that the European project was a project of integrating dignity and liberty. The concept of an inherent dignity of human life was present in the European tradition from Pico della Mirandola to Kant and Sartre. These philosophers ascribe the choice of oneself to the idea of inner dignity which was the foundation and origin of human dignity. In this concept of freedom there is an essential and important link between dignity and freedom.

In his philosophy of freedom, Dierksmeier distinguishes between quantitative and qualitative freedom and dignity. What is the relation between these concepts? Together they produce a strong concept of freedom for all. A qualitative concept of unified freedom for all aims at optimizing freedom for all stakeholders of society. This means that we should not ignore morality in economics but look more closely into the business and society interface. Accordingly, it is argued that we need to discuss business ethics in the light of a qualitative and more comprehensive concept of freedom.

With this combination of freedom and dignity it is important to introduce diversity into the very notion of unity in Europe. This implies the distinction between formal and informal freedom and the concept of a unity of shared principles in a variety of practices with an underlying convergence of normative orders. Accordingly, Dierksmeier argues that we must find structural mandates that are inclusive of all.

This means that it is important to promote the values of dignity and liberty in the managerial contexts. However, we should not forget that things get complicated when we are talking about the promotion of human dignity. Reflective judgment is needed. Accordingly, what is required is continuous redesign of the business model. Dierksmeier sees his philosophy of freedom as defining a new role for business ethics as an inspiration for corporate strategy, leadership, and organization culture. Strategy should focus on this concept of qualitative freedom, implying a dignified freedom for all where the corporation takes the freedom of employees and other stakeholders seriously. The humanistic vision of management implies a battle against opportunism and quantitative maximizing freedom. The challenges of management are to accept that management is also about freedom and human dignity. Corporate governance is about enabling human freedom. It is about problem-solving and negotiations on the basis of respect for common freedom and dignity in society beyond a mechanistic model of management. With this we can say that the global economy searches and defines a cosmopolitan perspective for the global of the European idea. Europe for the future searches to guarantee autonomy through respect for human dignity and freedom. Accordingly, the business of business is not business, but ultimately society. This implies a thick description of the cultural specific implementation of shared responsibility in European business ethics.

Critical theory of economic markets

An important critical position is proposed by Peter Seele from Lugano, Switzerland. He argues that a problem with the European school formation is that these schools of business ethics are based in Germany, and many of the schools' theories have no importance outside Germany. In the younger generation today the German school-building system has been challenged from many perspectives. The younger generation, as suggested by Peter Seele, go to many different conferences and write in particular journals in order to develop their positions (Seele 2014a, 2014b). It could be argued that today it is no longer the schools of business ethics that are important but rather the work published in different international journals with emphasis on particular aspects of research. A further criticism of the schools is that they are epiphenomenal creations, a kind of ephemera of thought that are not reality in itself but pictorial creations of reality that have moved away from reality and no longer describe it (Seele 2014a, 2014b). As theoretical pictures of reality, the schools become images and self-fulfilling prophecies. The schools are rather "incommensurability creators" that actively create disagreements rather than help to find common solutions.

A new challenge to business ethics today could be to move beyond the schools toward a broader interdisciplinary approach to business ethics and ethics of economics. In this context we may move beyond a discipline-like business ethics and instead start to talk about "philosophy of management" or economic philosophy as the important discipline for integrating ethics and economics. With the concept of economic philosophy it is possible not only to talk about business ethics, but indeed also about the political philosophy of economics. With this approach, Peter Seele (2014a, 2014b) suggests opening up a new reflection on the foundations of economics with political philosophy.

Matthias Kettner, a professor at the University of Witten-Herdecke, has developed a critical theory of the market that is based on discourse ethics but also follows an economics of the good life based on new interpretations of the theories of John Stuart Mill. The economics of the good life is also a theory about the limits of the market. Kettner is close to Professor Axel Honneth from the Frankfurt School who discussed the concept of competition in the market and in relation to the concept of the market. The economics of the good life is about free and just conditions of the market. This is also what Honneth, in *The Law of Freedom* (2011), addresses in his theory of recognition of free subjects in the institutionalization of democracy in society. Honneth tries to show that there is an implied normativity in economic system that moves toward greater freedom. Here he argues against Habermas, who maintains that economics is an amoral system different from the communicative basis of ethics in the life-world. In contrast to Habermas, Honneth argues that a critical formation of ethical norms of freedom is possible on the basis of economic markets. With this approach, Honneth argues that there is a potential normativity and ethical *Sittlichkeit* in economic system that can contribute to the institutionalization of norms of freedom in modern society.

Cosmopolitan business ethics: Global ethos and corporate citizenship

We can now sum up the different parts in the context of cosmopolitan business ethics. What are the possibilities and limits of the different approaches to German and European business ethics with regard to developing a cosmopolitan business ethics as a global philosophy of management?

The cosmopolitan dimension of the ethics of responsibility of Jonas, Lenk, and Maring seems to be quite evident. The ethics of responsibility is an ethics for the whole planet and indeed also an ethics for future generations. Also when we look at the concept of collective and institutional responsibility we can argue that this approach has an important global and cosmopolitan dimension. The concrete ethics of humanity aims at considering each human being in relation to the future of humanity. As future-oriented the ethics of responsibility is a moral and political responsibility for the future of humanity. This ethics of responsibility goes beyond the different fields of ethics in order to establish a global and cosmopolitan concept of business ethics. With the ethics of responsibility for humanity we can say that corporate social responsibility becomes universal responsibility for the future of humanity in cosmopolitan society.

The cosmopolitan dimension of the system of ethics and economics of Peter Koslowski is less clear to define. The ethical economy can, however, be said to be a global approach where future institutions are defined as ethical institutions. From the cosmopolitan and global perspective there is a future-oriented dimension of ethics which focuses on the reflective and practical dimensions of decision-making and management. With this the proposal of an ethical economy becomes a proposal for a global and cosmopolitan ethical economy where economic ethics and ethical economy integrates ethical theory and economic theory in order to understand globalization and the future of global business. With this approach the concept of ethical economy can also be applied as the foundation of a global societal ethics suggesting global empowerment and social solidarity.

With regard to globalization and business ethics it is a big issue whether the concept of order from order ethics of Karl Homann and Christoph Lütge can be transferred to understanding globalization and cosmopolitanism. As order refers to an economic order at the national level it is an issue for discussion how the concept of order can be applied at the global level. The topic for discussion here is whether we can argue for the relevant conditions of the order ethics at the level of the global society. We need to define the basic rules and customs for society that are applied as regulation of the interactions in international society. A criticism of order ethics in this context has been the suggestion that order ethics is limited to the national limits of egoistic action because it is difficult to define general conditions of order in global society where there is not really a pre-established social order. In order to deal with this problem we can argue that order ethics, in order to be defined as global and cosmopolitan, needs to be based on a proposal for a global and cosmopolitan business order shaped by international institutions for economic cooperation. This is an attempt to avoid order ethics ending with the proposal of a global anarchy of business interactions without order.

The republican position of business ethics of Horst Steinmann can also be related to the idea of global ethics and cosmopolitanism. In fact, republicanism has been related not only to the nation state, but also to the federation of states in the international community. Concern for the common good in *res publica* can be moved from the local community to the international community. The republican position argues for the construction of an international community with rules and ethical norms that regulate the activities of international corporations. In this sense the concept of good corporate citizenship is supposed to be applied as global corporate citizenship at the level of international business (Scherer and Palazzo 2008, 2011; Scherer, Palazzo, and Matten 2014). In this context the republican position includes a universalist and rationalist foundation of international corporate citizenship. Accordingly, corporate citizenship as cosmopolitanism can be founded on discursive reason and universal moral norms.

Being close to the position of republican business ethics and to the concept of economics and ethics, the concept of integrative business ethics of Peter Ulrich is also open to cosmopolitan business ethics. Integrative business ethics aims at integrating ethics in the business of international business corporations. As means of formulating a global approach of practical reasoning and rationality in business, integrative business ethics also aims at developing business ethics for international corporations. Within the framework of deliberative democracy, integrative business ethics aims at international norms for civil society and deliberative democracy in the international community. Following Habermas, integrative business ethics searches to build deliberative democracy for international business institutions in order to promote discursive rationality in international business. With regard to the search for justice and equality the idea of basic income that is promoted by integrative business ethics scholars is also supposed to be applicable at the level of international politics.

The concept of governance ethics of Joseph Wieland can also have an important application to international business ethics. Governance ethics is about practical issues of management of international and global business corporations. Different programs of CSR and compliance should not only be limited to national business corporations but they have an international application. It is important that international business is focused on the use and application of relevant programs for good governance and values-driven management of business corporations. In this sense, in particular the Federal Sentencing Guidelines for Organizations in the United States and European programs of business ethics, CSR, and values-driven management should be proposed in a way so that they can contribute to improve the governance and management of business corporations. Accordingly, governance ethics has a direct cosmopolitan application to international business organizations and institutions.

Indeed, the approach of global ethics proposed by the Center for Global Ethics with Hans Küng and Claus Dierksmeier as representatives can be said to have an international and cosmopolitan approach to business ethics. The project of a world ethos aims at establishing cosmopolitan norms for business ethics in global institutions and organizations. In this context, the concept of global ethics includes norms of good corporate governance and standards of compliance for international business corporations. When combining freedom and global ethics in the framework of the tradition of global ethics this approach contributes to the definition of a cosmopolitan and intergenerational concept of responsibility which contributes to the solution of global problems. The universal dignity of all human beings in the global economy is based on these concepts of world ethos and global responsibility.

In addition, we can also build up a tradition of critical global business ethics based on the critical approaches in German business ethics by Matthias Kettner and Axel Honneth. The critical approach looks at international economics and globalization from the point of view of the criticism of the market. It is in particular important to criticize the problems of power structures at the international economic markets. The critical approach to cosmopolitan business ethics proposes a critical Marxist reading of the international economic developments in particular with regard to social and economic oppression with a perspective for analyzing structures of domination and lack of recognition in the international community.

Therefore, after this examination of the different schools of business ethics, the ethics of responsibility, ethical economy, order ethics, republican business ethics, integrative business ethics, governance ethics, global business ethics, and critical business ethics can be said to be applied from a perspective of global and cosmopolitan business ethics. With this presentation of European and German business ethics from the perspective of global business ethics we have moved toward a foundation of cosmopolitan business ethics from the perspective of the pluralist basis of the ethics of international business corporations.

10 What is corporate social responsibility?

In this chapter we will, on the basis of the previous presentation of business ethics and the ontology of responsibility, go into depth with the discussion of corporate social responsibility (corporate responsibility or CSR) (Idowu 2013) This approach is based on our earlier description of the ethics of responsibility (Maring 2001; Rendtorff 2016d). We can argue that CSR is sweet aspirational talk for cosmopolitan business ethics. By aspirational talk we mean that CSR expresses the wishes of a company to reach perfection in terms of ethics and responsibility (Christensen, Morsing, and Thyssen 2013). The definition of cosmopolitan business ethics as global corporate citizenship and universal responsibility is the foundation of CSR in the specific context of management of the company. A central issue is the definition of the term (Pedersen 2006, 2015). We then analyze the arguments for and against corporate social responsibility. Finally, we argue for an institutional theory of corporate moral responsibility as based on social responsibility (Goodpaster 2003; Carroll 2009).

Corporate social responsibility

Theories and principles of business ethics form the basis for the formulation of the concept of corporate responsibility, the responsibility of business (CSR) and its social and environmental responsibility, topics that the term of social responsibility usually covers. The definition of the concept of the responsibility of business is in itself a difficult discussion (Boyer 2001; Morsing and Thyssen 2003; Djursø and Neergaard 2006; Rendtorff 2009; Idowu 2013). In general, when we define corporate responsibility we deal with the topic of the company's basic existence as a responsible organization. This responsibility is based on the company's power and ability to act and take into account all the stakeholders. We can, however, criticize the term "corporate responsibility" for being too vague and too broad in comparison with the intention to define specific responsibilities of the company, particularly with a focus on an effort of business that goes beyond the already given responsibilities. This has been one of the arguments for using the concept of CSR, which has gained considerable ground, not at least because of the European Union's work with the concept of CSR in the *Green Paper on Corporate Social Responsibility* in 2002 as part of EU's official policy in this area of business (European Commission 2001). In recent times, many people have begun to argue that the concept of CSR is too narrow since there is a tendency to understand the concept of responsibility only as a concept that covers social conditions and relations. Therefore, some people prefer to use the term "social responsibility" to emphasize that social responsibility must be understood more broadly, so that it not only covers social issues, but also is directed more broadly to include all types of business's responsibilities and accountabilities in society.

This definition, can, however, be considered to be too broad with little focus, and therefore it can be argued that the concept of social responsibility in general or simply corporate responsibility with focus on social conditions really is better.

A possible solution could be to use the concept of social responsibility, while stressing that it should be understood broadly and always must be interpreted in close relation with companies' fundamental responsibilities in society, including the environment and all relevant stakeholders. The reason why it is necessary to distinguish between the company's basic responsibility and its social responsibility is that there has been a tendency to reserve the concept of CSR to a "voluntary action," beyond the company's basic legal and financial commitments (European Commission 2001). This has particularly been the trend in the EU's work with the concept, and they have made these distinctions in order to emphasize that the company's social responsibility is ethically justified and thus differs from its other accountabilities and responsibilities.

The argument for volunteerism is also based on the focus on inner motivation that characterize the values-driven approach to organization and management. Therefore, we can consider the movement for CSR as closely related to ethics and values-driven leadership. When it comes to getting the company to do something more in relation to its regular field of different forms of responsibilities, that is what it is economically and legally required of the company according to business and law.

However, there has also been criticism of this focus on voluntary social responsibility. One can say that if responsibility is voluntary, then there is no guarantee that the company will live up to its responsibilities. Without coercion, it is argued, responsibility will run off in the sand, and the company will refuse to be consciously aware of its responsibility. That argumentation seems to be reasonable, and it is important to see social responsibility in light of the impact of the company's basic ethical responsibilities so that social responsibility always reflects a basic ethical responsibility and in this sense cannot be reduced to a "voluntary" responsibility in the sense of an "arbitrary" responsibility that we without bad conscience cannot resist assuming. In this sense, CSR has four basic dimensions (Carroll 1979, 1993a, 1993b, 2009). Primarily comes the economic responsibility for running the company in a financially reasonable manner in relation to the involved stakeholders (shareholders, employees, customers, suppliers, etc.). Next comes the legal responsibility to always obey the law and follow society's regulations. Then follows the ethical responsibility that deals with the assessment of economic and ethical issues from a broader ethical perspective. Ethics must ensure that the economic and legal actions are ethically sound and not only serve to ensure the company's economic gain for shareholders or owners or prioritize specific stakeholder interests at the expense of others. Finally, the so-called philanthropic responsibilities must be mentioned. This is the responsibility to be philanthropic and to give gifts in a responsible manner. The European Commission's definition of social responsibility as voluntary can be described as close to the philanthropic responsibility, since the responsibility of the company is understood as something beyond the company's ordinary responsibilities.

The company's four responsibilities

We can define corporate responsibility dimensions as follows (Carroll 1979, 1993a, 1993b, 2009):

- *Economic responsibility.* The company must produce goods that can be bought and sold for profit at market. Being economical means to deal with the company well on a micro strategic level, but also in the long term be responsible as part of the national economy. The company must act in economic terms with concern for the bottom line and resources. This is the strategic dimension of corporate responsibility disclosed by Milton Friedman (1970) with a paradoxical statement that "[t] he social responsibility of business is to increase its profits."

- *Legal responsibility.* The company has a responsibility to follow society's laws, regulations, and rules of law and to live up to all its national and international legal obligations. It is important to follow the law with the utmost care at all society's levels, i.e. nationally, regionally, and internationally. Responsible legal actions should ensure that the spirit and intentions of the law are followed and that the company does not only apply rules nominally according to their own interest.
- *Ethical responsibility.* The company's ethical responsibility covers economic and legal responsibility as it determines both economic and legal action. At the same time the ethical responsibility is the institutional prerequisite for the proper exercise of responsibility in these areas. The ethical responsibility implies respect for common ethical values and codes of conduct, and it gets its legitimacy from the interests for the ethical principles of fair equality, integrity and dignity, etc.
- *Philanthropic responsibility.* The company's philanthropic responsibility deals with its philanthropic gifts and donations externally and internally. This responsibility is motivated by society's expectations that the company acts as a full member of the community; it implies responsibility to donate gifts and help the community in a way which also serves the common good.

Overlapping CSR between economics, law, and ethics/philanthropy

The relation between the four kinds of responsibility was later challenged by Archie B. Carroll himself. In fact, instead of making a picture of CSR in a pyramid of economic, law, ethics, and philanthropy it is much wiser to illustrate CSR in an overlapping Venn diagram where economics, law, and ethics/philanthropy are linked together in the space where the three circles or spheres of responsibility overlap in a Venn diagram. Accordingly, this is illustrated in Figure 10.1 (Carroll 2009).

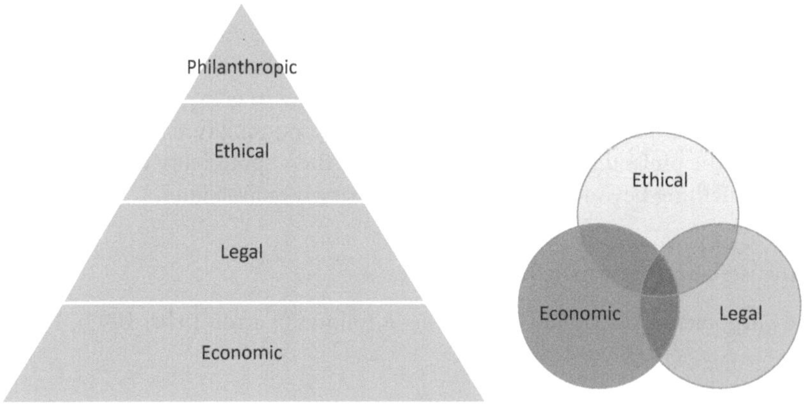

Figure 10.1 Two illustrations of CSR: as a pyramid and as a Venn diagram.

On the basis of the different approaches to CSR it is possible to distinguish four different concepts: instrumental approaches, political approaches, integrative approaches, and ethical approaches (Garriga and Doménec Melé 2004; Rendtorff 2009). In fact, these different approaches to CSR indicate the tensions between the instrumental and economic approaches in relation to the political approaches. Much debate on CSR has been concerned with the possibility of finding the right balance between these four approaches.

Criticism of corporate social responsibility

The American economist Milton Friedman, who was a strong supporter of free-market forces and critical of government monetary measures in the economy by limiting regulations, argues in his famous article "The Social Responsibility of Business is to Increase Its Profits" (1970) with a number of principled arguments against the thesis of companies' social responsibility (see also Schwartz and Saiia 2012). Friedman's point of view is a good expression of the neoclassical perception of corporate social responsibility that has long been dominant among the critics of values and ethics in business. The basic starting point is a criticism of the cultural and values-driven view of the company as an organic unity of meaning and culture, as Friedman assumes that the company is more than just a legal and economic construction to create economic and earnings and growth. His skeptical argument is therefore based on the premise that it is completely wrong to ascribe to companies such responsibility (Friedman 1970). The company is no more than a fictitious legal construction, due to different forms of ownership, i.e. sole ownership, partnership, or limited liability company. In the last case, the shareholders have limited liability, i.e. they are only liable for their contribution, while they have left the practical operation of the company to the board and management. Now Friedman emphasizes that only those individuals who represent the company, and not the company as such, may be responsible. It is therefore the board and management and part-owners of a limited liability company that have overall responsibility. According to Friedman, it is the executive's fiduciary duties, their important "moral" responsibility to enforce the rights of shareholders, i.e. to give them the greatest possible profit (Friedman 1970). If this does not happen, and, for instance, management donates all the money to charity, the company's management is according to Friedman's attitude bordering on the illegal, because it uses money for purposes other than intended. The result is that all talk about social responsibility can be considered a subversive doctrine, where the company is politicized in the direction of the "pure socialism."

Now you could argue that the money is used in the shareholders' long-term interest and thus appears as long-term shareholder value because the socially responsible business is expected to achieve greater acceptance and trust of the community, ensuring the company's survival in the long term. In this Friedman so far agrees, but the argument according to him adds nothing new in relation to the general economic understanding of the company, since it just expresses that social responsibility can be economically feasible. Friedman's argument for this is supported by management guru Michael Porter, who for many years has stood for a purely economic approach to business and organization theory, but who now argues for a strategic and efficiency-oriented approach to CSR, going from corporate strategic philanthropy, via strategic CSR toward creating shared value as the strategic aim of combining business and CSR (Porter and Kramer 2003, 2006, 2011). If we want to be a philanthropic and socially responsible company, he claims, we must develop an economically viable strategy for this by producing maximum profit, both for the company and for those who must benefit from the philanthropic donations. Porter argues that the idea of creating shared value (CSV) is the most rational interpretation of CSR since it combines strategy with responsibility for society in making the fusion of creating value for society and creating economic value for the firm. This idea has been contested by many scholars as an attempt to harvest low-hanging fruits, since it only works where there is correspondence between the interests of the firm and those of society (Crane *et al.* 2014).

Although such a strategic and economical approach to social responsibility can be seen as alluring, it is controversial whether profit maximization can be ethical. This is the core argument against CSV and economic CSR (Schwartz and Saiia 2012; Bosch-Badia, Montllor-Serrats, and Tarrazon 2013). This argument is a utilitarian cost–benefit analysis in which it is proposed that utility maximization ensures production of the best products at the cheapest price. Profit maximization occurs, taking into account consumers and society and therefore it is ethically acceptable. Being socially responsible is simply an integral part of this profit maximization, and there is no economic news or theoretical innovation in the case of CSR. The problem is that Friedman's defense of the relationship between social responsibility and the company's regular financial obligations is in danger of becoming meaningless. From a backward-looking perspective, the thesis of profit maximization is in danger of becoming a tautology when the profit and economic consequences only are deduced later, since the most profitable definition is always that which was found to be the most profitable according to the prediction. On the other hand, Friedman may be right that there are costs associated with social responsibility: administration and staff, reporting and auditing of financial statements and reports, development of codes of ethics, and other matters can be quite expensive. It is therefore important to think through the economic consequences of work with programs of social responsibility.

Arguments for and against social responsibility

The debate on CSR should be seen in a global context (Crane, Matten, and Spence 2008). Of the principal arguments for and against CSR that play a role in the discussion the following can be mentioned:

The case for CSR

1 The social responsibility of creating a better and more sustainable business is a good basis for long-term innovation and development. Social responsibility gives the company a good public profile.
2 The company will be a good citizen, contributing to self-regulation of society and create cohesion in society by being socially responsible.
3 Social responsibility is advanced "reputation" and "risk management" which form the basis for crisis management and gives the company a good reputation in the outside world.
4 The company will have greater social legitimacy and recognition through social responsibility.
5 By being socially responsible the company can keep good employees and get new and motivated employees while creating a more trusting relationship with customers.
6 The company is a part of society, and therefore we can hold it collectively responsible in relation to the whole of society.

7 Managers must not only be accountable to the company's shareholders or investors, but take into account all the company's various stakeholders in its decisions.
8 There is a close relationship between CSR, long-term stable investments, and financial gains. CSR is a sophisticated form of "long-term shareholder value."
9 Companies cannot avoid being political. To be socially responsible is to take the political side of the business economy seriously and reflectively help to define the values and ethics of business in society.
10 Social responsibility is an expression of a necessary burden that businesses should help to carry in a democratic society that will combat social exclusion and give the weakest in society proper living conditions.

Arguments against CSR

1 Only human individuals, not companies and things, may be responsible. Talking about social responsibility can never be more than marketing of the company.
2 Social responsibility means that managers use the money for their own purposes rather than in the interest of the company. Therefore, it is illegal.
3 Social responsibility leads to socialism, where the manager no longer seeks to achieve profit to shareholders, and the company becomes a political actor.
4 Social responsibility is nothing else than a form of economic thinking that involves what any good leader is doing anyway when the manager makes the company maximize its profits.
5 Social responsibility dissolves the capitalist economic system and leads to the institutionalization of a new and not very efficient economy that no longer follows market forces.
6 Social responsibility is undemocratic because it leaves the leaders, not the employees, to determine what is responsible in society. Social responsibility can therefore be determined as a dissolution of democratic decision-making.
7 Social responsibility is ideology and religion. It has nothing to do with the actual business of the company.
8 It cannot be demonstrated that social responsibility gives the company economic and financial gain. It is pure philanthropy, where money is not invested rationally. Moreover, high costs are associated with developing social responsibility, e.g. in connection with administration, staff training, and accounting, reporting and development of codes of conducts.
9 Social responsibility is not tied to real ethical intentions but is a strategic concept, which only serves to give the company a good public reputation. The aim of CSR is "window-dressing" and "green-washing."
10 Social responsibility is not in favor of the weak, because it creates an artificial philanthropic economy where the real competitive businesses cannot break through.

Is the company a moral person?

Friedman's criticism shows that the discussion about corporate responsibility masks a more fundamental debate about who and what is ethically responsible. When we talk about a change in the company's role in society toward a good corporate citizen who also is committed to the common good, we perceive a moralization of the company, where the company should be understood as a moral person with a real ethical and political responsibility (Goodpaster 2003; Matten and Crane 2005). To be ethical an organization needs to establish a close connection between moral conscientiousness and corporate culture (Goodpaster 2007). In a criticism of Friedman, professor at Harvard Business School in Cambridge, Massachusetts, Lynn Sharp Paine, in the book *Value Shift. Why Companies Must Merge Social and Financial Imperative to Achieve Superior Performance* (2003), writes that ethics expresses a change in the values of the economy. Today we have reached a situation where we not only perceive the company as an amoral financial instrument or a "fictitious legal person" but also as a "morally responsible agent" with its own values, principles, and attitudes (Paine 2003: 243ff.). The business is from this perspective no longer a purely economic actor, but an ethically responsible agent that can be attributed motives, actions, and intentions. The most comprehensive defense for the company as a moral person can be found in the works of the US business ethicist Peter French, who in the book *Collective and Corporate Responsibility* (1984) defends a so-called collectivist argument for the thesis of the moral and legal responsibility of the business corporation. French believes that ethical and legal responsibility requires that the business corporation is regarded as a moral person, i.e. as someone who can be assigned responsibility and guilt (French 1979, 1984: 30). The prerequisite for assigning responsibility and guilt to businesses must be that one can observe behavior and intentions of the company to do certain things. Talking about collective intentionality is nonetheless difficult because we usually only can ascribe to individuals intentions and motives. Still French thinks that we can operate with a level of collective action and intentionality in the company where individuals' joint actions are more than the sum of individual actions. As members of the company, individuals do things as part of a collective action structure where they jointly follow certain motives and values. French describes this as the company's "Corporate-internal-decision-making-structure" (French 1984: 38). It is this complexity of the structure which means that it makes sense to attribute to the company responsibility for its actions. With these considerations, French is inspired by the US discussions about responsibility for various military massacres in the wake of the Vietnam War. Although the individual soldiers acted under orders, and even if it was maybe just a mad captain who had issued the order, the military as an institution is still responsible for the massacres. It was the military's internal decision-making structures that were morally problematic, and in addition to working with the individual responsibility, what the organization could work to improve is its awareness of responsibility for the collective decisions and actions.

French argues against the individual-based criticism that only individuals and not organizations can have moral responsibility. He provides an illustrative example of an air disaster which occurred on Mount Erebus in the Arctic. On a clear day, a plane crashed into the mountain. Everybody blamed the captain for the accident, as it was not possible to detect any technical reason for why he flew too low. Subsequently the accident investigation board did not agree. Not only the captain, but the airline company as such could be regarded as responsible for the accident. The reason was that there was not a sufficiently developed internal decision-making structure that could have helped the captain to understand his mistake. The internal regulations, safety rules, and maybe also the codes of ethics were simply too deficient. Focusing on the company's internal decision-making structures is therefore the tool that can help to increase the understanding of the company's good citizenship while making the company more closely aware of its ethical and social responsibility. We can say that the company has responsibility to contribute to ethical awareness, and accordingly understanding of morality becomes an integral part of the organization. But how can you say that a business can have a soul or rather a moral conscience? Is this not abstract word quibbling?

In the article "The Question of Organizational Consciousness: Can Organizations have Values, Virtues and Visions?" Peter Pruzan (2001) addresses precisely this question. He discusses what it really means to say that the company has a consciousness that manifests itself at the collective level of the organization. Pruzan also stresses the importance of values-driven management and ethics for cultivating company consciousness and soul. The point is that values objectify the organization's core vision as a basis for joint action in the company. When they become the basis of a consensus-oriented dialogue, values create the basis for the organization's identity and integrity, which can also be described as a prerequisite for an ethically functioning governance. We can argue that the common dialogue on values, virtues, and visions, so to speak, creates the organizational identity. It is important that the organization's leadership contributes to such value dialogue, which can be said to represent the company's active self-reflection.

If one wants to create the basis for social responsibility and ethical awareness, values-driven management is necessary for cosmopolitan bussiness ethics as an alternative to power-based management methods of modern post-bureaucratic organizations. We can say that values-driven management in the form of written visions, values, and ethical principles will be part of the firm's moral consciousness and conscience when values and ethics are the basis for the internal decision-making structure. This implies a reflexive form of organization based on a democratic dialogue and culture. Here the business corporation is viewed as a whole with a common vision of the good life. But there is not always agreement about the company's vision and basic values. Therefore, working with values-driven management is also quite difficult: there may be major conflicts between different views of value and values-driven management when all groups within the organization meet. Values-driven management nevertheless contributes to formulating the organization's ethical awareness, because it goes beyond profit maximization as the only consideration and ideally involves all the various stakeholders of the company. For example, this takes place when values-driven management is linked to a theory of ethical accounting that can measure the values that are at stake, or when we make an effort of organizational development of the company as a learning organization.

Values-driven management and the company's collective decision-making structure

The philosopher John Searle, in *The Construction of Social Reality* (1995), has developed a theory of collective intentionality that can help us to understand the concept of corporate internal decision-making structure as the basis for collective action. The provision of the company as a moral person can be conceptualized from Searle's constructivist concept of institutions as social objects that are "ontological subjective, although they are epistemic objective" (Searle 1995: 63). Searle's perception of intentionality can be used to justify the view that notions of corporate interests, goals, plans, and objectives of action in concert with the company's rules and values for strategy and tactics as a whole constitute the company acts as representative of a group of individuals. Thus the level of common action constitutes an intermediary between the individual and the collective, based on the experience of being together in a collective "we," which is the starting point for the idea of a collective intentionality. It is possible to explain the groups' actions from individual intentionality, because the groups will have to assume others' intentions and perceptions as part of their individual intentions and views. Collective intentionality can be explained by individual intentionality, but it would also presuppose the collective intentionality, because one cannot act as an individual without the basis of previously given collective action patterns. The collective intentionality is a part of the individual intentionality, even if it cannot be reduced to this. This means that we cannot ignore the existence of a collective intentionality that understands the company as a moral agent. We can therefore say that organizations are responsible for their actions, both on the individual and at the collective level. Individuals are, in other words, responsible for the way in which they take part of the company as a collective whole, by being part of or improving the group's collective actions. Individuals can be held responsible as members of the company, even though they are not directly behind certain actions as initiators of these actions. As a moral and legal person the company can therefore be considered as an independent entity whose intentionality includes the following elements: there must be (1) a number of agents whose actions and intentions relate to each other in such a way as to constitute a company; (2) agents, whose status in the organization is that their actions and intentions coincide with the organization's actions and intentions; (3) aspects of organizations, for example policy goals and practices, that not only reflect the sum of the individual intentions, but also characteristics and circumstances in the organization, that allow agents to collaborate and act in judicial problematic ways (Laufer and Strudler 2000: 1309). It is this intentionality that means that we can attribute to the organization responsibilities at the collective level.

The various arguments for and against values-driven management testify that the process of values, ethics, and social responsibility must be thoroughly thought through. There is a close relationship between the notion of organizational identity and the context of the company that is developed by working with the company's values. The strategy aims at creating an identity of the company that which turns out well in behavior and actions, and symbols and images. Social responsibility can here serve as an instrument for developing the organization's cohesive identity. Such a strategy integrating social responsibility, ethics, and values of the organization and management should be carefully planned. The company develops such a strategy by defining values and social responsibility. Stakeholders must be defined. Objectives and means must be determined. A timetable and action plan will be developed. The key stakeholders are determined and the company formulates a strategy with emphasis on thinking about integrating responsibility and ethics into the company's other activities.

On this basis, the company must develop a vision and a mission, and the company's specific ethical guidelines are formulated. They must focus on both internal and external stakeholders who meet in preparation of strategies for objectives for the company. This should be followed up with a definition of objectives and performance criteria for goals and criteria to document stakeholder satisfaction. This is reported internally and externally, e.g. in connection with the annual report. Finally, the company determines a possible strategy and future initiatives to build values and corporate social responsibility and defines follow-up of the company's liability in policy and strategy. Ethics, values, and social responsibility are all expressions of a strategic approach to business management and business operations, which has great development potential, if applied systematically and thoughtfully.

Based on the company's identity and collective unity with a common moral responsibility, corporate ethics and values-driven management is an instrument both to enhance sustainability and improve the company's competitiveness and economic earnings. A strategic use of values-driven management combines the ethical considerations for society with focus on how ethics and values can strengthen the company's business strategy and future activities. In contrast to a purely economic or performance bureaucratic strategic planning (Mintzberg 1994: 3), values-driven management implies a holistic leadership that transcends traditional disciplinary divisions and combines elements of the different approaches to strategic planning. There can be both elements of innovation and environment adaptation, but also political considerations that come into play in values-driven management. From a strategic point of view it is important that the company rethinks its ability to act as a good corporate citizen in the light of its financial capacity and its competitiveness. In this way, values-driven management and ethics contribute to economic strengthening of the organization, for example in the form of enhanced reputation, greater sales and earnings, or capacity to attract better employees. It must however, be emphasized that the economic gains and income cannot stand alone as purposes of values-driven management, but must be proposed as an integrated result of systematic efforts to take care of the organization's integrity, values, and social and basic moral responsibility.

11 Sustainability, social responsibility, and corporate governance

Having thus rehabilitated the notion of the company as a moral person with a collective responsibility and conscience we can now analyze the relationship between business ethics, social responsibility, and sustainability in the global community as the perspective of cosmopolitan business ethics (Cannon 2012). We also need to look at guidelines of business ethics in the US and EU. Sustainability forms the basis for the triple bottom line, which specifically realizes business ethics in a strategic direction. In this context, we can establish a close relationship between ethics, social responsibility, and corporate governance in the framework of cosmopolitan business ethics (Rendtorff 2009; Simpson and Taylor 2013).

Sustainability and responsibility

A milestone for development of business ethics and corporate social responsibility has been the UN's work to make the concept of sustainable development the basis for international politics and global development. This happened with the so-called Brundtland Commission, a UN Commission on the environment, who in 1987 published a report, *Our Common Future: Sustainable Development in International Politics*. The report considers need for sustainability on the basis of the global problems of overexploitation of natural resources, the greenhouse effect, global warming, social problems, the population explosion, and global poverty. The report proposes sustainability as the central principle for world development. By sustainable development, it is understood above all that present generations of humanity have the responsibility to leave the Earth and its resources in good condition for future generations (World Commission 1987).

Sustainable development is challenged by the fact that we have entered the Anthropocene age. This is a recent geological concept signifying that the impact of humanity on the environment of the planet has become more serious, because of climate change and other modifications of the natural environment by humanity. The Anthropocene age may have started in the 18th century, when human beings started to act as a collective force in evolution that modifies its natural environment with its thermo-industrial revolution. Since that time the expansion of the global human geography with the increase of the human population has contributed to this modification of the natural environment.

It may be argued that the concept of human responsibility as an indication of what it really means to be human has become particularly important in the Anthropocene age. It is implicit that concept of responsibility is the key notion in understanding the ethical duty in a modern technological civilization. Therefore, the concept of sustainable development does not only have to focus on the future in terms of utility, but rather sustainability should be based on this fundamental responsibility to preserve the Earth for future generations.

Although the Brundtland Report has been interpreted as an expression of a pragmatic utilitarianism to allow the maximum use of land resources, as long as it does not diminish the possibilities for future generations, one can on closer inspection rediscover the ethical principles of autonomy, dignity, integrity, and vulnerability as the foundations of UN development policy. The report focuses on autonomy and self-determination by arguing for people's democratic and economic freedom (World Commission 1987). Human rights in the form of respect for human dignity and the sanctity of life also play an important role in the report. Integrity, which is also prioritized by the report, refers to the importance of ecosystem integrity and to the importance of support of indigenous people's life forms in the light of solidarity and justice between the planet's populations. Finally, we can say that the principle of vulnerability is present as defining the whole living world and accordingly is behind the entire report, since the report's basic aim is to develop principles for protecting the environment and life on the planet.

By proposing the basic ethical principles as the principles of the whole living world we can say that the Brundtland Report makes a bridge between the human and the non-human field of ethics. This is underlined by the focus on sustainability analyzed from the perspective of human responsibility for future generations and based on ethical, cultural, and aesthetic resources (World Commission 1987). It is also important that the sustainability report is understood globally so that sustainable development is not only directed at individuals or states, but is also understood as an address to the global community and its organizations. The ethics of the Brundtland Report can be summarized as a defense of democratic self-determination, the human right to a dignified life, respect for ecosystem integrity, respect for the living world and vulnerable nature, integration of man and nature, as well as strengthening of international justice and solidarity.

We can say that the ethics of the Brundtland Report with its focus on international justice, democratic self-determination, the right to respect for human dignity, and respect for ecosystem integrity and vulnerable nature contributes to the integration of man and nature; it not only sees ethics as anthropocentric, i.e. centered on people, but contributes to a close integration of human ethics with the ethics for animals and nature. Accordingly, the Brundtland Report opens up a view of the relationship between man and nature that can be termed "bio-humanism," where the idea of the organism's self-organizing development is a key aspect for the justification of a recognition of an independent moral status of animals and non-human nature (Rendtorff 2009).

However, it is man's moral sense, awarding animals and nature a moral status, which by virtue of human judgment is capable of "putting ourselves in the other's place." By this we recognize that animals from the point of view of duty ethics may have interests and rights, and that from the perspective of utilitarianism one must avoid causing them unnecessary suffering and pain. Stakeholder theory can in this way be said to include animals and nature, and sustainability ethics has a practical application in relation to complex problems related to themes such as interference with ecosystems, genetic modification of organisms and of food, guidelines for experiments, and guidelines for the use of transgenic animals or treatment of animals in agriculture (Rendtorff 2009).

When it comes to animals, ethics takes into account the possible cohesion between them and people, including animals' own worth and integrity, i.e. whether they feel pain or live in conditions that do not suit them. One can in general say that human dignity depends on how we treat animals, and therefore we can never completely overlook animals as possible stakeholders. As regards nature, it can also be pointed out that there is a link between human bodily existence and ecosystem integrity. Our respect for nature's survival comes not only from utilitarian interest, but from a fundamental concern for living integrity, i.e. the relationship between human society and its basic natural conditions. From this point of view, ethics of sustainability is a unique event in the international community because it has managed to formulate some principles of the world's global development that integrate social, environmental, and economic issues in an overall conceptual framework (Rendtorff 2001c). The question now is what this means for businesses and whether we can use sustainability as a guideline for business ethics.

Sustainability and the triple bottom line

1 The Brundtland Report sustainability principles (1987):

- Sustainable development focuses on nature and the environment, but involves economic and social conditions.
- The Brundtland Report focuses on the links between nature conservation and community development.
- Sustainability needs not to be interpreted as a purely utilitarian and instrumental concept.
- Sustainability can be combined with the ethical principles of autonomy, dignity, integrity, and vulnerability. These should be understood within the framework of the principles of solidarity and justice.
- The ethical principles can also make sense in relation to animals and nature. They can be thought of as values expressing concerns for stakeholders.

2 Sustainability and organization theory: John Elkington's *Cannibals with Forks* (1997)

- In his book, Elkington integrates sustainability and the notion of "the triple bottom line." Businesses have a new responsibility after the Cold War and with the emergence of the global consumer society, where it is important to integrate environment and economy.
- Companies have a huge responsibility in a globalized economy: the notion of sustainability puts forward community-oriented business in contrast to free market forces.
- The ethical principles can be integrated into "the triple bottom-line." Social responsibility is to promote sustainability in relation to the triple bottom line.
- New sustainability accounts and reports, which integrate social, economic, and environmental concerns, contribute to this. A sustainability accounting approach provides, like an environmental report, a description of the company's consumption of energy and the environment.
- The company works in this regard to develop a stakeholder- and sustainability-oriented life-cycle that respects the environment and nature.

The English environmentalist and business consultant John Elkington has helped to make the concept of sustainability central to corporate activities. In his book, he developed a framework for business strategy and value management that makes sustainability the central guiding principle of business management and business development (Elkington 1997; Rendtorff 2009; Cannon 2012; Idowu, Kasum, and Mermod 2014). This strategy builds on the already mentioned famous triple bottom line, where the company aims to make a profit within the social, economic, and ecological conditions in the organization. Elkington generalizes the notion of the company's sustainability and contribution to sustainable development in accordance with the principles of the triple bottom line in respect for the three P's, People, Planet, and Profit (Elkington 1997; Cannon 2012). By focusing on the triple bottom line the company can contribute to the ethical principles included in the organization of the company, business organization, and development. A sustainable business strategy therefore aims to ensure that economic, ecological, and social conditions become a part of a productive interaction in the company. This can be done by developing sustainable technologies and ecological effective strategies. For example, the business could include green accounting, life-cycle analysis and altogether a long-term strategy of the company, which is based on sustainable development. In addition to this focus on sustainability in international policy, John Elkington's work has affected businesses strategy development, and the UN adoption of the Global Compact principles.

Kofi Annan's Global Compact principles

The world economic summits in Davos in 1999 and 2000 contributed to materializing sustainability in relation to companies' specific strategies. At these meetings were discussed the Global Compact principles adopted later by the UN at the initiative of Kofi Annan, UN Secretary-General. The UN Global Compact principles can be considered as the most important ethical principles for international business and cosmopolitan business ethics (United Nations 2003, 2015). These principles emphasize respect for human rights, protecting the environment, and combating corruption as central themes for business ethics. Following the formulation of the principles, an international network of companies that wanted to follow the principles was founded (United Nations 2003). The Global Compact principles emphasize that companies should contribute to the protection of human rights, including within their own organizations (Rasche and Kell 2010). They must respect the trade unions and labor rights and refrain from the use of forced or child labor. Companies must avoid any form of discrimination. With regard to the environment, businesses must be prudent and take a responsible approach, and the use of environmentally friendly technologies must be ensured. Finally, it is emphasized as a fundamental principle that companies must combat all forms of corruption.

The UN Global Compact's ten principles are derived from: the Universal Declaration of Human Rights, the International Labour Organization's Declaration on Fundamental Principles and Rights at Work, the Rio Declaration on Environment and Development, and the United Nations Convention against Corruption. The principles are defined as follows:

Human Rights

Principle 1: Businesses should support and respect the protection of internationally proclaimed human rights; and

Principle 2: make sure that they are not complicit in human rights abuses.

Labor

Principle 3: Businesses should uphold the freedom of association and the effective recognition of the right to collective bargaining;

Principle 4: the elimination of all forms of forced and compulsory labor;

Principle 5: the effective abolition of child labor; and

Principle 6: the elimination of discrimination in respect of employment and occupation.

Environment

Principle 7: Businesses should support a precautionary approach to environmental challenges;

Principle 8: undertake initiatives to promote greater environmental responsibility; and

Principle 9: encourage the development and diffusion of environmentally friendly technologies.

Anti-corruption

Principle 10: Businesses should work against corruption in all its forms, including extortion and bribery.

The Global Compact principles and the UN Office of the Global Compact have been very important for cosmopolitan business ethics in the years after they were accepted by the UN governments. More than 8,000 companies have signed the Compact and we can therefore talk about institutionalization of a global framework for business ethics with the Global Compact (Rasche and Kell 2010; Rasche and Gilbert 2012).

Business and the 17 UN development goals

A recent sustainable development-oriented political decision in the UN has been its 17 development goals. These development goals, which were adopted by world leaders in September 2015, came into being in January 2016 (www.un.org) and should be substantially met by 2030. The 17 development goals are the following:

- No poverty
- Affordable and clean energy
- Climate action
- Zero hunger
- Decent work and economic growth
- Life below water
- Good health and well-being
- Industry, innovation, and infrastructure
- Life on land
- Quality education
- Reduced inequalities
- Peace, justice, and strong institutions
- Gender equality
- Sustainable cities and communities
- Partnerships for the goals
- Clean water and sanitation
- Responsible consumption and production.

The UN is committed to work for these goals in order to build a sustainable planet for future generations. The combatting of poverty is essential for meeting the other goals. The cosmopolitan agenda includes working to create better opportunities for all, and reduce inequality and raise better standards of living globally (www.un.org). Moreover, the action to tackle climate change is essential to meet the goals and combat poverty. The global development goals also include people, planet, and profit, referring to economic growth, decent jobs, sustainable consumption and production, and peace and justice (www.un.org). The UN recommends that everybody globally adopts and takes ownership of these development goals. Governments should integrate the development goals into their national strategies, and the UN recommends that all civil society stakeholders contribute to the realization of the goals. This includes, of course, business corporations. Together with governments and civil society, businesses must get involved in meeting the UN development goals. This is essential for the development of a cosmopolitan business ethics based on sustainable development.

Ethics and values-driven management in the US

Parallel to the UN's work to establish principles for business ethics, there has been, both in Europe and the United States, increasingly greater focus on the area of CSR and values-driven management (Goodpaster 2012). In the United States the Federal Sentencing Commission introduced in 1991 the so-called Federal Sentencing Guidelines for Organizations, which encourage companies to voluntarily establish ethics programs to avoid high penalties if lawlessness is committed by the organization (US Sentencing Commission 1995). These guidelines also contain some requirements for a well-functioning ethics program that after the commission's opinion should be introduced in US companies. After the Enron scandal the guidelines were supplemented by comprehensive legislation called the Sarbanes–Oxley Act of 2002, imposing requirements for companies to have financial reporting and transparency in management, which clearly complements efforts to strengthen ethics in American business.

Seven formal requirements for ethics and compliance programs according to the Federal Sentencing Guidelines

With a somewhat convoluted legal language the US Federal Sentencing Guidelines describe requirements for functioning ethics programs with the following points (US Sentencing Commission 1995):

1. Standards and Procedures: The organization shall establish standards and procedures that reasonably are able to help reduce the likelihood for criminal/unethical behavior.

2. Leadership and Oversight: Specially selected individuals among employees at high level should be attributed overall responsibility for ensuring compliance with these standards and procedures.

3. Individuals with Substantial Authority in the Company Cannot Have a Propensity to Act Criminally or Unethically: The organization must be aware not to give broad powers to individuals that the organization knows or should have known through performance of its obligations, tended to engage in illegal activities.

4. Communication and Effective Training: The organization should take steps to effectively communicate its standards and procedures to all members and other agents, e.g. by requiring participation in training and educational programs or by issuing publications, which handily explains what is required.

5. Monitoring, Auditing, and Disclosure: The organization must take reasonable steps to get compliance with its standards and procedures, e.g. by using monitoring or accounting systems, suitably designed to detect criminal/unethical behavior among employees of the organization and other agents and by developing or already have a reporting system in place through which employees and other agents without fear or punishment can report criminal or unethical the behavior of other members of the organization.

6. Discipline and Incentives: The standards should be strengthened through enforcement disciplining mechanisms that adequately include mechanisms to take disciplinary action against individuals who have broken the law. Appropriate disciplining of the individuals responsible for discovering violation of the law, is a necessary part of enforcement, i.e. of the discipline imposed on employees in the specific case.

7. Corrective Action: After discovering a breach of the law organization should take the necessary steps to respond appropriately to the violation of the law and avoid similar cases – including a necessary modification of the relevant ethics and compliance programs.

The adoption of the Federal Sentencing Guidelines for Organizations has been important for the development of business ethics and values-driven management in the USA. The centerpiece of these guidelines is that society needed some new ways to relate to organizations that had broken the law. One can say that the courts were in a dilemma between judging the criminal business so hard that it also affected innocent stakeholders (such as employees who not involved in the fraud or shareholders), or to give the company a harmless fine that really did not have any impact on the business and would count as a necessary business expense (Rafalko 1994; Wulf 2011).

As a way out of the dilemma the legislator has decided to attempt to take a kind of crime prevention approach to ethics by introducing values-driven management as a possible basis for reduction of the fine. The key to this approach to regulation is that companies that are willing even to declare themselves ethically, socially, or environmentally responsible, can get a reduced fine. The punishment-reducing factors are: (1) that the management acted in good faith and did not know about the crime; (2) that there is a meaningful ethics and compliance program within the company; (3) that there has been a rapid reporting of the crime or cooperation with authorities in exploration of this action; (4) that the company helps to solve the problems arising from the crime, by disciplining individuals or providing compensation for the damage it has caused. Companies that follow these guidelines may have their fines substantially reduced, for example from 1 million US dollars to just $50,000 (Rafalko 1994: 627 ff.; Rendtorff 2009).

This means that the Federal Sentencing Guidelines for Organizations can be described as a legal strengthening of the requirement to introduce business ethics programs in the United States. Even though this regulation does not use direct force, it is obvious that it is advantageous for businesses to introduce codes of ethics and be socially responsible as good corporate citizens. Companies with an ethics program will be much stronger in the legal action after an indictment if they have an ethical code. That is to say that it can be a direct advantage to have codes of conduct and reporting systems, as these will in any case act as an insurance policy for the company if it is dragged to court (Rendtorff 2001b).

Indirectly, one might also imagine that the company will be able to avoid serious crimes if it has already educated employees with regard to acting ethically. There has thus been a legal dimension in the development of business ethics in the decisions of the Federal Sentencing Commission in 1991. One can go so far as saying that any business that does not have a business ethics program runs a high risk. It would be unwise not to appoint a senior officer who is responsible for ethics, and install a reporting mechanism about ethics in the organization. There is therefore a great interest in introducing ethics programs in US companies.

A good example of how wrong things can go if you do not have values-driven management is the company Daiwa Bank, which kept secret that an employee had committed fraud in order to manipulate stock prices. The bank was ordered to pay 340 million US dollars. Had the bank had a meaningful ethics program (compliance program) which informed employees on ethics and law, it would have been able to get a reduced fine. In addition, business ethics reporting procedures and values-driven management could help to be an "early warning" of ethical problems and dilemmas both externally and internally in relation to the company. The characteristic of the American concept of values-driven management is such that ethics largely becomes a matter of practical ethical leadership. It is about introducing ethics in organizations, which is why ethics is seen as "compliance with a code," i.e. to obey company rules or codes of ethics. The motivation for introducing an ethics program in the company is therefore not just good will, but the company is forced thereby to avoid a greater evil. There is no talk about an idealistic ethics because the Federal Sentencing Guidelines reflect a pragmatic approach to the problem where you have to use both law and power to help to ensure ethics and corporate social responsibility.

Main features of the Sarbanes–Oxley legislation

The Sarbanes–Oxley legislation, which was conducted as an evident extension of the Federal Sentencing Guidelines, has been feared and strongly debated among auditors. Some have seen it as a means of creating greater transparency in companies, while others have been more critical and perceived the law as an expression of strong bureaucratization of corporate accounting matters. However, it is certain that it is far less susceptible to fraudulent accounting, since many of the provisions in Sarbanes–Oxley are quite extensive. Here are some of the most important (McAlister, Ferrell, and Ferrell 2005: 63):

1. The law establishes some public watchdogs to monitor implementation and compliance with the rules for accounting and financial management.
2. The law requires that the directors and accountants sign that the accounts and financial reports are true and do not conceal information.
3. The law requires the board and accounts committees to include panels of independent members who do not have any financial interests in the business.
4. The law prohibits companies to give loans to employees or board members.
5. The law requires that there is a code of ethics for accountants and accounting managers. The code of ethics must be officially registered by the authorities.
6. The law prohibits accounting firms that perform both accounts and consultancy for the same companies without approval of the company's accounting committee.

7 The law requires that the company's lawyers report irregularities to senior management and, if necessary, to the board. If executives and board do not respond to these reports, the lawyers should stop representing the company.
8 The law demands protection of "whistle-blowers," i.e. persons who draw attention to the irregular situation.
9 The law requires that financial analysts must sign that their recommendations are based on facts.
10 The law requires that employees in investment funds must be open about how they serve the interests of investors and how the investors' portion of company shares affects the decisions of the company.
11 There shall be 10 years of prison for crimes of internet use and misuse of electronic communications.
12 Legislation requires that the company's two highest accountants do not work with company accounts for more than four years. Other accountants are prohibited from working with a financial account for more than seven years. Audit firms must therefore move their employees around various companies now and then.

Although the Sarbanes–Oxley Act came into force after the scandals of Enron, Arthur Andersen, and WorldCom, it became important in the context of the financial crisis after 2007 and 2008. The credit crunch of the financial crisis with the risky investment in mortgages and financial products needs strong regulation of transparency and responsibility. The worldwide financial crisis with different forms of risky, unethical, and even illegal behavior needs strong global regulation (Rendtorff 2016a).

Ethics and values-driven management in Europe

Ideas about values-driven management and corporate social responsibility have not been as developed in Europe as in the US. It is true that in recent years there has been much debate about the relationship between ethics and economics and the ability to develop ethical orientations that breaks with the traditional economic values based on private property, profit, and shareholder value. In this context people often used interchangeably terms as the political consumer, ethical investments, corporate social responsibility, ethical accounting, and values-driven management in European industries.

Yet there has not been introduced the same legislation and institutional basis for the company's ethics in the US, and business ethics has only through the last two decades begun to have an impact in businesses and teaching in business schools and other higher education institutions (Gilbert 1999). Work on the European policy for business ethics can be said to reflect the different European perceptions of values-driven management expressed in the implicit values of management and ethics in European companies. Progress toward a European policy on CSR began when Jacques Delors as head of the European Commission appealed to European business to help to take care of the problems of social exclusion in European societies. In 2000, the European Council in Lisbon invited European leaders to prioritize better working conditions, lifelong learning, involvement of socially vulnerable groups, and sustainable development as key elements of corporate strategy (European Commission 2001). At the same meeting, they worked to encourage companies to take on social tasks that were beyond ordinary legal and social standards, and they asked companies to contribute to environmental and social development in the European Union. This was the background for the commission's draft of a Green Paper on CSR.

The EU has in this context regarding its activities on social responsibility established a multi-stakeholder forum, which contributes to developing the European policy of social responsibility. This is part of the Commission's policy on open communication and transparency. This gives rise to a new form of "governance," a stakeholder dialogue that prioritizes those with the greatest interest, but risks ignoring the common good, i.e. public interest. It can therefore be emphasized that stakeholder dialogue must always be considered in relation to representative politics and democracy if it is not to be perceived as undemocratic.

The EU Green Paper makes social responsibility and ecological sustainability basic components in the formation of new partnerships both locally and internationally. It highlights in this context that not only multinational companies but also small and medium enterprises (SMEs) can help to build commitment to CSR of European businesses (European Commission 2001). The Green Paper is part of the EU's focus on social benefits that were central to the Lisbon meeting. The emphasis on social responsibility must be seen in the context of the EU's overall goal to become "the most competitive and dynamic knowledge economy in the world" (p. 1), thus creating a stable economic growth with a focus on more and better jobs and greater social cohesion.

The European Commission called for a broad debate in which all society's various stakeholders, including businesses, should help to create both economic growth and social and ecological sustainability. Thus, attention to social responsibility should be seen in the context of a greater focus on values in European populations. The Green Paper emphasizes globalization and the increasing technological development as a cause of the need for greater social responsibility as part of its effort on economic growth.

The European Commission defines social responsibility as corporate voluntary contributions beyond what is legally required of them (European Commission 2001). In this way to be responsible should not only be understood as an alternative to regulatory legislation, but as a contribution to the company's social development. The Commission finds that there is no conflict between good earnings and social responsibility, but that the responsible business in the long run will ensure greater sustainability and competitive advantages. This has firstly to do with the fact that better working conditions and good values in the company can help to create more motivated employees and greater confidence among customers, investors, and consumers. Secondly, companies that are not working with social responsibility could take significant risks with respect to maintaining a good reputation and image. The European Commission stresses commitment to community as an important part of the social responsibility that contributes to enhancing local social capital. Responsible environmental behavior can create win–win situations where companies can gain competitive advantage, while taking into account their stakeholders (European Commission 2001). Similarly, social responsibility can help to ensure respect for human rights, and the European Commission calls on businesses to formulate codes of conduct, including human rights, and go beyond the minimum legal standards for ethics.

The European approach to CSR is based on a holistic and voluntary approach where businesses according to industry and market situation are encouraged to make an effort for social responsibility that refers to their specific relevant stakeholders. We can admit that many traditional management strategies have become obsolete in terms of capturing social responsibility. It is important to work with alternative models for accounting, reporting, and measurement of the company's services to capture social responsibility. Here many European countries, including Denmark and France, are in the process of adopting new rules for drawing up these alternative accounts.

Perhaps the European Commission, as is the case in the United States, should refrain from operating with a very rigid distinction between legal and social responsibility, and instead try to integrate social responsibility in the legal liability and responsibility. On the whole, it could be discussed further how law and legislation supports social responsibility. Instead of voluntary ethics, we may better talk about corporate "self-regulation" and the changing role of businesses in society as responsible citizens (corporate citizenship). In this context we could apply the concept of the company as the good citizen, contributing to social justice as the foundation of the concept of social responsibility. Why not, as in the United States, do more to create legal and regulatory support for CSR, for example, by supporting the development of such initiatives, economic, social, and political, not only from the nation states, but also on the general EU level?

However, one can say in summary about the legal regulation of companies' social responsibility in the US and EU that the US employs the legal system to actively push companies to self-regulation, while the EU takes advantage of the political system. The US approach is characterized by a combination of an appeal to enlightened self-interest and the idea of the company as a moral person with ethical accountability. In both cases, the important insight is calling for self-regulation and self-management of business ethics and compliance through ethics programs and values-driven management (Wulf 2011). Seen from the state's point of view one can consider regulating social responsibility based on a broad definition of the law and good corporate citizenship, where ethics is developed in the general framework of just institutions in democracy.

Corporate governance based on corporate social responsibility

Corporate governance based on CSR implies that management and the executive board acknowledge their responsibility for good corporate governance. This should in particular happen in relation to the company's stakeholders. The management is exercised by using a program for values-driven management, ethics, or compliance that relates to the company's stakeholders. This program must be formulated from international guidelines and rules on CSR and the triple bottom line. These are based on human rights, sustainability, and profit: People, Planet, Profit (Idowu *et al.* 2014). From these are formulated concrete strategy and policy plans for business development of good governance. To ensure good corporate governance we can refer to the following questions as fundamental for stable development of the company:

1. What are the shareholders' rights, and will they be respected?
2. What are the directors' wages, and they are reasonable?
3. How is the board composed? Is it professional and independent of conflicts of interest?
4. How does the company's audit and accounting controls function? Does accounting take place on an independent and objective basis?
5. How do we select top executives? Will it be done by merit or by non-professional standards?
6. Is revision and financial reporting credible and truthful?
7. Are the company's stakeholders participating in the financial decisions? Are they informed?
8. Does the company have the appropriate compliance programs and ethics rules?
9. Are investors professional and do they follow their recommendations?
10. Does the company periodically communicate its books?

11 Does the company follow a well-reflected economic strategy?
12 Does the company discuss the business relationship between shareholders and the interests of others?

From ethics and responsibility to corporate governance

The development and the debate about business ethics and values-driven management is accordingly characterized by very different approaches to social responsibility and programs of values-driven management which in the United States more than in Europe are grounded in law and not only in ethics (Simpson and Taylor 2013). In Europe, more emphasis is put on social responsibility as an expression of intrinsic motivation and as an expression of an element of competition. One can say that the American discussion about ethics programs has been linked to the debate about good corporate governance to a larger extent than in Europe. However, this debate is not unknown in Europe. Following the Sarbanes–Oxley Act of 2002 (SOX), on May 21, 2003 the European Commission adopted a plan for modernization of company law, strengthening the rules on corporate governance and audit guidelines (Schans Christensen 2004).

Corporate social responsibility was initially aimed at a wide range of stakeholders, concentrating the debate of corporate governance on strengthening boards and management, and in particular giving owners, shareholders and investors more certainty and transparency and the possibility to inspect the company's financial state. In addition, an effort to ensure better use of corporate resources and strengthening their competitiveness was initiated. It is, however, an implicit premise in the efforts to improve corporate governance and ensure more competitive companies, namely that it does not only strengthens shareholders, but also other stakeholders. The EU has started to work with corporate governance, reflecting an understanding that the need of regulation and increased focus on these issues is not only an American problem, but also applies to European companies (Schans Christensen 2004).

In the action plans, the EU emphasizes the need for clear international principles to be usefully adapted to the different countries in Europe. The key element of the European guidelines for corporate governance is to go beyond strengthening of shareholders and competitiveness with transparency and disclosure on business accounts as a priority (Simpson and Taylor 2013). The EU has no desire to develop a common set of guidelines for the companies of member countries, but instead tries to strengthen and support the work that is going on in each country. Each country is invited however, to propose a set of guidelines that companies can use in order to realize the action plans. The EU has, in connection with the action plans, adopted a number of recommendations communicated to member countries with focus on the realization of the action plans.

Among specific requests from the EU is the "comply or explain" approach, which means that companies must meet guidelines or explain why they are not able to do so (Schans Christensen 2004). Listed companies must account for their corporate governance in the annual reports, and they need to strengthen their electronic communication with shareholders. The EU must endeavor to make it easier for companies in the member countries to use electronic means, such as electronic general meetings of shareholders, to give greater opportunities to participate in the general meeting without being physically present. EU guidelines on corporate governance also include some requirements for company boards. Nominations for boards and appointment of auditors must be made by a majority of independent members. The board of directors as a whole should be responsible for the company's annual reports. Principles for remuneration of senior management should be clear and available, and could be taken up at the company's general assembly. Any institutional investors should also have the right to inspect general principles and policies, as well as the salaries paid.

One can say that several governments have tried to see a connection between ethics, corporate governance, and CSR. For instance, the government of Denmark set up the Nørby Commission, which from March to December 2001 worked on guidelines for corporate governance. The committee report is in line with other Danish and international reports on the subject, for example, the English Cadbury Report on the financial aspects of corporate governance in 1992. In the summer of 2005, the Danish Corporate Governance Recommendations were revised in cooperation with the Copenhagen Stock Exchange. The Nørby Report focuses on operational recommendations to ensure good corporate governance. The Commission's recommendations can in this respect be considered as a basis for further possible concrete developments of a strategy for corporate governance in the European context (Nørby Committee 2001; Thomsen 2004). Following the OECD Guidelines, the Nørby Committee's report emphasizes that openness, transparency, accountability, and equal treatment of shareholders should be important principles of good corporate governance. The committee also set out seven recommendations for corporate governance (Nørby Committee 2001):

1 Focus on shareholders' role and relationship with the board and management
2 The role of stakeholders and importance for the company
3 Openness and transparency
4 The tasks and responsibilities of the board
5 Responsible selection of board members
6 Remuneration of directors and management
7 Risk management.

Moreover, we can add the recommendation on good communication and use of information technology to provide shareholders with insight into the company's work on making it easier to participate in general assemblies and having procedures for information about important decisions that the board is facing. It is also considered as important that the members of the board are independent, and the report suggests specifically that only six members of the board can be elected at the company's general assembly, so there is also room for the appointment of independent board members. In addition, the management and board members should have a reasonable remuneration, and there must be clarity of how and by what criteria the company assigns salaries to board and management. Finally, the report highlights that it is important that the company establishes systems for risk management, i.e. that it has ethical procedures for how the company handles crisis situations, i.e. mismanagement or other problems regarding the company's activities.

Corporate governance in a small EU country

It is important to be aware of the difference in corporate culture and ownership when Denmark is compared with other countries (Thomsen 2004; Parum 2006; Rendtorff 2009). The Danish business sector consists of relatively few large listed limited companies, a number of foundations and family-owned businesses, and a large number of small and medium-sized enterprises, some of which are private limited companies and cooperatives, which is slightly different from other countries with many listed companies.

In addition, Denmark – conditioned historically by the wishes of many foundations and family-owned companies on defense against hostile takeovers – distinguishes between A and B shares, where only the holders of Class A shares have voting rights at the general meeting. Denmark, unlike in many other countries, since 1972 has had claims for employee representatives on the board, which many think discourages international investors because it may hinder the owners' free disposal. The international focus on corporate governance and the Nørby Committee recommendations have had a mixed reception from Danish business (Thomsen 2004: 81; Rendtorff 2009). Business leaders commonly place emphasis on the importance of good morals in management, but for many rules and bureaucratic procedures it can have the opposite effect and make management less efficient. Danish industry has been skeptical of more legislation on corporate governance matters, and has been concerned about European standardization. The Danish Industry Federation believes that there is a risk that strict rules deprive owners of responsibility, and it stresses that the law is not enough for creating good governance. Critical voices have also claimed that the Nørby Committee's report is too rigid, and that it is characterized by too many bureaucratic instructions without really addressing the problem. The report perceives Sarbanes–Oxley as a political ideological Act which does not contribute to solving the problems. However, concerns are not shared by all in Danish business. Others emphasize the need for internationalization and professionalization of Danish boards. There is a close correlation between good ethics, CSR, and corporate governance and this is needed for cosmopolitan business ethics in Denmark and other countries. It is wrong to restrict corporate governance to a relationship between the owners and management, since in the future there will be greater coherence between corporate governance and social responsibility. The development of new external and internal communication and management practices strengthens the company's competitiveness. Good ownership is important and it can be strengthened through rules for corporate governance. Similarly, it should not be seen as an obstacle but as a strength that there are employee representatives on the board, and it is time to pay attention to the problems of the division between A and B shares. Seen from this perspective, the debate on corporate governance is a necessary step toward the globalization of Danish companies. In Denmark, values, openness, transparency, decency and equality are central to the debate on corporate governance in large as well as small and medium enterprises. Companies have achieved much by communicating their work with corporate governance. In sum, Danish companies' attitudes to this task are divided into the categories of the "waiting and arrogant, the selectively communicating and the holistic group" (Parum 2006: 34; Rendtorff 2009). The communication of corporate governance aims to create confidence and the necessary credibility of the company's annual report. From a communication and public relations perspective, it is important to go from a unilateral unidirectional public relations propaganda or from a condescending way of communication toward a two-way symmetrical form of communication based on dialogue and understanding rather than manipulation and bias. This shows that good corporate governance is essential for the move towards cosmopolitan business ethics.

12 Business ethics as stakeholder management

We have repeatedly touched upon the discussion of stakeholder management or stakeholder theory as a very important management strategy for business ethics and corporate social responsibility (Stieb 2009; Philips and Freeman 2010; Freeman *et al.* 2010; Bonnafous-Boucher and Rendtorff 2016). Stakeholder management is essential for governance of the corporation in cosmopolitan business ethics. We will now introduce the stakeholder model and come up with a suggestion as to how management should prioritize relationships with its various stakeholders. Finally, we will discuss the definition of justice and fairness in relation to stakeholder management from the perspective of cosmopolitan business ethics.

The stakeholder model

The stakeholder model can be seen as an instrument to realize corporate governance and CSR in the practical management of the business firm (Freeman 2004; Philips and Freeman 2010; Freeman *et al.* 2010; Bonnafous-Boucher and Rendtorff 2016). The stakeholder theory can be used to steer the company with communication and dialogue with its shareholders and other interested parties. The aim is to formulate company strategy from a continuous "listening" to stakeholders, who must also be involved actively in shaping the company's values. By involving stakeholders in the formulation of corporate strategy and business plans, etc., management can ensure sustainability of the company in the long term. Stakeholder theory is based on the view that not only shareholders and investors, but also a wide range of stakeholders are contributing to value creation in the company. The stakeholder-driven management of the company is based on the perception that the involvement of internal and external stakeholders – shareholders, owners, management, employees, customers, suppliers – improves economic viability of the firm in the globalized economy. The assumption is that it provides economic returns to involve stakeholders. R. Edward Freeman (2004), described as the stakeholder model's father, highlights in this context that we must understand the business's social responsibility and corporate governance as responsibility toward stakeholders, i.e. as "corporate stakeholder responsibility." Being socially responsible means including corporate stakeholders, and it is in the interest of the firm to have stakeholders included in the strategic planning and formulation of the company's vision and mission. Stakeholder management breaks here with neoclassical economic theory, which follows Milton Friedman's idea that CSR can be reduced to a responsibility to obtain financial gain for the shareholders. Companies must not only use their power to make money, but they must also be politically and socially responsible in the community (Wheeler and Sillanpää 1997: 33).

The strong and powerful position of business in modern society is the background for this need for a broader stakeholder engagement. The enormous power that management and shareholders possess over the company in processes of globalization requires greater focus on a broader range of stakeholders. According to the stakeholder theory we need greater attention to stakeholders' requirements and needs, so that the one-sided power relation between management and the environment does not have negative consequences for employees, customers, suppliers, and society as a whole. If a company must work well in a modern society, it cannot be reduced to an economic agent in a perfect market, but must also be seen as a political organization that should involve all relevant stakeholders in production, accounting, and financial and strategic planning. A business corporation should not be constructed as a closed device, but as an open system in constant interaction with the outside world.

Stakeholder management manifests a departure from classical theories of management (Stieb 2009; Philips and Freeman 2010). The company can no longer be controlled by Frederick Taylor's principles of scientific management and production-oriented theories of perfect competition, such as those proposed by economist Michael Porter. These theories perceive the company as a production machine and do not regard the need to check and benefit stakeholders in management. This can, in turn, be the case of the human relations school or human resource theories of business management that are based on employees' needs and loyal affiliation to the company. Despite important insights about personal development at work and self-management in the corporation, this approach also has imperfections relative to the stakeholder theory, because it tends to perceive customers and employees as mere instruments for the financial profit of the company.

By contrast, the stakeholder model aims at respecting all stakeholders' autonomy, dignity, integrity, and vulnerability. Stakeholder theory is based on the fact that the company is part of a complex interaction with the outside world (Bonnafous-Boucher and Rendtorff 2016). To survive in the long term the organization should be aware of these internal and external interactions and engage in continuous dialogue with all stakeholders. This dialogue forms the basis for reflection, action, and decision-making that sees the company in close conjunction with its economic, political, and social environment (Wheeler and Sillanpää 1997: 126). Seen in this light, it can be perceived as a concrete expression of the new institutional approach to organization theory. The stakeholder perspective can be regarded as an organizational ecology, where the organization, rather than acting as a bureaucratic and hierarchical structure with rigid order and control, stands as an open system which is in constant interaction with its surroundings.

Stakeholder dialogue is a progressive process of reflection where the company will be able to observe itself in relation to its surroundings and become a learning organization, with the best basis for achieving sustainability and interacting with its surroundings. Stakeholder theory does therefore not just imply a strategic definition. Stakeholders cannot be reduced to instruments or reasons for the company's actions. We cannot settle for the instrumental stakeholder theory (Jones 1995). In light of the company's work for sustainability and the good life at the community level, stakeholder requirements must be evaluated from the vision of the common good, which is implicated in the company's values. This is evidenced by Freeman's claim that the stakeholders' interests converge over time beyond their individual preferences; in spite of the starting point of their own interests they point beyond themselves to a common solution acceptable to all. By focusing on the common good, we can now assert that ethical stakeholder management must be universally acceptable and ultimately cannot come without accounting for the common good of society (Argandoña 1998). Freeman (1984: 46) claims that "A stakeholder in an organization is (by definition) any group or individual who can affect or is affected by the achievements of the organization's objectives." All stakeholders, even those who do not shout out for their rights, are therefore in principle entitled to be consulted and involved in the company's strategic decision-making process. Stakeholders are further defined by Freeman as any group of individuals or organizations that can benefit or suffer from the company's actions, or whose rights may be violated or granted (Freeman 1998: 250).

Accordingly, together with Velamuri, Freeman has proposed the following ten principles of company stakeholder responsibility (Freeman, Velamuri, and Moriarty 2006; Freeman and Velamuri 2008):

1. Bring stakeholder interests together over time.
2. Recognize that stakeholders are real and complex people with names, faces, and values.
3. Seek solutions to issues that satisfy multiple stakeholders simultaneously.
4. Engage in intensive communication and dialogue with stakeholders, not just those who are "friendly."
5. Commit to a philosophy of voluntarism – manage stakeholder relationships ourselves, rather than leaving it to government.
6. Generalize the marketing approach.
7. Never trade off the interests of one stakeholder versus another continuously over time.
8. Negotiate with primary and secondary stakeholders.
9. Constantly monitor and redesign processes to better serve stakeholders.
10. Act with purpose that fulfills commitments to stakeholders. Act with aspiration toward your dreams and theirs.

The socially responsible business

Traditional perceptions of stakeholder theory and of the stakeholders themselves tend to put business at the center of the stakeholder chart (Figure 12.1). The company's other stakeholders will be placed around it. A more progressive way of expressing the idea of the company as socially responsible and serving society, however, is not to place the company at the center of the diagram, but at the same level as the other stakeholders. Here the company no longer presides over the stakeholders, but rather is a responsible agent that contributes to the common good in line with society's other actors. The Danish company Novo Nordisk has on various occasions worked with a model for self-representation, which tentatively places the company and its mission as one of many actors in community. One can say that the stakeholder model acts as a network diagram, where the company will be part of civil society's network relationships.

Dimensions of stakeholder theory

Freeman's ten principles clearly show how stakeholder theory can be considered as a network-based, communicatively oriented theory, working at placing the company in a social context, and this approach aims to promote both individual interests and the concern for the community without sacrificing the profit-oriented business economic foundation of corporations. In this regard, we can distinguish between: (1) voluntary versus involuntary stakeholders, such as owners versus non-owners; (2) primary stakeholders

Figure 12.1 The responsibilities of business for society: the different stakeholders in the community.

(those who have direct and effective links with the company, e.g. owners or employees) and secondary stakeholders (whose relationship with the company is more peripheral, such as occasional customers). This is closely related to the distinction between internal and external stakeholders, such as employees or customers.

Thus, we can propose a limited definition of the relevant stakeholders in an organization that can be used to distinguish the importance of the company's various stakeholders. From this perspective we can define a stakeholder as: (1) any group or person who is indispensable for the organization's survival, success, and prosperity, or (2) is important for the definition of the organization, its mission and purpose, and affects or is affected by the organization and its activities. Stakeholders occupy differing roles and positions within and outside the company (Mitchell, Agle, and Wood 1997).

However, the question of the definition of stakeholder status in relation to reflections on corporate ethics and social responsibility becomes more complicated when we analyze the various dimensions of stakeholder status. The problem is whether one can distinguish between instrumental, normative, and descriptive elements of stakeholder theories when relevant stakeholders must be identified (Donaldson and Preston 1995).

Instrumental stakeholder theory is not necessarily beyond the traditional business model, but considers the company's interest in maximizing profits as the basis for the analysis (Jones 1995). Descriptive stakeholder theory is content with identifying groups or individuals that can actually be described as stakeholders from the applicable border definitions without making any ethical prioritization of these stakeholders. The normative theory, however, goes further to include in addition to the description of actual stakeholders the question why certain people or groups must be taken into account by the company with a focus on CSR and corporate governance. The normative theory also seeks to answer the question about who from an ethical point of view basically can be counted as stakeholders of the firm (Mitchell, Agle, and Wood 1997).

Stakeholder theory is not only descriptive but also instrumental and normative to the extent that it consists exclusively of determining the relevant stakeholders. Mitchell *et al.* have given an account of both a descriptive and a normative determination of stakeholder status, which is suitable as a basis for integrating stakeholder theory with CSR and corporate governance (Mitchell, Agle, and Wood 1997: 862). This approach is about how leaders should relate to and prioritize between different stakeholder requirements. It is argued that there are three concepts of prioritization between stakeholders (stakeholder salience), which is common in stakeholder theory, and which must be regarded as relevant to include in the definition of stakeholders: (1) stakeholder power to influence the company; (2) the legitimacy the stakeholders to the company; and (3) urgency of stakeholder's claim on the company (Figure 12.2).

One can point out that the differences in relation to stakeholder theory do not to any great extent concern the determination of the actual stakeholders. There is great consensus on the distinction between a limited and extended provision of relevant stakeholders, and some commentators admit that it is difficult to establish once and for all who the company's stakeholders are. It is part of CSR and corporate governance in a complex globalized society that various, often unexpected, persons, groups, and institutions may be relevant as stakeholders (Mitchell, Agle, and Wood 1997). Likewise, external stakeholders can in some cases be internal and vice versa.

A company that acts inclusively in relation to its stakeholders is working to define its stakeholders in order to enhance its activities and its relationship to the environment. Following this attempt to define relevant assumptions for prioritization of stakeholders in corporate governance, we can highlight the following internal and external groups that should be involved in formulating business ethics and CSR:

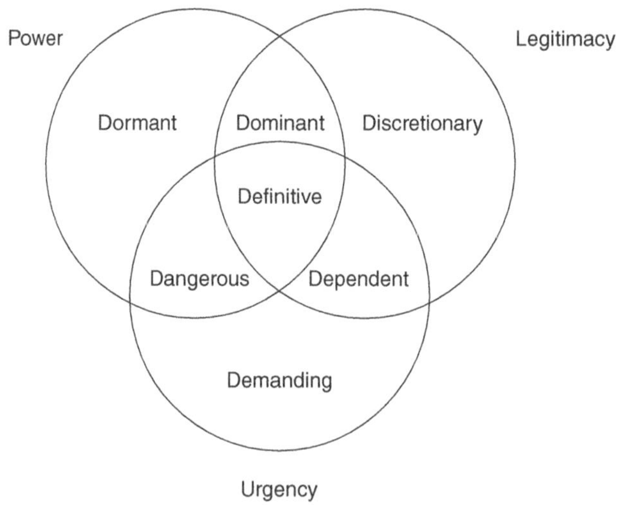

Figure 12.2 Managing stakeholder challenges: stakeholder salience model.

1 Investors and shareholders contributing to the company's financial activities
2 Leaders in charge of the company's strategy and management
3 Employees who contribute to the production with their labor
4 Business partners that the company works with
5 Customers who guarantee its existence
6 The local community, which supports and benefits from the activities of the company
7 Civil society, including NGOs and political organizations in the community
8 The environment, including the interests of future generations, animals and nature, and their representatives in the form of various lobby groups and organizations.

Based on this broad definition of the company's potential stakeholders it can be critically argued that it is impossible to take into account so many different groups, and that it is therefore impossible to define a broad area of responsibility of the company. In addition, the relations between the various stakeholders represent potential conflicts that make it impossible to reach a consensus between these groups.

This tension between the stakeholders' power, legitimacy, and pressure on the company can provide the basis for a definition of a typology of relevant stakeholders:

1 Sleeping (dormant) stakeholders (those who do not become active)
2 Discretionary stakeholders (those with authority and power)
3 Demanding stakeholders (those with high stakes)
4 Dominant stakeholders (those who have all the power)
5 Hazardous stakeholders (those who may pose a threat)
6 Dependent stakeholders (those who are deeply attached to the organization)
7 Crucial (definitive) stakeholders.

But we can also mention:

8 Non-stakeholders; and not least
9 Latent (implicit) stakeholders (those who can suddenly become relevant (Mitchell, Agle, and Wood 1997: 873), but do not at the present time seem to be important to the company).

So there is a close link between legitimacy, influence, power, and the pressure that each stakeholder can put on businesses when it comes to prioritizing different concerns and objectives of the firm. Therefore stakeholder theory is an important tool for improving corporate ethics and social responsibility, because the theory helps to make decisions far more strategically sound. From an ethical perspective, stakeholder theory needs, however, a direction pointing out of the isolated prioritization of individual interests. Strategic management with a focus on stakeholders is also about how to find a solution that everyone involved can support. Therefore we can find a justice-oriented element in stakeholder theory, combining its instrumental, descriptive, and normative elements as the basis for companies' ethics and responsibility. This will be discussed in the next section.

Definitions of the term stakeholder

The literature contains many different definitions of stakeholders. From Mitchell *et al.* we find a summary of some of the definitions. They introduce a distinction between three main groups of requirements: power, legitimacy, and urgency (urgent requirements). A strong stakeholder is of course one who has both power and legitimacy, and requires fast action by virtue of urgency. In addition, we should not forget the so-called non-stakeholders who may become stakeholders very quickly and therefore cannot be completely ignored. Among the other definitions of stakeholders appearing in the literature, Mitchell *et al.* mention the basic idea that a stakeholder is someone who has some relation to the company, whatever it may be. It may be a participant involved in a joint process or some kind of interaction with the company (Mitchell, Agle, and Wood 1997: 860), or a person who in some way relates to or who is affected by the business. A more classical and less broad definition of a stakeholder is that the company relies on a stakeholder who has power over it. One stakeholder can be a person or group that can determine whether the company must exist, but a stakeholder may also be a person over whom the business has so much power that it can decide everything about that person (Mitchell *et al.* 1997: 860).

Others talk about stakeholders as being part of a common power relation with the company and that stakeholders are important as an integral part of the company. This definition is close to a definition where business and stakeholders form a symbiosis and where stakeholders have legitimate claims in relation to the firm's activities. This is closely linked to the notion that a stakeholder also can have a legitimate moral claim over the company. This may also involve the idea that the company should be aware of its special moral respect to selected stakeholders. Based on these definitions, we can with Mitchell *et al.* (1997) summarize and clarify Freeman's definition of a stakeholder as someone who affects and or is affected by the company, with the notion that stakeholders may have power structures, specific legitimacy, or urgent relationships with the company that need to be taken into account when dealing with them.

Stakeholder management and fairness

The ultimate point of reference for priorities between stakeholders who are affecting and being affected by the organization can, in an ethically normative sense, be determined as reasonable in relation to the processing of their claims.

Justice between stakeholders can be conceptualized by the principle of fairness that helps to establish a close link between social responsibility, corporate governance and good corporate citizenship. By the fairness principle we understand that stakeholder analysis is based on an impartial and fair treatment of all stakeholders of the company. But what does fairness and reasonableness mean concretely in an organizational context? Here we can find important insights from Robert Philips in his book *Stakeholder Theory and Organizational Ethics* (2003). In his endeavor to define the basis for organizational ethics, Philips combines stakeholder theory with John Rawls' moral philosophy and political theory. Rawls' theory is based on a conception of justice as fairness that, as already mentioned, can be understood from two basic principles of justice: (1) political freedom for all citizens; (2) the difference principle, which means that social inequality can only be justified if it is in favor of the most disadvantaged in society (Rawls 1971).

From Philips, we find an effort to transfer the fairness principle from political philosophy and democracy theory to organization theory. The concept of "justice as fairness" functions in Philips' account as the foundation for corporate ethics and social responsibility by being a fundamental management principle of legitimate processing of stakeholders. As an ideal for justice within the organization, fairness and reasonableness can help to choose among the normative constitutive stakeholders of the firm, i.e. the narrowly defined core stakeholders on the one hand, and the derived and secondary stakeholders on the other. In addition we can mention the company's openness to non-stakeholders and potential new stakeholders, an openness that fairness is helping to create. In the interests of business ethics and social responsibility we can emphasize that stakeholder theory must be considered as a part of the effort to seek a convergence over time for all stakeholders' requirements which can be expressed in the concept of sustainable development. To argue for fairness as the basis for fair treatment of stakeholders in the light of corporate ethics and responsibility may not mean that all stakeholders should be treated equally, but that there must be a minimum of fairness in corporate decision-making procedures. Following Philips (2003: 51), it may therefore be emphasized that the interpretation of fairness and reasonableness as that all stakeholders should have an equal share in the firm would be wrong.

Fairness as a basis for prioritizing between stakeholders is on the contrary based on just and equitable treatment in the decision-making process and not primarily on equality in the distribution of goods and services from the company. Justice as fairness implies that constitutive stakeholders such as shareholders, customers, suppliers, employees, and local communities should be treated equally and fairly, and that inequality can only be justified if it demonstrably improves the conditions of the most disadvantaged in society. This means that the application of the principle of justice as fairness as the basis for ethical action within organizations and financial markets can be concretized by means of the concept of treating others properly in doing business with them, and of the concept of fair play, referring to just interaction between business partners. Philips (2003: 86) examines the roots of the concept of fair play, dating back to John Stuart Mill, and expressing a cooperative interaction with other people who create new obligations for cooperation and moral responsibility in the business firm. In an ethical sense the interests of fair play thus express an ethical response to the opportunistic challenge of profit maximization as the only objective of business. According to Philips the concept of fair play was already developed in John Rawls' early articles, when Rawls argued that fair play implies requirements for mutual benefit and provides a basis for fair competition and cooperation between people who let their freedom be restricted by organizations or by the financial markets.

Under these conditions, an obligation arises to cooperate to everyone's advantage. We can thus argue that justice as fairness expresses a duty of fair play and involves a responsibility to work for the common good and for equality in relation to the various stakeholders' demands. Justice as fairness implies therefore a mutual commitment of management, shareholders, and society to work for the common interest, and that is the core of the application of stakeholder management as a basis for corporate governance and CSR. On this basis, management with focus on stakeholders can be considered as an attempt to deal with social expectations to the company's good citizenship and as an expression of the company's efforts to help to promote the common good of society. But stakeholder theory is also legitimate from the perspective of strategic management, because stakeholders have legitimate demands to be treated fairly and justly by their organizations and companies. Different groups of stakeholders are from this perspective legitimate stakeholders if they have well-founded rights to be treated fairly and equitably by the organization.

According to good corporate citizenship of business corporations, it is necessary, in the interests of sustainability, social responsibility, and corporate governance that all stakeholders are equally recognized as the basis for fair treatment of all interests of the involved parties. It may be that the stakeholders who do not have a direct affiliation to the company, and therefore do not have an obvious normative legitimacy as core constituents nevertheless have a clearly articulated requirement to be taken into account. Therefore, we must in extension of Philips emphasize that civil society organizations and social activists may have legitimate claims against the firms if they in some way may be able to arise as the company core constituents, such as employees, customers, or representatives for the local community.

Social responsibility of some Danish companies as cosmopolitan global actors

A number of international companies have done a lot in order to stress their values, ethics, and social responsibility. Here are some distinctive examples of how companies communicate with their surroundings and appeal to their stakeholders.

Carlsberg Breweries, Denmark's largest brewery, has since 1876 been supporting Danish art, culture, and society. The business corporation is majority-owned by the Carlsberg Foundation, linked to the Danish Royal Academy for Science and Letters. This foundation is very important for supporting art and science in Denmark. CSR has also been important in the campaign "Drink responsibly" where Carlsberg seeks to promote an ethics of responsible drinking. Moreover, Carlsberg deals with CSR in order to implement care for the environment and responsible use of resources by the company (www.carlsbergdanmark.com).

Danisco/Dupont, a food production group that, among other things, produces sugar, highlights on its website the company's commitment to social issues, global objectives, and business integrity. The company sees itself as committed to learning and understanding of the social and cultural implications of its operations and to enhance long-term business such that it contributes to increasing the quality of life. The business stresses that it perceives CSR as part of its values and that it will work with social responsibility through active corporate citizenship (www.danisco.com).

Danfoss Group, known for the production of thermostats and other heating and cooling products, highlights confidence, safety and reliability, and technology, as well as global, local, and environmental responsibility as core values. Stakeholders must be provided with customer-oriented and environmentally friendly production, and the company emphasizes that it will work responsibly, both in Denmark and internationally, to enhance the communities in which it plays an active role. The company also mentions compassion and respect for employees as key values (www.danfoss.com).

Dong Energy, a large energy company, producing energy for Northern Europe has since 2006 moved from being a carbon company to being among the best of the global carbon-clean energy companies. From being a coal-intensive energy company, Dong has made a transformation toward green energy, working with establishing off-shore wind energy. In recent years the company has become market-leading in constructing such wind energy off-shore constructions. The company considers itself as a prime mover toward CO_2 reduction and production of carbon-clean energy following the world summit on climate change, COP21, in Paris in 2015 (www.dongenergy.com).

DSV, a global provider of transport and logistics solutions, is a Danish company with local businesses in more than 80 countries in Europe, North and South America, Asia, Africa, and Australia. DSV emphasizes that the company aims at integrating sustainability and CSR into its leadership and core business to provide sustainable logistics solutions to customers. The company subscribes to the UN Global Compact principles with engagement in CSR, focusing on resource efficiency in transportation, zero-tolerance toward corruption, and focus on labor and employee rights (www.dk.dsv.com).

Grundfos, a company that produces pumps, is often mentioned as one of the pioneers of business ethics and social responsibility. The company emphasizes soft values such as social responsibility and concern for the weak in society as a part of corporate culture. Grundfos is sometimes associated with the Danish theologian and philosopher Nikolai Frederik Severin Grundtvig's view of life; he emphasized the role of living human historic and popular communities for the future of humanity. It should be noted that the company as a global player wants to contribute to sustainable development by developing better technology to manage global water problems (www.grundfos.com).

Lego, the global toy company, has also tried to link CSR with the core business of the company. The company proposes a responsibility ambition stating that Lego wants all children to have fun, as well as creative and engaging play experiences. The company links playing with learning and innovation. Moreover, Lego has a focus on earning trust from stakeholders. Lego combines CSR with a strategy for environmental leadership dealing with climate change and reducing emissions in the use of resources and material for the sake of future generations. Lego also proposes transparent business and care and concern for human and labor rights (www.lego.com).

Lundbeck, a global pharmaceutical company specializing in psychiatric and neurological disorders, focuses in their approach to CSR on the UN Global Compact principles. The company emphasizes that in order to be fair, transparent, and accountable, it monitors best practices and business standards. Moreover, it follows the precautionary principle in order to minimize environmental impact. The company aims to give employees good working conditions and it respects labor rights. Moreover, part of the profits to the company is donated to the Lundbeck foundation, supporting health and natural sciences in Denmark.

Maersk is a company that is generally associated with very traditional business values. The company manufactures its philosophy based on A.P. Møller's letter to his son Mærsk Mc-Kinney Møller, where it is claimed that "My old saying 'No loss should hit us as can be avoided with constant care' should be a watchword through the entire organization" (December 2, 1946). These words "constant care" are considered as to be essential to the values of the Maersk Corporation (www.maersk.com).

Vestas, which manufactures wind turbines, is also trying on its website to portray itself as a company that connects sustainability, social responsibility, and ethics. By developing products that reduce CO_2 emissions and promote renewable energy, the company has the best means to present itself as socially responsible. The company is not blind to the potential aesthetic and environmental problems of producing windmills, as it promises to relate to this (www.vestas.com).

The William Demant Holding Group is a company that manufactures and sells products and equipment designed to aid the hearing and communication of individuals. This involves hearing aids, diagnostic instruments, and personal communication. The company emphasizes that it considers high ethical standards as an integrated part of its mission. This involves complying with the Danish legal regulation for CSR. The company has adopted principles of business ethics, environment and work environment, human rights, and good corporate governance. The company also joined the UN Global Compact in 2010 and has formulated an extensive business ethics policy, including guidelines for the environment and relations with suppliers (www.demant.com).

Coloplast describes itself as a company that develops products and services that make life easier for people with very personal and private medical conditions. The business focuses on solutions for intimate healthcare, including ostomy care, incontinence care, wound and skin care, and urology care. The company includes respect and responsibility as essential for customer relations and it searches for medical solutions that minimize trauma for the patients. The company integrates social concern with respect for the environment (www.coloplast.com).

13 Shareholders, management, and employees

On the basis of presentation of the stakeholder model, we can now develop an analysis of the relationship of the firm to key internal and external stakeholders from the perspective of cosmopolitan business ethics. In this chapter we look at the internal stakeholders, while the external stakeholders will be discussed later in the next chapter. The main internal stakeholders are shareholders, management, and employees. These stakeholders are closely related to each other and often have identical preferences, but are also sometimes in tension with each other due to conflicting interests.

Finance ethics

An important problem concerning the internal stakeholders, as already mentioned, is the relationship with owners, investors, and shareholders. This has been in particular the case after the financial crisis in 2008 (Rendtorff 2009; Bruin 2015). The corporate governance debate touches upon this issue, when it seeks to guarantee the principles for the protection of these groups and to ensure clarity and transparency in the company's financial statements and reports. With stakeholder theory we meet a critical attitude toward the dominant view of the company's duties as exclusively based on the obligation to maximize profitability and value creation for owners, investors, and shareholders (Crowther 2004).

This discussion about whether the company's obligations only include shareholders or must include a wider number of stakeholders goes way back in history. In a famous case from 1919 in the United States called Dodge versus Ford Motor Company, the question was whether the Ford Company could avoid paying dividends to its shareholders (Schans Christensen 1992: 35). The court ruled that the company obviously had a duty to ensure the return to shareholders by pointing to the so-called "fiduciary duties," i.e. special duties of the company to the shareholders, but at the same time the concept of fiduciary duties must be interpreted more broadly, so that the management has a duty to ensure the company's general welfare, which can be defined not just as the duty to give the shareholders the highest profit in return for their investments.

This broader understanding of the objectives and duties of business means that we must perceive companies not just as agents for principals, i.e. shareholders or owners, who use the company as an instrument for increasing their wealth. With such a broad concept of economic rationality, the company can be seen as a social system that is not just an opportunistic instrument for ensuring welfare, but as mentioned in the light of transaction cost theory also a kind of "nexus of contracts" where the company's actions are not conceived as perfectly economically rational, but rather embedded in and dependent on complex social relationships.

The company is not as in principal–agent theory (see the work of Michael Jensen, former professor at Harvard) a legal fiction, but in the light of the stakeholder theory rather it is to be understood as a political-economic system, which manifests itself as a venue for various conflicts of interest between different rights holders, shareholders and stakeholders (Jensen 1976). With John Boatright's extension of the term contract, as previously mentioned, to be applicable also to more-or-less formal contracts with the stakeholders of the firm, i.e. employees, managers, customers, suppliers, and the local community, we can argue that the narrow property rights-based view of the company has been broken up and is no longer absolutely valid.

In this light, ethics in the financial sector is not confined to protection of the shareholders' and owners' rights (Boatright 1999b: 16–18). Ethics becomes an integral part of economic behavior, because investors, stock companies, owners, private equity, etc. in the financial sector and on financial markets are held accountable for their ethical as well as economic behavior and performance. It will be an integral part of the strategic management in trading companies, banks, and capital companies to think of the company's ethical conduct and good reputation (reputation management). To ensure harmonious interaction between shareholders and stakeholders it will be necessary for businesses in connection with their economic financing to focus on ethics as a strategy for integrated rationality that helps to develop trust in the company's honesty and good citizenship.

Thus financial ethics includes questions of ownership, good relations with shareholders, transparency and fairness in economic control of the companies, and, on the whole, a focus on ethics throughout the finance and money industry, including general ethical questions about trust and honesty in financial markets. In view of the stakeholder model we can highlight the so-called "stakeholder paradox" (Goodpaster 1991) as central to the financial sector. The paradox comes from the contrast between stakeholders and shareholders, namely that the company has special obligations to earn money for its shareholders, while also having obligations at least as strong to its other stakeholders. Important factors which should be handled in this context are compliance with the rules of law, security of reasonableness and fairness in the contracts that the company takes part in, confidentiality of contracts, development of codes of values-driven management for the financial industry, and, in general, ethical rules about the financing of the company, prohibiting insider trading and not least ensuring equity and fairness in the financial markets. These are important areas that are highly regulated. But the legislation cannot stand alone, and ethics helps to make businesses more aware of their behavior and endeavor to live up to the requirement of good citizenship.

Corporate governance and good corporate governance in boardrooms and on the executive board is a key area of financial ethics and of the relationship with shareholders of the company (Boatright 1999b: 26). One of the reasons of the increased focus on corporate governance is as mentioned the increasing number of "institutional investors" who have begun to affect the company's strategy and values, and through a higher degree of shareholder activism they wish to have a greater influence on the financial market.

In addition to this focus on corporate governance in order to get ethical security and financial guarantees for investments, finance ethics also deals with ethical issues related to corporate financial solvency, insolvency, or bankruptcy. When a company shuts down or goes into receivership, there is great attention to the economic and legal consequences, but less so on how payments and redemption of the claims of creditors, etc. must be handled with justice and fairness to all involved parties and stakeholders. The employees are rarely taken into account in connection with bankruptcy. It is usually the strongest parties who get the most and the lawyer handling the estate is usually getting a good profit. To focus on the ethics of corporate bankruptcy is to see how this affects the company's stakeholders, and investigate how it is possible in a reasonable manner to support them.

Other financial ethical issues we can mention are the ethical questions in the case of mergers and hostile takeovers of companies (Boatright 1999b: 149). Here the tension between shareholders, owners, and other stakeholders is in particular expressed because those who have taken over the company have the power to press their views over the minority, which is often done without listening to the former management. If the takeover is hostile and exclusively done to make the company passive or to milk the capital, ethical issues about the responsibility for the internal stakeholders in the company emerge. On the whole, ethics of purchase and sale of companies concerns how to avoid actions that are close to cheating and fraud because the firms are in the gray area between ethics and law. It is important to ensure equality in relation to information and as a precondition for negotiations. This must also imply an effective and fair pricing in connection with the takeover of businesses between different people and companies.

The many ethical problems within the financial sector and the financial markets demonstrates the necessity of rules for corporate governance. From a somewhat broader perspective we also need codes of conduct, codes of practice (best practice), and ethical guidelines for financial markets as a whole. Such a set of rules can help to ensure that stockbrokers, stock-exchange companies, private equity funds, and institutional and non-institutional investors respect the rules of fair competition and ethical values. One could also call for these rules to be combined with the use of values-driven management in companies in the financial markets. Companies can in this connection require clearer and more informed formulations and evidence of their financial principles and policies, in connection with acquisitions, mergers, bankruptcy matters, purchase and sale of shares, etc.

The company's finance and ethics

The theoretical basis for values-driven management and ethical companies is very much a challenge to earlier perceptions of the company in economics and finance. We can say that the company's owners, through their ethical commitment, show their commitment to society. Here are some of the tensions with the traditional theory of finance:

- Business ethics is based on a community-oriented view of the economy that breaks with the notion of the utility-maximizing individual actor as the foundation for finance theory.
- It is possible to manage the company's finance with corporate social responsibility. This approach integrates CSR as socially responsible behavior in contrast to pure profit maximization in the core of the business corporation (Crowther 2004).
- The market is not perceived as a pure economic system, but as a subsystem of other social systems in which economic actors interact in a social context, with culture and society.
- The shareholders' power is not absolute, but is limited by both internal and external stakeholders' concerns. This challenges our conventional thinking about the relationship between company management, owners, and other stakeholders of the business firm.

- The company's commitments to other stakeholders mean that its legal personality, i.e. the company's rights and obligations, is not exactly the same as the interests of owners. There are a number of interests in relation to third parties, which the company should take care of, such as environmental concerns, social considerations, concerns for the local community, etc.
- We can no longer perceive the relationship between company and shareholders as monistic, but as dualistic, because there is always a possibility of diverging interests, for example in relation to the other whether the firm must have a strategy to ensure profit in the short or long term.
- We are forced to combine contract theory about the company's financing with stakeholder theory, which places the company in a broader social context.

Ethical investments

A strong expression of the need for ethics in the financial sector has emerged in discussion of ethical investment (socially responsible investment, SRI). Ethical investments means that you only invest in companies that comply with predefined ethical values and principles concerning, e.g. environmental, consumer, and human rights (Sparkes 2002: 40). General requirements are such that a business to be considered in the category for ethical investments must not produce weapons, pornography, or tobacco, use child labor, underpay workers, or pollute the environment.

The discussions about ethical investments have a long history, dating back to the 1920s, when religious movements in the US fought against the so-called "sin stocks," i.e. companies that made their profits selling tobacco and alcohol. The movement for ethical investment is also primarily an Anglo-American movement that has historically been dependent on personal, political, and ethical initiatives and thus has been more or less tightly organized dependent on specific communities or groups in society (Vallentin 2003: 114; Rendtorff 2009). In recent years, however, there has been more focus on ethical investments, and a stock index has been created for socially responsible and sustainable companies, e.g. the Dow Jones Sustainability Index and the Boston Based KLAD Organization for Measurement of Social Responsibility, both of which contribute to providing investors with information about the ethical and socially responsible companies they invest in.

The arguments for ethical investment strategies are, first and foremost, that these are necessary to ensure that businesses are ethically and socially responsible. Economic investment pressure is a firm instrument to ensure good corporate citizenship. Ethical investments are necessary because the institutional investors who typically are pension funds or mutual funds, often represent broad groups of community members who more or less explicitly expect their money to be invested in socially responsible companies. Therefore, investors have become more interested in ethical companies, and companies do more to raise awareness of their corporate governance policy and social responsibility.

The idea of ethical investment is that you can follow the conditions of the market economy and invest money in a private capitalist company, earning money from the investment while doing something good and ethically right for society (Boatright 1999b: 111). This presupposes, however, as many investors have tried to prove, that ethical investments also provide economic benefits. Studies have shown that ethical investments may well be profitable, even though they may not always provide the greatest dividends.

While CSR is often considered a voluntary and generous action that goes beyond what the law requires, ethical investments concern the company's financial foundation, since the financial contribution depends on the company's ethical commitments. One can therefore argue that the consequentialist and utilitarian justification of ethics is an even stronger invitation to ethical investments when compared with activities related to CSR. In relation to CSR, that is not only justified economically, but also from the perspective of more broad concerns for society, the relationship between ethics and economics in ethical investments is more pronounced because ethics in this context does not make sense unless it is economically viable.

Ethical investment lies at the financial basis of the company by not perceiving profit maximization as ethically neutral, but rather as related to the question of ethical and unethical ways to make money. Steen Vallentin (2003: 117) mentions four basic approaches to ethical investments:

1 The negative approach, i.e. refusal to invest in companies which do not meet the criteria that have been set for ethical investments. Here the investor will not invest in arms production, pornography, alcohol, or tobacco, or in companies which violate human rights or the environment.
2 The positive approach, which defines some criteria for what is ethically right, and chooses specific companies based on the criteria, which the investors have set up. They decide, for example, to invest in organic products, environmentally friendly production, or companies that do something extra for employees.
3 The activist approach, based on shareholders' active participation in corporate decisions (shareholder activism), where ethical investments depend on shareholders' attitudes and perceptions of the values that play a role for the company.
4 The index-based approach to ethical investments, where the investors select the companies that they invest in, based on their place in the rankings among leading investment indexes, e.g. the Dow Jones Sustainability Index. This approach is very much based on expert screening of corporate ethics and social responsibility, considered from the perspective of various predefined criteria.

The motivation for ethical investments defines, to a greater or lesser degree, which investment approach is chosen. From the above distinctions we can point to some basic values-driven attitudes that explain why people choose to invest ethically. A common attitude is founded in fundamental ethical or religious beliefs, which implies that certain products and production methods cannot be accepted. It may, as already mentioned, be alcohol, tobacco, pornography, or weapons, but the selection may also depend on views of life, and basic values among different groups such as vegetarians and activists for animal protection, who are against slaughterhouses and cosmetics companies that use animal testing to develop their products.

A second type of motivation is more political and relies more systematically on active ownership by shareholders who engage with the company's respect for the values that help to ensure sustainability in the world. Here shareholders not only reject certain products, but they contribute with active involvement in the company's activities to improve its values and community engagement. In addition, we can mention a pure economic argument for ethical investments, which claims that profitable ethical companies are also the most economically viable, because they have a long-term approach to sustainability in society. One variant of this is the institutional motivation for ethical investment, combining ethics and interest in safe financial return, which we find in pension companies and pension funds. Because of their many members with democratic attitudes they need to ensure that their investments are made in companies with socially responsible attitudes and products.

Should large companies have an ethics employee?

It is an important part of the development of ethics and values-driven management, and of ensuring leadership with integrity in both financial and other decisions, that both small and large organizations, and in specific cases small companies, delegate responsibility for ethics and values to specific individuals. In the US Federal Sentencing Guidelines for Organizations it is, as mentioned, required that the company employs an ethics officer, a senior employee with an office and subordinates who can act as a kind of rapporteur on ethical questions to top management. We could describe this position as a "corporate secretary for ethics" (US Sentencing Commission 1995; Rafalko 1994).

Such an employee is a person who feels especially responsible for the company's ethical profile. It is someone who knows the business well, and has an experienced judgment, is motivated, and by virtue of her or his position holds sufficient power to implement their decisions. The employee and their office also take specific initiatives for development of ethics, codes of values-driven management, and ethical guidelines in the organization. This can include for example the identification of ethical problems in management of the company; development of special ethics programs; and solving the company's internal ethical issues, which could include ethical issues in relation to top management, management problems, issues related to shareholders, and finally ethical problems in relation to the other stakeholders. It must of course be possible to impose decisions and suggestions for ethical development of the organization that such an employee might have.

Many employees have been strongly opposed to this model because they perceive an ethics officer as a kind of thought police or unacceptable internal monitoring and control of the organization. Therefore, an ethics officer must be aware of a number of requirements that must be satisfied for such a person to be fit for the job:

1. The ethics officer must make clear to which extent he or she has a large degree of influence in the company.
2. The ethics officer must consider whether he or she gets enough respect and trust both from colleagues and from the leaders.
3. The organization should think about whether it has sufficient resources to carry out internal investigations and procedural change in the company.
4. The organization should also consider whether it can get access to information and support mechanisms that will contribute to early warning, etc., about ethical issues.
5. The organization should evaluate whether employees would approve the creation of an ethical officer.

Management with integrity

One of the main problems with regard to internal ethics is how we can get good leaders with a strong understanding of ethical problems. The impression quickly gained from reading the newspaper headlines and from radio and television is that the morale of the leaders in the large companies is declining. In the 1980s, it was the financial scandals of the businesses, and in the 1990s and 2000s came, for example, greater focus on highly paid leaders' salaries and stock options, which also accrued to the European top executives. It has been shown that the wages of managers in the largest companies have increased exponentially in relation to the employees, and that poses the question whether the top leaders in terms of their ethics and social responsibility also live up to their salaries, or whether they simply have become more opportunistic and better at promoting their own interests.

An important concept of managers' ethics is the principle of high moral integrity, including the ability to have ethical formulation competence and moral judgment (Paine 1994a; Rendtorff 2011b). As previously mentioned, integrity can be defined as a unity and wholeness of a person or organization, defined by moral person's moral identity, which is determined by the person's ability to make good and well-founded ethical decisions (Table 13.1). A person who has high moral integrity and who is aware of the importance of values and ethics is extremely important for developing ethics and responsibility as a basic element in a company's history, culture, and values. Therefore the leader is an important figure in the development of social responsibility. Leaders should help take initiatives for values-driven management, ethical strategies, and ethics programs, but they must first and foremost through their own actions demonstrate commitment to the company's development of stakeholder management, public credibility, and trust and in relation to good corporate citizenship.

Lynn Sharp Paine has several articles focused on the need to improve the ability of managers to moral thinking, integrity, and ethical judgment (Paine 1994a, 1994b, 1997a, 1997b; Rendtorff 2011b). She bases management ethics on the principle of integrity as "integritas," meaning wholeness, perfection, or purity. Integrity is here understood as a moral virtue and as the basis for the individual's good life and actions. Integrity expresses that the employee wants to do the right thing, and also to receive trust from his or her colleagues. We should be able to count on the person. Integrity is psychologically associated with a high degree of self-control and self-respect. Integrity is closely related to the specific and sustained commitments, duties, and obligations. It expresses a moral firmness in decision-making, even if the individual is not dogmatic in his or her view of life. Integrity is the manifestation of a sustained moral coherence of individual and organizational behavior (Paine 1997a, 1997b). There is a close link between principles and practice. Integrity is also essential for a coherent personality and identity. Paine rejects a possible objection that integrity as a concept is just formal, and as such should be grounded in any moral virtue. She believes it is part of the concept of integrity that it is inconsistent, for example, to mention the fact that a mob or mafia boss should have integrity, although there is consistency in his or her actions.

Table 13.1 Dimensions of decision-making

Performance of the moral action	*Judgment and integrity*	*Decision-making*
Social consensus	Organizational aspects	Determine the action's ethical intensity
Influence from society	(e.g. culture)	Assess the act with judgment
Temporal immediacy	Power relations	Formulate action ethical objectives from
Proximity and remoteness	Socialization	the perspective of the integrity strategy
Moral intensity	Conditions	Go ahead with moral action
	Individual motivation	Result: ethical or unethical behavior, i.e.
	Personal values	with high or low integrity

For Paine, integrity is grounded in Kant's moral principles that an action to be moral should be made into a universal law. We can say that the leader by virtue of his or her integrity comes close to incarnating the organization's identity and actions. Therefore, there is a close correlation between individual integrity and the integrity of the institutional level of the entire organization. Integrity is key for development and formulation of values-driven management, and the company's various codes and rules help to strengthen the integrity of the individual. That is why good leadership implies combining high moral integrity with the development of an ethically coherent organizational culture.

In the article "Managing for Organizational Integrity," Paine (1994a) emphasizes that an integrity-based approach to business ethics does not see any contradiction between the considerations of the company's rules and regulations and manager's personal ethics. To focus on integrity means that the company not only focuses on the manager's ethics, but also on the values that the company develops in different programs of ethics and values-driven leadership. Programs for value-driven management are accordingly organizational means to influence individual behavior internally in the company. That this implies an organizational basis for the understanding of ethics must therefore not be interpreted as a weakening of the personal responsibility of leaders and employees, rather the contrary (Paine1994a: 109; Rendtorff 2011b).

Integrity, judgment, and ethics

An ethics program can serve as an organizational pressure and help to create consensus in the organizational culture concerning specific norms and values that are considered as ethically right. Developing strategies and programs for ethics and values-driven leadership expresses a "hope for the good practice for the individual." Ethics must therefore not only be understood as "to obey the law," but rather as a quest for virtuousness in the individual's common practice (Paine 1994a: 109).

However, it is important that a theory of organizational integrity and values-driven leadership does not leave out the importance of the manager's judgment and the ability to act and express themselves ethically. In "Law, Ethics and Managerial Judgment," Paine (1994b) argues that good management ethics should imply a close relationship between law and morality. Managers must be aware that something is not necessarily ethically right, just because it is legal. But at the same time the legally oriented ethicist understands the importance of jurisprudence as a necessity for ethics (Paine 1994b). Law and morality are not totally separate, as the law expresses an attempt to universalize and institutionalize morality with important ethical principles.

The law cannot capture all aspects of the decision, and it is still the manager's job to evaluate decisions in the light of the reflexive thought, which is the basis of good deeds. An understanding of judgment and ethical formulation competence based on organizational integrity can be said to mediate between ethics and law, without yielding one discipline to the other. The management decision is based on an acquired specialized ability to understand the complex relationship between personal and organizational integrity and to involve all the company's stakeholders in the ethical decision-making (Brown 2005; Rendtorff 2011b).

Good corporate citizenship is also about developing "the organization's integrity" so it helps to create connections between the individual and the organization's ethical awareness that mutually promote and support each other (Solomon 1999). There is a close correlation between the leader's ethical consciousness and the struggle to formulate a common platform for values-driven management in the company, and thus it is the function of managers' ethics to ensure the good corporate citizenship of the organization.

Corporate ethics and ethical formulation competence

A number of characteristic problems arise in connection with ethics in relation to employees in the workplace. These may be summarized as various forms of stress, based on the employees' lack of sense of dignity and recognition as equal, e.g. in connection with illness, old age, injuries, or cuts and restructuring of budgets and organizations. Additionally, we can mention the need to handle issues and problems in connection with the change, organizational breakdown and multicultural confrontations in the business organization. A key aspect of the business manager's integrity is in this context the manager's ability to moral thinking and judgment (Paine 1994b), what we may call "ethical formulation competency." This consists in the identification, analysis, reflection, and understanding of ethical issues, dilemmas, and problems. By defining words and concepts of ethical dilemmas and problems the ability to have ethical formulation competency can create an operational framework for an otherwise abstract, emotional, and inaccessible area. At all levels of ethics in public and private organizations managers need to be able to evaluate and formulate the problems, solutions, and dilemmas concerning ethical issues. This applies to investments, accounts, ownership, consumers, employees, and other stakeholders that influence the company's culture and function. A leader must therefore be aware of and able to take into account in decision-making the ethical dimensions in all parts of the management function, namely: (1) to be able to identify ethical issues that matter to the business; (2) to capture and justify the ethical implications of management decisions; (3) to use ethics in the implementation of values and development of corporate culture. The importance of having trained for the task a highly developed ethical formulation competence will soon be felt in: (1) work on implementing (cultural) values; (2) the ability to capture the ethical aspects of the daily management; (3) the capacity to wider legitimize and justify decisions. The ethical formulation competence expresses itself in this connection in the ability to engage in a responsive dialogue process with the company's various employees.

Employee ethics

Efforts to strengthen management ethics become more complicated, however, when we look at the reality of life in the company. In everyday life there is always the possibility of a potential conflict between the most powerful of the company's internal constituents. Respect for human dignity is increasingly important for resolving conflicts in organizations (Hicks 2011). Management can come into conflict with both shareholders and employees. At the same time, management is constantly in tension with the other two groups, where one can imagine various alliances, for example between shareholders and employees or employees and customers facing management and directors.

The tension comes from the possible split in the ethical commitments of management ethics. On the one hand, it must prioritize strong economic returns to shareholders, and on the other, it must think about development of the company and about the employees' working conditions. In this connection, management can benefit greatly from developing the relationships with employees, and this is where employee ethics comes into consideration as a means of developing good relationships with the employees and to ensure a good and fair treatment of the employees in the firm (Crane and Matten 2004, 2016).

The relationship between management and workers has historically been seen as a conflict between employers and workers. The employment relationship was not considered as a question of mutual understanding or what is ethically correct, but as a relationship that was characterized by struggle about the privileges and money. The workers have organized themselves into unions, and employers have formed their employers' associations as interest organizations through which their demands could be formulated.

This contradiction between workers and employers has largely determined the ethics in relation to employees, defined primarily as a matter of protection of employees' fundamental rights at work. Workers' rights are about strengthening the universal human rights in the employment relationship. The focus was previously on the protection and promotion of rights, such as the right to freedom of association, to good wages and working conditions, to unemployment and health insurance, to protection of privacy, and to freedom from discrimination. The ethical justification for these rights can be found in the basic ethical principles of taking into account the consideration of the person's autonomy, dignity, integrity, and vulnerability. These principles are found in many international conventions and declarations about workers' rights, such as the UN Universal Declaration of Human Rights 1948, developments in the political and social conventions (positive rights including the right to health, housing, education, etc.), ILO standards for workers' rights (freedom of association, occupational health, and prohibition of forced labor and child labor) and the Global Compact, but also in standards for measuring corporate social responsibility, such as SA8000, which focus on the protection of labor rights (Djursø and Neergaard 2006: 136; Buhmann 2014).

In connection with the growth of the welfare state and the emergence of a well-ordered labor market in many Western countries, employee policy has a more basic and fundamental dimension which in addition to consideration of fundamental rights of employees also puts the issue of the good life at work at the center of personnel policy. The focus is in this context the concept of work, and what can be done so that employees feel that the work becomes more meaningful and motivating for life (Cuilla, Martin, and Solomon 2007). One can say that the staff policy provides a basic question about the relationship between personal identity and work, namely, "Why do we work at all?" This shows that in many cases we not only attach importance of money to work, but also in late modern society we are increasingly using work as part of our self-realization and realization of the vision of the good life.

From a historical perspective, this new concept of work is quite unusual (Ciulla 2000). In classical Greece it was perceived as unworthy to work. Work was something done by slaves while the free aristocrat discussed policy at the Agora, the marketplace of the city state. Work was not an end in itself and was not meaningful to the lives of free citizens. This aristocratic attitude toward work was dominant in the Greek and Roman slave society, but with Christianity in the Middle Ages was created an understanding of work as a duty, and a portion of it was to live a godly life. This view was, however, a long time in the shadow of the aristocratic belief and with the Renaissance, which celebrated the creative human being, it came into conflict with the monks' discipline. Therefore it is only with the philosopher Hegel's description of the battle between masters and slaves, and his emphasis on the fact that slaves get their identity by reshaping nature, that there emerges a focus on work as part of human self-realization. This development continued with Karl

Marx when he asserted that the working man overcomes his alienation through real work, i.e. where workers themselves manage their work and master the means of production. Max Weber also connected work and identity by considering work as a vocation that is followed by the Protestant human working animal (Ciulla 2000).

In late modern society such a criticism of work hardly exists. We no longer strive for the utopia of the work-free society (see the work of the philosopher André Gorz) or the leisure society, but rather we see work as the goal of life. Money is not everything, but companies have the task to give people meaningful work. Work will more and more become the predominant basis for our self-esteem and self-respect. Work provides the identity, self-respect, self-realization, and recognition that is necessary to be a good person. The previously mentioned developments in theories of organization and management from Taylorism and Fordism to human resource management to values-driven management is prompted by the growing need to motivate employees, reinforce their self-management and allow for the development of the personality through work (Lipovetsky 1992, 2006).

It is also important to note that values-driven management and ethics programs in companies are introduced to support management and the business environment's calls for more ethics and responsibility in the company and also to mediate between the requirement for strengthening worker's rights and the requirement for increased employee motivation. From this perspective, we can normatively summarize some of the requirements that we can ask for in an ethics program in a business that combines consideration for the interests of management with the need for staff development.

We could thus highlight the need to focus on the role of the employees in values-driven management, and account must be taken of the internal social responsibility for employee welfare and wellbeing. At the heart of values-driven management is a concern that values should help strengthen the employees' intrinsic motivation to work. This is the basis for creating loyalty and trust in work and a basis for involving employees in company management, which eventually also helps to reduce potential conflicts between employees and management. It is also important to create legitimate channels for the employees' freedom of expression and whistle-blowing, i.e. channels through which employees can inform management or the public about ethical issues in the company.

Whistle-blowing is a hot topic in contemporary society. We can refer to the leaking of confidential information from governments that was undertaken by Julian Assange and his WikiLeaks team, or the infamous scandal concerning Edward Snowden, who publicized classified information about the US government surveillance of private citizens, and as a consequence had to flee his country and go to Russia. We can also point to Bradley (now Chelsea) Manning, who in the US also publicized classified government information, and initially received a severe prison sentence.

Nevertheless, even before these cases the topic of whistle-blowing created much controversy and fascination. We can mention here the many cases of whistle-blowing in relation to business firms and private organizations. Often such cases refer to situations where individuals feel moral responsibility to make public any wrongdoing and fraud in their organizations. Indeed, from that perspective, whistle-blowing emerges as a potential weapon against corruption, mismanagement, and general non-compliance with legal obligations by a broader public (Thüsing and Forst 2016). In the United States, famous cases where whistle-blowing was important include the Enron and WorldCom Scandals with the collapse of the accounting firm Arthur Andersen, which led to the Sarbanes–Oxley legislation.

The problem of whistle-blowing provides an important example of the conflict between employees' loyalty to the company versus their obligations to society or others outside the company. It is about protecting employees who by virtue of their affiliation with the company have obtained information on the company's damaging activities toward others. The employee believes that the public has a right to know about these conditions because of their unethical or abusive nature. Here it can be argued that the employee has an obligation to come forward with the information when it can be said to be in the public interest.

This is illustrated in the American film *The Insider* about a chemical researcher in a tobacco company who finds that the company with full knowledge has made its cigarettes become more addictive. The researcher chooses at great risk with the help of a journalist to make his knowledge public. His information is essential to a lawsuit concerning the actions of the company, which mean that more people die of lung cancer. In this case the employee has reason to suspect that it is of benefit to the public to obtain information about the damage that the company has caused, and we can argue that the employee's information leakage therefore can be ethically justified. This does not remove the risk of job dismissal and other reprisals that an employee runs if he leaks confidential information from the company to the public.

Therefore, whistle-blowers are often in a very difficult situation. They can be bound by all forms of contractual ties to the company, which means that they can be prosecuted if they break their confidentiality. It is true that the employee's contract with the company includes a certain loyalty and commitment, but this cannot be unlimited, and the company has no right to put strong political and social constraints on their staff. Although one can say that values-driven management and ethics may require a certain acceptance of the common standards, this of course does not imply a blind acceptance of the organization's norms and values. In the light of the ethical principles the concern for the individual's autonomy, dignity, integrity, and vulnerability should imply that the employee, in cases where public and societal interests are at stake, must go beyond his or her obligations toward the company and rely on their rights to freedom of expression.

It remains a question whether values-driven management can be used to address the fundamental conflict between workers and employers, which is rooted in the contradictions of the employment relationship. This tension between values-driven management and the conception of the employment relationship as a conflict between employees and management manifests itself to a particular degree when we discuss possible democratic dimensions of values-driven management. In many cases it seems impossible to overcome contradictions and tensions without agreeing to create real political democracy in the workplace, which is the same as leaving companies to the workers, and therefore this may appear on the edge of the principles of a private capitalist free-market economy. The problem is just what to do next; we cannot return to Taylorism or to a more hierarchical organization. There is nothing else to do than to work seriously and honestly with values-driven management, so that we come as close as possible to the democratic ideal of a workplace with mutual respect and understanding between stakeholders.

The banality of evil in organizations

The necessity of focusing on employee ethics can be illustrated by a problem in organizations where employees become part of an institutionalized evil in the company. The concept of the banality of evil in organizations comes from the German-American political thinker Hannah Arendt (1906-1975) in her philosophy of judgment and responsibility. In the book *Eichmann in Jerusalem. A Report on the Banality of Evil* (1964) she analyzed the Nazi criminal Adolf Eichmann, who was partly responsible for the organization of the Holocaust, as an expression of the banality of evil (see also Laustsen and Rendtorff 2002; Rendtorff 2014b). Even though it is a part of totalitarianism as radical evil, Eichmann's evil is not evil in the ordinary sense, but rather it is evil of the administrator, official, and organization man. In her analysis, this evil administrator was an obedient bureaucrat with no personal involvement in his work. He was an ordinary person with a particular intelligence who showed ambition as a bureaucrat without any ethical awareness of the morality of his actions.

Arendt characterized the personality of Adolf Eichmann by emphasizing that:

1 He was unable to think critically.
2 He had no moral sense or reflective judgment, and had little memory of his awful acts.
3 He did not understand ethically what he had done.
4 He had no ethical formulation competency.
5 He was an ordinary employee and officer with ambitions to make a career in the system.
6 He did his "duty" for his superior in the system without considering the moral implications of the system's actions.

According to Arendt it is characteristic that the bureaucrat does not take responsibility for political decisions, but just implements those decisions. Moreover, the victims collaborate in their own extermination. The duty of obedience is the first virtue of the bureaucrat. The bureaucrat considers the norms of the system as the universal morality. It is a characteristic of the bureaucratic system that it makes opposition look useless and meaningless. Eichmann should be considered as the paradigm of the "organization man" who simply fulfills his role in the system to the letter. With these dimensions of the actions of the bureaucratic administrator in the totalitarian system Arendt ends by sarcastically describing Eichmann going to the gallows "with great dignity" and performing all his clichés of the Nazi system. Arendt ends the description by saying "It was as though in those last minutes he was summing up the lesson that his long course in human wickedness had taught us – the lesson of the fearsome, word-and-thought-defying banality of evil" (Arendt 1964: 252). With this description of Adolf Eichmann, Arendt helps us to understand the dimensions of moral blindness that we need to avoid in private business and public administration (Rendtorff 2014b).

After Arendt, different interpretations of moral blindness, power, and domination from the perspective of the concept of systemic action have been presented. The sociologist Zygmunt Bauman pointed to the organizational rationality in the Holocaust. Stanley Milgram pointed to total obedience as systemic rationality of ordinary men. Philip Zimbardo talked about role-playing in organizational systems. Bauman argues that the Holocaust shows the hidden potentialities of modernity. Auschwitz is, according to this point of view, similar to the modern factory but with people as the raw material and death the final product. Auschwitz is the essence of modernity because of the rationality of the Holocaust. Bauman points to the fact that the bureaucracy of the Nazis was based on well-defined calculations of aims and means. The system of the Holocaust was therefore extremely rational, based on strict administrative and organizational discipline and structures. The moral blindness of the system was happening in a very efficient and goal-rational organizational system. Violence and dehumanization were authorized and accomplished in modern organizations. The American psychologist Stanley Milgram tested Eichmann's theses empirically in a professional and organizational context in his famous obedience experiment, published in *Obedience to Authority* (1974). Milgram's experiments showed that ordinary people as members of a hierarchical order system under pressure are able to perform immoral acts. The subjects were in many cases able to inflict suffering with a sense of innocence in their eagerness to fulfill their job and role in the system (Laustsen and Rendtorff 2002; Rendtorff 2014b). Milgram refers to it as a cybernetic-organizational approach to obedience. Following Milgram we can say that moral blindness does not lead to a feeling of the loss of morality, but that instead it receives another focus. In contrast to unconditional moral sensibility, the dominating morals become the feelings of loyalty, discipline and honor that are motivated in the wish of the individual to be a part of the instrumental role community of the organizational system. Milgram's experiment demonstrates the need to have employees with ethical formulation skills, high integrity, and abilities to make good and right decisions through reflective judgment.

More recently, Philip Zimbardo, with his Stanford Prison experiments in social psychology, described in *The Lucifer Effect. How Good People Turn Evil* (2007), has emphasized role-playing and role identification as essential for cybernetic obedience in organizations. These experiments are about the transformation of character from good to evil. The experiments started out as fun, but soon the borderline between reality and fantasy started to blur. Certain prisoners had a strong personality transformation. We can say that a certain alchemy of character changed their personality. Even Zimbardo was taken in by this system of evil. He was enthusiastically working on his experiments and he did not see the evil he produced. Only his girlfriend and later wife made him see by her immediate reaction how evil his actions were. That made him stop the experiment after a week. In his interpretation of the experiments, Zimbardo emphasizes the close relation between good and evil as two sides of the same coin. He shows how evil can be a part of good and vice versa. He also shows how good can produce evil. However, the most important element in this production of evil is role-taking within systems. We adopt certain roles and we aim at realizing these roles without reflecting on their general impact on human beings. Evil is a part of this general role production. Evil is in the system. Zimbardo can interpret the events of the Abu Ghraib Prison events based on his prison experiments. It is the same personality transformation that we experience in the cruel behavior of the guards in this prison. It is the essential achievement of Zimbardo to demonstrate how role-playing in systems can create evil and change personalities. Personalities are dependent on systems and people act within the systems. It is difficult for individuals to resist the pressures that they are exposed to in such systems.

On the basis of these theories of moral blindness we can deduce the following elements:

> 1. Moral blindness implies that the administrator or judge has no capacity of moral thinking. 2. The administrator or judge only follows orders and justifies his or her actions by reference to the technical goal-rationality of the organizational system. 3. The administrator or judge is strongly influenced by the ideology, principles or instrumental values of the organization. 4. This attachment includes an abstraction from concrete human needs and concerns in the legal or administrative system. 5. In many cases the moral blindness strangely enough includes collaborations from the victims of the harm. 6. The victims follow the rationality of the system and they identify with their roles either motivated by pure obedience or rather motivated by

> an attempt to minimize a greater harm. 7. Moral blindness contains a dehumanization of the victims and people or stakeholders implied in the process. They are considered not as human beings but as elements, things or functions of the system. 8. Moral blindness relies on total obedience by the administrators of the system. 9. Technology and instrumental rationality is an essential element in the administration of the organization or legal system. 10. Each participant in the organization is accomplishing a specific work function with a specific task but he or she has no general overview of the organizational system. 11. Judges or administrators may behave opportunistically to follow their own interest with regard to the main goal of the instrumental system. 12. Judges or administrators may act irrationally beyond common human understandings of morality in order to serve the instrumental rationality of the organizational system. 13. The administrative obedience to realize the organizational aim becomes the central interest of the administrators of the organization. 14. Obedience, role identification and task commitment remains the central and ultimate virtue of the commitment of members of the organization to the organizational system. 15. Each member or administrator of the organizational system commits themselves to the values of the organizational goal of the system.
>
> (Rendtorff 2014b, 58–59)

In particular, Frederick Bruce Bird, in his book *The Muted Conscience. Moral Silence and the Practice of Ethics in Business* (1996), has contributed to the definition of moral blindness in organizations. This book provides the most comprehensive recent attempt to define the application of the concept of moral blindness in business ethics, but it can also be applied to public administration. In fact, Bird extends the concept of moral blindness to include moral muteness and moral deafness. Moral muteness is defined as the inability of people to defend their ideas and ideals. In Bird's analysis we can say that moral blindness is a sort of covering notion that includes the concepts of moral muteness and moral deafness. As indicated, Bird defines moral blindness in the following way: "People are morally blind when they fail to see or recognize moral concerns and expectations that bear upon their activities and involvements" (Bird 1996: 85). This shows how moral blindness is present in business administration. We can also find an attempt to apply Hannah Arendt's philosophy of the banality of evil to systems of contemporary public administration in the book by G.B. Adams and D.L. Balfour, *Unmasking Administrative Evil* (2009).

Research in business ethics emphasizes the importance of moral imagination (Werhane 1999) and ethical formulation competency in order to deal with moral blindness, muteness, and deafness in organizations (Bird 1996). We need to be able to relate critically and reflectively to our mental models (Werhane *et al.* 2011). It is a question of integrating moral consciousness and corporate culture (Goodpaster 2007), and in order to overcome evil in administration we need to unmask it from the perspective of moral imagination in the context of deliberative democracy (Adams and Balfour 2009).

14 Consumers, public relations, and ethical accounting reports

On the basis of the analysis of the ethical obligations in relation to the company's internal stakeholders, we will now turn to the relationship with the external stakeholders, such as consumers, communities, and the general public, from the perspective of cosmopolitan business ethics. Ethics toward consumers is built on trust and social responsibility. In an era of globalization and communication, legitimate public relations become particularly important, and the company's ethical accounting and supplementary reports are an important dimension of the effort to establish good public relations and manage corporate legitimacy in society.

Consumer ethics

Consumers and customers are among the most important external stakeholders in relation to corporate social responsibility and ethical obligations of the business firm (Crane and Matten 2016). Usually, we may argue that the commercial relationship between seller and buyer is purely a legal contract, and that the company has no other obligations to consumers other than what the purchase contract says. The definition of the consumer as a stakeholder, however, means that it goes beyond the purely formal relationship and considers consumer and business as being in a much closer social relationship.

This means not only that the company can consider consumers as objects of profit maximization or to increase its power, but that consumers and purchasers of the company's products must be described as key stakeholders that ultimately are fundamental to the company's survival. Therefore, the company must pay attention to the consumers as a part of the company and help to protect their independence, autonomy, dignity, integrity, and vulnerability, that is, on the whole their basic rights.

At the same time, consumers, like shareholders, have changed status from being passive buyers and recipients of the company's production to manifesting themselves publicly and critically in relation to the company products. Today, companies are selling products, but they also sell attitudes, feelings, and lifestyle, as we saw in the sociological analysis of the late modern society (Lipovetsky 2006; Rendtorff 2014a). Every product includes a production history, signals determined values, and is marked by brands, values, meaning, and a significance content, that help to give the buyer identity, appealing to his or her attitudes and lifestyle. You can say that the company's values cannot fail to express themselves in the product and that the consumer, by rejecting or selecting different products, takes a position regarding the firm's attitudes and values (Jensen 1999). In this sense, the concept of the political consumer has been generalized, so that all of us, more-or-less voluntarily or knowingly, have become political consumers who signal attitudes, lifestyles, and values through the products we buy and appreciate.

Marketing and ethics

A fundamental problem is how to sell products in an ethical manner. In marketing ethics, there are four basic conditions that need to be analyzed: product ethics, the ethics of price, the ethics of distribution, and communication ethics (Brenkert 2008). Product ethics deals with whether it is ethical to market products based on manipulation with consumer satisfaction and enjoyment. The ethics of price deals with the price level in terms of product quality, but also with manipulation of the price by the company. Distribution ethics is about how products are distributed between the rich and poor, and communication ethics is about how businesses can communicate advertising and sales of the product in an ethically acceptable manner (Boyer 2001).

This whole problem can be understood in terms of the figure of Hermes from Greek mythology, whose name means messenger. Hermes was the god of thieves, but also of merchants, while being the messenger of the gods to the humans. The merchant traditionally had a bad reputation as someone who wanted to cheat the buyers and was therefore considered no better than a thief. As the ethics of sales and marketing is considered as a matter of communication, the figure of Hermes is therefore of interest for understanding the tensions in marketing ethics. It is Hermes who helps to create a consistency in the communication, which is a prerequisite for the successful exchange of goods and money (Boyer 2001).

The concept of the political consumer is commonly known from large international conflicts, such as the boycott of Shell Oil in 1995 in connection with the crisis when Shell announced the dumping of a drilling platform in the North Sea. Here Greenpeace started an action where some of their activists chained themselves to the drilling platform in the North Sea (M. P. Sørensen 2004; Rendtorff 2009). Shell's arrogance in connection with the case created a chain reaction where thousands of consumers across the world in protest did not want to buy Shell products. Although there was good scientific evidence that the dumping was probably the most environmentally friendly solution, and although it was approved by the British government, Shell had to stop the dumping in order not to incur a historic economic loss. The business was not good enough to communicate with its customers, and it had no understanding of customer values. The Shell boycott shows very clearly that there is a relationship between ethics and values and choice of products, even though it is very difficult to give a precise determination of the motives and extension of the ethical dimensions of consumer choice compared with, for example, price or quality.

Consumer ethics and political consumption deal with the company's responsibility to its customers, i.e. the responsibility to produce good products which respect the basic quality requirements, are economically viable, have the desired value for the consumer, and are not environmentally harmful (M. P. Sørensen 2004; Rendtorff 2009). Increased consumer awareness in late modern society has led to consumers and the general public being much more focused on whether the product meets with ethical requirements regarding respect for sustainability, and this is not an erosion of social cohesion in society. It implies that the conditions under which the product is made, namely production history, are becoming more important, and it is required by the company that it can provide a coherent and ethically sound production history (Coff 2005; Rendtorff 2016a) about the conditions in which the product has been made, including whether the workers have received a good salary, and if the products are imported, whether the product comes from a country that has democratic governance and respect for human rights. There are also demands on companies that they can demonstrate that the product is not harmful to humans and does not violate general moral standards in society. Finally, in the context of the increased environmental and health awareness, there is extra focus on whether the product can harm the environment, animal, or plant life, and in general the future of human life on the planet. So there are good arguments for bringing consumer interests into the spotlight and to involve consumers in the development of values concerning the company and its products. In a globalized experience society, these values increasingly affect the competitiveness of products in the market.

Politically conscious and active consumers are no longer a marginal phenomenon in society, and today there is much more focus on ethically and politically focused consumption, which according to the Institute for Future Research in Denmark can be defined as "a behavior where consumer choice of products and producers puts emphasis on conscious attitudes or values that targets community" (M. P. Sørensen 2004: 14). Consumer ethics has become a dominant parameter in understanding consumers' behavior, since it is our values and attitudes that more or less consciously guide our choices. Attitudes and values are present in our consumption behavior, either negatively when we reject certain products, or as in the ethical investment where consumers positively select certain companies that show that they do good with their products, e.g. with their ecological profile, fair trade products, or environmentally friendly production.

Especially in relation to protection of the environment and following the international focus on sustainability, climate change, and world environmental problems, the ethical consumer has been labeled as the green, ecological, or environmentally friendly consumer (Devinney, Auger, and Eckhardt 2011). Ecological values represent a great concern that products do not pose a threat to health or to the environment. This consumer requires that the production must be friendly to nature and animals. There should be control of the ecological life-cycle and waste problems, and the products and production methods should respect international conventions on sustainability and biodiversity. With the development of the theory of the triple bottom line with respect for economic, ecological, and social dimensions of production, environmental quality requirements for the products have been generalized not only to be about the environment, but to include social production circumstances, such as respect for workers' human rights.

Thus, we can say that the ethical and political consumer has made their concern for the community an integral part of their buying behavior. Despite the fact that it may seem paradoxical that all goods should reflect political and ethical considerations, value preferences have become an integral part of the perception of buying and selling in today's economic market (Devinney *et al.* 2011). Critical voices argue that we have thus been confronted with an unfortunate politicization of the private economy and the private market, as consumers now cannot be perceived as value-neutral economic agents, but rather function as actors who assess the company's products and services not only economically, but also politically (M. P. Sørensen 2004). The trend is not surprising if it is analyzed as a part of the growing interest in CSR.

Instead of reducing consumers to pure utilitarian actors who always maximize the benefits of their buying behavior at the lowest possible price, the trend toward integration of attitudes in consumption documents that emotions, preferences, and values are integrated into our purchasing behavior so that the economic value of products cannot be measured only on the economic market, but also depends on the feelings and emotions and esthetic quality which influence our evaluations of the products. We can say that there is a close relationship between ethics and economics, where an economic preference in the end cannot be separated from the values and politically and esthetically conscious preferences of the consumers. The company's politicization and the performance of the company's good citizenship responding to consumer demand for products which reflect environmental and social attitudes requires companies to be aware of their values and articulate and have a strong value foundation values: issues of sustainability, human rights, product authenticity, esthetic liability, etc. In this sense we can perceive the emergence of a kind of extended consumer responsibility in cosmopolitan world society.

The company and the local community

A key aspect of CSR is the active contribution of the firm to the local community. This can be done by creating partnerships or otherwise integrating into the local community through different business activities or philanthropic engagements (McIntosh *et al.* 1998). Partnerships with the local community and its organizations are based on integration of the business company into the community so that it can achieve legitimacy and engage in good relations with its neighboring communities and with the countries or regions in which it operates, such as through contributions to support local activities and protection of employees and their families or with support for education or health promotion activities. However, it may also include help to local non-profit organizations and partnerships with local firms and NGOs.

In general, this has been regarded as an expression of corporate philanthropy or charitable contributions to community. While this may be welcome, it is important to emphasize that the community may need more of the firm's active involvement in the community and would prefer partnerships based on mutual recognition rather than passive financial contributions to the community.

We can say that the company by engaging in the community can express its gratitude for the help it has received through the community's contribution to its activities. But if the company should engage in local community problems in a constructive manner, it is important that it understands and identifies the problems that affect the local community. These can involve serious social or economic problems such as poverty, crime, or discrimination. Once the company has begun addressing the problems, it is important that a strategy for the company's social contribution to the community is formulated, for example, in collaboration with various interest groups and stakeholders.

It is an integral part of European policy on CSR that companies should engage in the community to combat social exclusion and thereby contribute to creating greater social cohesion. European governments, e.g. in Denmark and in the UK, have endeavored to make partnerships and social responsibility in the community a central element in the development of the company's local roots and of a sense of belonging. It is therefore considered very important for the company to engage in dialogue with relevant stakeholders in the community, so that the company becomes an integral part of its society.

Public relations and legitimacy

The increased focus on corporate ethics and responsibility toward consumers has made ethics an integral part of modern marketing, advertising, and branding of the company.

When we have to deal with the company's external stakeholders, we can observe an increase in the degree of reflexivity and ethical awareness of the firm, going from the classic view of the company as a legal contract to today's ethically reflected company that works to develop and manage legitimate public relations in a complex, polylingual, and polycentric society with many different requirements and reference points and demands from the various stakeholders of the company (Jensen 2000; Holmström 2004).

Managing legitimacy and the public sphere

The concept of legitimacy has become central to understanding business ethics and CSR (Le Roy and Marchesnay 2005: 77). Where the classic concept of organizations from the 1960s understood organizations as closed rational systems, the increased focus on the company's ethics involves a new understanding of the company as being in close interaction with its surroundings. Organizations are now considered as open systems, where it is not the material or technological circumstances, but ethical values, cultural norms, symbols, and cognitive performance in the company's external environment that are essential for its development (Suchman 1995). The concept of legitimacy is fundamental to this new organizational understanding. This concept comes from the sociologist Max Weber who distinguished between traditional, charismatic-authoritarian and rational identification forms. Modern organizations have thus largely been determined by rational legitimacy concerns, which is the basis for the classic business economic theories of strategic planning, goal-rational management, etc. Gradually, the rational identification form has been criticized, and thinkers like Habermas and Luhmann have conceptualized alternative legitimacy concepts. Habermas claims that legitimacy is based on the force of the better argument and its freedom from coercion, which points toward a democratic view of business ethics. Likewise Luhmann has emphasized that legitimacy is dependent on the company's various communication media in various communications systems.

Mark C. Suchman has in organization theory done much work in providing a description of various forms of legitimacy in the light of institutional theory. He distinguishes between strategic and institutional legitimacy theories which have not necessarily been in dialogue with each other. The theories have either had a pragmatic action-oriented, normative-moral, or cognitive-epistemological perspective. Common to these theories, however, we can formulate a definition of legitimacy as the process by which an organization justifies its right to exist to other subordinate or equivalent organizations (Suchman 1995: 573). Organizational legitimacy is based on values and cultural conditions that justify the organization's right to exist. To gain legitimacy implies an effort to create the conditions to perceive and evaluate the organization according to a number of desirable values and standards. Legitimacy is first of all a cultural construction, but may be more or less embedded in society's basic perceptions. Organizations today follow a purely administrative and technological form of leadership and management without thinking through their legitimacy conditions, and are highly vulnerable to their environment. Therefore, there is increasing focus on pragmatic, moral, and cognitive legitimation of the business corporation's activities. Business ethics is an important instrument for developing and influencing this legitimacy, and values-driven management contains elements of an effort to pragmatically make the interaction with the environment to function better, morally to do the right thing, and cognitively to make the outside world perceive the company's actions as "natural," i.e. take them for granted in the community and thereby ensure a high degree of legitimacy of the firm in society.

The classic business organization in the 19th century and at the beginning of the 20th century saw itself as an economic organization of production, which did not have the task of relating to its legal, political, and social environment. After World War II there emerged a new business understanding where the firm was conscious of its impact on the external community, but it was not common to propose that the firm should act strategically in order to investigate this issue. A more reflective variant of understanding the role of business in society arose during the 1950s. According to this view the company should be aware of the external influences and the need for good public relations, and therefore contribute to lobbying to influence its environment.

Finally, one can mention the ethical reflective and socially responsible company, which has emerged over the last 30 years and which also considers relationship to the outside world as a question of legitimacy, ethics, and responsibility (Jensen 2000). This business does not just do marketing and advertising for itself but wants to create itself as a business with legitimate public relations. Such a business firm considers branding, storytelling, corporate identity, and values as an integrated part of legitimate public relationships where the business firm is working strategically to be a good corporate citizen.

In this concept of the quest to create good public relations that converge with the company's ethical and socially responsible profile, for critical reflective consciousness, ethics and social responsibility are not just empty "window dressing" approaches. Legitimate public communication is not just about spin or instrumental communication but manifests itself as the company's honest interest in promoting ethically consistent values, responsibility, and identity.

Therefore, public relations is not just a matter of marketing, but serves management function at the highest level in the company. Legitimate public relations with a focus on stakeholder relations, values, ethics, and responsibility is essential for the development of the company. Legitimate public relations includes a wide range of external stakeholders who affect or are affected by the company. It concerns relationships with local, national, and international public authorities and administrators (local, national, EU, and UN), the local community, and civil society with consumers, interest groups and other stakeholders. From this perspective, public relations appears as the "continuous and systematic management function with which companies, private and public organizations and institutions are trying to get attention, sympathy and support from members of the public, which they are in contact with" (Nielsen 2001: 60f.).

By virtue of this definition the ethics of public relations aims at making the company appear as honest and proactive as possible in order to show the company in the public space as an ethically responsible economic, political, and social actor, who as a good citizen will contribute to the sustainability of society and thereby strengthen its legitimacy as a serious participant in the public debate and decision-making of the community. Jürgen Habermas in one of his early works, *Structural Transformation of the Public Sphere* (1962), has described this ideal of a public sphere as a common space in society where society's various citizens could meet in an open and serious discussion about society's political and social conditions.

Each citizen is considered as a moral person who will contribute to the common good of the community. In continuation of our determination of the company as a moral actor in society, it must be a requirement that the company is also contributing to this debate from its responsibility and values. This especially in a time when many critics argue that the ideal of serious public debate with economic and technical system dominance has been replaced by mass media and spin doctors who do not contribute with serious arguments and ethics-related policy discussions, but just try to manipulate and convince to achieve power and financial gain.

The ethical business needs to take hold of the ideal significance of legitimacy, which is to search for truth and action that is based on practical reason and moral wisdom. As part of the strategic management, highly developed public relations aims at having an open and reflexive two-way communication with the outside world. This view is based on Habermas' ideal of communicative reason based on respect for the coercion-free force of the better argument and on preparedness to listen to all voices in the debate: the public sphere must not only be subject to strategic and instrumental communication in order to promote self-interest and profits. In view of Habermas' theory, deliberative arguments may be the key to the company's successful public relations.

At first glance, many commentators may argue that this is idealistic and very far from the suggestive and ideological elements of advertising and marketing, which are central to corporate efforts to sell their products or services. However, thanks to rising consumer activism and awareness of corporate ethics and responsibility in civil society, there will be less contradiction between sustainable business management and a strategy for legitimate public relations, accepting the communicative reason's basic principles.

The ethics of public relations aims at basing corporate communication on fundamental respect for truth and making honesty and moral integrity central features of the company's basic image. The rhetorical means ethos, pathos, and logos can only be meaningful on this fundamental basis of trusting communication with the company's stakeholders.

This requirement of serious and genuine communication becomes no less important in a time when companies are challenged by many different actors, such as consumer groups or NGOs or state institutions. These organizations often see themselves as the critical public's representatives, to uncover shameless corporate hypocrisy. Often public relations include therefore also crisis communication when aggressive stakeholders are critically campaigning against the company's activities.

We need truthful and honest answers to the charges, if companies do not want to lose face in public. The requirement for truthful public communication is therefore also justified from the fact that public relations in mass media society is very floating and difficult to control. The temptation to manipulate the public and follow the spin doctor's rhetoric that communication can be fully controlled and determined represents a very risky communication strategy. For despite a possible short-term economic gain this will in the long term be dangerous for the company and definitely not in line with ethics in stakeholder management and social responsibility. If a company gets a bad image and loses public confidence, it can take decades of good deeds before it can regain the lost goodwill.

Construction of public relations in different companies

Inger Jensen, in "Public Relations and the Public Sphere in the Future" (2000), has developed a very good chart showing the different ideal-typical forms of corporate public relations. A similar scheme is made by Verstraten in the book *Business Ethics. Broadening the Perspective* (2000: 175f.), which also highlights some ideal-typical understandings of CSR. Table 14.1 combines these two tables. The table shows the development from an economically responsible company to a company that is proactive and economically, legally, and ethically responsible (Jensen 2000).

Table 14.1 Legitimacy challenges: construction of public relations in different companies according to systemic requirements

Behavioral features	*The economically and legally responsible company*	*The company that recognizes the need for social responsibility*	*The ethical and proactively socially responsible business*
Agents who define values	The market	The market and the state	Market, state, public discussion, institutionalized stakeholders
Objectives and means	Economic success on the basis of compliance to minimum legal rules	Economic success in society's economic and legal rules and general customary morality	Economic success, liability, and legitimacy and respect in society
Management focus	Rational strategic planning in relation to economic markets	Bound rationality from traditional strategic and economic methods. However, has a certain openness toward new methods	Values-driven management, internal and external negotiations, values are defined by the triple bottom line
The search for legitimacy	Legal and economic criteria	Is willing to look at problems and issues that are beyond the economic market	Accepts the role that it has been given in the public and the social system
Ethical standards	Considers the economic market and the company as value-neutral	Defines standards from a community-oriented perspective. Avoids doing things that are against the prevailing social norms	Has conscious attitudes to the topics discussed in public
Social acceptance of the company's actions	Considers its actions as limited to what the shareholders and owners can accept. Does not go beyond this framework	Takes into account the legal and economic requirements, but also goes beyond them and relates to the stakeholders who are affected by the actions	Is willing to be accountable for its actions with other groups, even those that are not affected by company actions
Strategy for action	Seeks economic profit and adopts defensive adaptation to ensure that costs are externalized	Reactive adaptation. When possible, identifies externalized costs. Compensates victims of these costs (e.g. pollution)	Proactive adaptation. Takes leadership in the development of new technology. Evaluates the company's actions. Is proactive toward future social change
Reply to social pressure	Maintains a low profile if the company is attacked, uses PR to make its public image better, rejects errors and public discontent, publishes information only when it is legally required	Accepts responsibility for solving specific problems. Admits mistakes in previous practice and tries to convince the public that current practice is better	Communicates openly and self-critically with government and the general public. Works to improve existing legislation and business practices. Protests against conditions that do not serve the public good

(Continued)

Table 14.1 (Continued)

Behavioral features	*The economically and legally responsible company*	*The company that recognizes the need for social responsibility*	*The ethical and proactively socially responsible business*
Legislative and political activities	Seeks to maintain the status quo, actively opposes laws, internalizes costs that the company has previously avoided. Tries to keep lobbying activities secret	Is willing to work with external parties for better regulation. Less secret in lobbying activities	Avoids meddling in politics and does not seek to influence laws that the company has a special interest in; helps contrast the state with making relevant laws Tries to be open and honest about lobbying activities
Philanthropy	Contributes only when it is of direct benefit, or sees the company contributions as the responsibility of individual employees	Contributes to non-controversial and well-established purposes, which are also supported by the employees	Contributes additional support for controversial purposes of groups whose needs cannot be covered

Ethical accounting and sustainability reports

An important aspect of the company's environment relationships is the attempt to obtain goodwill and confidence from the outside world. This is done through the effort to integrate the company's stakeholders into the external activities of the business firm (Zadek, Pruzan, and Evans 1997). One such company, which is open and willing to be change-oriented in relation to the environment, uses a so-called balanced scorecard (Kaplan and Norton 1996), i.e. an measurement of value-added material and immaterial value (in various fields such as economy, customer satisfaction, business processes, learning), or ethical and social financial and sustainability reports to describe the relationship of the firm to the community and to its environment. This is part of the efforts of the company to show how ethics and values are integrated into the company's activities (McPhail and Walters 2009).

Ethical accounts and sustainability reports describe and chart the company's social, environmental, and ethical performance as a part of the annual reports of the firm. With this in mind, it is important to distinguish between ordinary accounting ethics and the new and broader approach, which manifests itself in the company's additional comments and reports (Pietras-Jensen 2005). The traditional accounting ethics deals with more limited ethical questions to the company's financial accounting and auditing.

Accounting officers and auditors are responsible for ensuring that they follow the profession's basic rules, which must be based on honesty, objectivity, and respect for the law. Here, the auditors and accountants appear as an ordinary profession, who should be aware of integrity and responsibility in their accounting policies. Transparency, objectivity, truthfulness, compassion, and concern for the public interest are here important principles. The Enron scandal, not least the defunct accounting firm Arthur Andersen's contributions to blurring the accounts, with the resulting Sarbanes–Oxley Act and the rules for accounting and corporate governance, focuses on the type of accounting ethics where the independent accounting profession serves as the basis for accounting practices and accounting policies (McPhail and Walters 2009).

The new accounting policies with ethical and social accounts and sustainability reports are based on these principles of independence, transparency, and objectivity, and this implies a significant extension of the concept of accounting. Financial accounts and reports consist not only of an economic or financial accounting and budget, but should also include a wider set of indicators and supplementary comments and reports. The idea is that corporate ethics and social responsibility should appear in the accounts. The financial statements and the supplementary report should inform about the company's successful efforts to work consciously with ethics and responsibility, and it must also give an idea of the problems and dilemmas that the company faces. When we include both the financial and economic, but also the ethical, social, and environmental conditions in the financial statements and reports, we get a much broader concept of corporate ethical accounting practices than was previously the case.

Ethical, social, and environmental reporting are at the same time oriented to internal and external stakeholders (McPhail and Walters 2009). They thus reflect the company's new position in society as a corporate citizen with cosmopolitan responsibilities who must report in relation to shareholders, employees, customers, suppliers, and also to society as a whole (McIntosh *et al.* 1998). All relevant stakeholders should be involved in the reports in order to judge the company's sustainability and progress toward better use of resources. In contrast to the financial accounts, it may be difficult to judge the qualitative aspects of company's development. In general it can be a problem to judge whether the company has good development and contributes to society's long-term sustainability from the principles of the protection of autonomy, dignity, integrity, and vulnerability.

The difficulty in making quantifications of these conditions means that alternative reporting must work with softer accounting procedures for measurement and verification of data concerning the company's performance on ethics and responsibility. Conversely, also the financial and economic accounts have many sources of error, and therefore it is important to supplement them with environmental, social, and ethical reports. But that does not make the measurement of values-driven management, ethics, and responsibility more objective, and it is important that attempts are made to verify by means of alternative accounting models that are also based on the external independent auditors and accounting staff.

The supplementary reports should not be seen as mere historical accounts. They are important instruments for the company's self-reflection and strategic development. There need not be a contrast between the economic and financial accounts and the social, ethical, and environmental description of the company's performance. The social report provides information about the treatment of employees' working and health conditions, and it can also be used to clarify community relations. Ethical accounting can in addition be said to focus on the effects of ethics, values-driven management, and CSR both externally and internally, while environmental accounting can provide more information about the company's contribution to environmental sustainability.

If the company is only evaluated on the financial bottom line, it can give a false impression of its sustainability and long-term performance, and a true picture of a company requires an integrated description of its financial, social, and environmental relationship and performance. In this way the supplementary reports contribute to stabilizing the company's activities and to gaining greater knowledge about their social legitimacy. The supplementary reports and accounts are therefore extremely important to develop ethics and social responsibility. It is one of the reasons why companies are so actively involved in constructing voluntary external accounts. In addition to the legal requirements for companies and corporations, annual reports with voluntary non-financial accounts document the company's willingness to be open and dialogue-seeking about fundamental strategic issues. Often, the non-financial accounts are also published outside the mandatory annual report or as leaflets and brochures that complement the annual reports (Pietras-Jensen 2005). These reports often appear with an impressive layout like a mixture of marketing and a serious report about the company's work, and much is being done to describe corporate values and management philosophy as an expression of the contribution of the firm to society.

It is characteristic that the corporate alternative accounts combine the attempt to capture the company's ethics and responsibility with an effort to describe the company's identity, history, and basic vision for its business and its relations to society. This applies to knowledge management accounting, presenting hidden knowledge or value resources of the company, and this is also documented by the many different names that companies provide for their supplementary reports, i.e. in addition to the terms ethical, social, and environmental accounts also are quality, stakeholder, holistic reports etc. Many accounts also refer to international standards for alternative accounts and supplementary reports such as SA8000 international labor standards (ILO) or professional ethics codes that can be used as widely known standards of accounting. It is characteristic of these types of reporting that the accounts are used for communication and for reporting on the company's non-material values, so that the companies can better position themselves in an effort to appear as socially responsible as possible.

Ethical accounting as a strategic management tool

The ethical accounting and reporting tool is largely a Danish invention. It was developed in the 1980s by researchers from Copenhagen Business School, Peter Pruzan and Ole Thyssen, who had received a Social Sciences Research grant and worked closely with the Spar Nord bank in Jutland, Denmark, to define and develop ethical accounting in conjunction with values-driven management and employee involvement in the formulation of the company's values. The starting point for this work on ethical accounting was stakeholder theory combined with Habermas' philosophy of communicative action (Morsing 1991; Bak 1996).

The idea has since been used by many municipalities and public institutions in Denmark. The original concept was to work with ethical accounting based on qualitative interviews and meetings with employees and other stakeholders in a longer process of dialogue that was started by a project group, which formulated questionnaires and started a number of dialogue meetings. Today, Spar Nord also works with ethical accounts, but they have been integrated into work on storytelling and values-driven management, and the company does not use the same degree of ethical accounting as at the beginning of the project.

We can say that Thyssen and Pruzan succeeded in managing to combine values-driven management with stakeholder dialogue and focus on CSR. The justification of ethical accounting was not only pragmatic, i.e. that cooperation between the various stakeholders in the company would be better through working with values, but it was also justified by communicative ethics, since it was claimed that the open dialogue about the company values would strengthen employee motivation and influence. This was coupled with a fundamental belief in democracy and in the need for democratizing the company through employee involvement in the value formulation processes (Morsing 1991).

Ethical accounting was built on the stakeholders' values, which later had to be assessed in the accounts. The ethical accounting project was seen as an instrument to map expectations to company and allow for the different groups in the organization to voice their values. The foundation of the use of ethical accounting is based on the idea that by listening to employees' perception of values through an open and democratic dialogue, the business organization can define the values that can improve the organization, so that at the same time it becomes more efficient and more able to meet stakeholders' expectations. Accordingly, the accounts aim to measure progress toward ethics with respect for the implementation and development of these ethical values in the culture of the organization.

15 Cosmopolitanism, religion, and legitimacy

We will now look at corporate ethics and responsibility from a broader perspective with a focus on the relationship between religion, ethics, and values. The chapter begins by presenting the relationship between Protestant ethics and corporate values. At the level of cosmopolitan business ethics, deep religious values play an important role in understanding business in contemporary capitalism. It then discusses the values behind the idea of social responsibility of business. Finally, the chapter presents the legitimacy issues from the perspective of the relationship between religion and business ethics.

Protestant ethics and business

The basis for the question about the ethics, values, and social responsibility of business can be advantageously considered in the light of the relationship between economics and religion, i.e. the correlation between the economic organization and society's spiritual or spiritual values. Perhaps there is a closer link between work and religion than we usually think (Lindhardt and Uhrskov 1997; Rendtorff 2013a, 2013b, 2013c, 2013d). This question is actualized by the emergence of a multicultural society, where employees may not share the same fundamental religious values.

Often corporate values are not completely determined rationally, but depend on basic ideological and religious beliefs. If we are to understand all dimensions of business ethics, it is also necessary to consider business values in the light of the relationship between economics and religion. Max Weber documented convincingly this connection in *The Protestant Ethic and the Spirit of Capitalism* (1904-1905). Weber studied the emergence of modern capitalism and showed that there is a close relationship between the modern organization of the economy and morality in the different types of Protestant church (Pietists, Calvinists, Puritans, etc.).

Weber believed that Protestantism's idea of work as a vocation and a duty was consistent with capitalism's self-understanding. Success and wealth at work was considered as a sign that they were about to earn God's eternal salvation (Weber 1904-1905). The money should not be squandered, but austerely reinvested so that the capital could accumulate and provide even greater assurance to the capitalists that they were among the elect.

This peculiar work ethic is not made so clear by the Reformation father Luther, who had a notion that faith alone, not work, determined destiny. By contrast, the follower Calvin emphasized that work wages may be a sign from God. Calvin can be considered a founder of Protestant and Puritan business ethics, based on truthfulness, sobriety, trust, and righteousness. Even in today's secularized society we rediscover elements of this Protestant ethics in economic organizations. The rational legitimization of the economy is based precisely on demands for a lot of work, and the individual must work to make sense of his life and be recognized as a good citizen in society (Lindhardt and Uhrskov 1997; Rendtorff 2013b).

The Puritans, who were settlers in New England in the United States, founded American capitalism and are also highlighted as representatives of the Protestant ethic (Frey 1998). Their infamous ideologue Benjamin Franklin stressed that "time is money" and that work should rationally be utilized to create greater prosperity. For the Puritans the personal call and self-interest in living according to frugal life ethics were a prerequisite for salvation and eternal life.

At the same time the individual's effort to live a life in faith and respect for God was the basis for the common good of society where everyone contributes to the development of society. Puritan morality was based on strict vocation, discipline, hard work, temperance, personal responsibility, trust, credibility, and honesty.

We can therefore consider Protestant ethics as a religious justification for capitalism's ideas about humanity's activity as rational actors on the financial market, whose task is to accumulate wealth to the community. Secularization of society means that many people today consider economic action as a matter of self-interest and profit maximization, which is contrary to Protestant ethics, which rather combined the adherence to religious values with a strict work ethic and rational economic action (Weber 1904–1905). The task was to create more welfare and prosperous flourishing in God's creation. As in the work of Adam Smith, the search for self-interest represents in fact a contribution to the community's happiness. And it is presupposed in the various Protestant beliefs that we must not only keep the money we have acquired, but as far as possible give it away to charity.

Protestant ethics thus integrates a stong work ethic and rational utility maximization of self-interest with an understanding of the duty to be benevolent toward other people. In business companies this implies a respectful and caring relationship with the company's employees and a willingness to give money back to the community in the form of charity, when great wealth has been achieved. Protestant ethics can be considered as the kind of paternalism and social accountability that has traditionally characterized many companies, and it is precisely this form of ethics that, because of society's secularization, seems partially to have been lost in favor of the morally indifferent company, focusing on the economy and not on the moral and ethical dimensions of working life. Likewise, the need for ethics and values is justified by an increasing loss of meaning in the workplace, where it is more and more difficult for the individual to find a vocation and a meaning in his or her work (Lindhardt and Uhrskov 1997; Rendtorff 2013b). The current quest for corporate ethics, values, and attitudes can, on this basis, be described as a response to this crisis of Protestant ethics.

Protestant ethics and secularization

Protestant ethics shows the close relationship between religion and economy, since the religious values actually are found as central in our organization of the economy. These religious assumptions are well described in Weber's analysis of Protestant ethics, where the basics of the modern capitalist economy are located in the asceticism of monastic monks. The ascetic mindset dictates that work requires deprivation of enjoyment and postponement of one's own needs for sleep and food.

Although one can describe the modern world as secularized, where the Protestant ethic has been weakened, it is characteristic that Protestantism still works at full strength in the company, for example, when one understands the company as a common destiny and a pact between employees and management. Here we experience the relationship with management as an integrated relationship where everyone is responsible for the company's future, and this conception of the community clarifies the relationship between Protestantism and corporate social responsibility.

A typical example of making such a fusion between religion and business in the Christian tradition is found by consultants who are trying to make the Bible important for business (Futtrup and Rydahl 2005). It is argued that the Bible's parables and stories, i.e. biblical wisdom, illustrate real dilemmas in working life, and such a "Management by Bible" uses Protestant Christianity in company management.

This view of the possibility of uniting employees and management in work in the sense of piety appears to conflict with opinions of the critical theologians and Christians who claim that there is a total contradiction between Christianity and the capitalist system. These critics highlight for example, that the Bible says that "it is easier for a camel to go through the eye of a needle than for a rich man to be saved." With this rejection of capitalism, the Bible cannot be used as a management tool. Historically, the rationalist work ethic of following one's vocation and doing our duty has been of great importance for the development of capitalism, exactly because of the strict boundaries between work and religion: Sunday is the day of rest, sharply distinct from the work day. Such a difference manifests a fundamental separation between economics and religion, where the economy is based on a strong material utilitarianism, while religion is considered a private matter which deals with the individual's vocation and personal relationship with God. Protestant ethics thus continues to live on as an integral part of our rational understanding of our working life.

The religion of the economy

To understand this relationship between religion and legitimation of economic action we can take a look at the religious background of the economy. The US economist Robert H. Nelson, in the book *Economics as Religion* (2001), distinguishes between two religious traditions in economic science: the optimistic Catholic tradition and the pessimistic Protestant tradition. The optimistic view includes thinkers like Aristotle, Aquinas, Claude Saint-Simon, and John Maynard Keynes. The pessimistic tradition has as its starting point the philosopher Plato, who prioritized ideas of the spiritual world and therefore looked down on the economy's tangible reality. A later variant of pessimism was developed by Luther, Calvin, the Puritans, and Social Darwinism, who claim that mankind is selfish and sinful, and that the economy is an expression of this hell on earth. The optimistic tradition does not look down on economic life, but emphasizes that economics is about the common good, and that it is possible to realize an economically just society. Nelson argues that these two concepts have shaped Western culture and that they still affect the modern economic science (Nelson 2001: 9; Rendtorff 2013b, 2013c).

Nelson further argues that even though economists see themselves as value-free scientists, they cannot avoid being influenced by morality, ethics, and religion. The idea of economic efficiency, which is one of the most important ideas in the modern capitalist society is not value neutral, but arises out of a particular religious view of the world. This relation may be formulated by means of the so-called market paradox, where economic action does not happen in mathematically perfect markets, but instead cultural and social conditions determine economic behavior.

The market paradox thus deals with the relationship between economic values and other social values. The economy contributes to science with visions of the best organization of society. One can say that economists, depending on their view of humanity, come with a pessimistic or optimistic proposal for the organization of human happiness on Earth, with Nelson's words "how to reach heaven on earth" the aim of economics. Therefore economists can be described as the worldly philosophers who decide which morality and ethics other human beings must live by.

This means that the modern economy in the 20th century was a response to the problems of Protestant ethics. The question is how to promote self-interest and at the same time be serving the community. Two prominent schools of the modern economy, the Chicago school and Cambridge school, represent two opposing answers to this problem.

The optimistic Cambridge school is represented by the famous Nobel Prize winner Paul A. Samuelson, who wrote an important book, *Foundations of Economic Analysis* (1947), which sold over five million copies in more than 15 editions. Samuelson inscribes himself in the optimistic tradition from Aquinas to Keynes with a project to develop a modern welfare state, creating material and social welfare, and considering the financial market as an instrument to promote the common good and develop social institutions for the benefit of all.

Samuelson's economic theory can be seen as Catholic economic thinking that criticizes the Protestant ethic. One can consider this project as a secularization of the Catholic economic project where the constant investment in market development and the common good create society as an integral unit between the individual and community. Against this background, Samuelson formulated his progressive view of the economy as the welfare state science. Samuelson's book was based on a combination of Keynesian ideas, a belief in the market economy and in the principles of scientific management.

Markets were important for economic development, but at the same time it was important to have a government that had a strong regulatory social function. The market was still the core of the scientific economy, which was based on mathematical analysis (Nelson 2001: 110; Rendtorff 2013b, 2013c). A scientific understanding of modern business organizations and of the financial market should be a way to construct the best society. We can say that Samuelson introduced economic sense as the basis for a good society. It was scientific management in a society with a mixed economy that combined the state and private markets. In opposition to the Puritans, Samuelson would, however, realize the utopia of the good society in this world here and now, not in the hereafter. The instruments for this were supposed to be rational science and utilitarian ethics. The economy should contribute to the common good, solving the collective action problems and combatting opportunism and egoism (the free-rider problem). The economy is thus considered by Samuelson as a scientific tool for generally creating rising living standards and improving conditions for the worst off, while letting businesses flourish.

The Chicago school represents, in contrast to this, an individualistic and ultra-liberal criticism of the welfare state project and of Samuelson's vision of state, of the individual, and of the market (Nelson 2001: 121). They perceived Samuelson's argument in favor of a mixed economic system as ideological and without any scientific basis. The Chicago school highlights the market's superiority from Social Darwinism's idea of evolution as a selfish struggle for survival and the right of natural property as the basic of economic practices.

We can mention an early economist of the 20th century, Frank Knight, as a key founder of the Chicago School. For Knight, the financial market is based on self-interest and freedom. Knight proposed in extension of Calvinism and Puritanism a view of man's sinful nature. This was based on a generalization of a secular version of the Christian concept of the sinful man. According to Knight, the free market is necessary because of humans' selfishness, opportunism, and hunger to always follow their own interest. The market has a social function of bringing people together even though they as egoists have different values and conceptions of life. That the market is effective as a social instrument is, according to Knight, because it works without power relations, and therefore it constitutes the real basis for a radical pluralism. On the market, Christians can exchange goods with other religious groups without compromising their faith, because exchange on the market is a matter of self-interest and profit.

Knight was the teacher of a number of very important economists such as Milton Friedman, who represented the next generation of the Chicago school. Friedman was also influenced by the notion of the sinful humanity. He introduced himself as an economic technician who argued for the free market as the basis for progress. His works highlight, like Knight, the importance of the individual's own interest and freedom, and his already mentioned criticism of corporate social responsibility in the article "The social responsibility of business is to increase its profits" (1970) shows how marked Friedman is by the ideal of market efficiency. The state must not intervene in the free market, which is central to economic activity.

This generalization of the neoclassical economic approach was followed by other Chicago economists such as Gary Becker and Richard Posner, who use this economic approach in other areas of social sciences, for example, sociology and anthropology. They highlight the fact that social agents can be defined exclusively by self-interest and utility maximization. Becker believes that this kind of economic behavior is found everywhere in social life: the family is analyzed as an economic entity, and social phenomena like discrimination, theft, and robbery are analyzed as strictly economic. Becker, who won the Nobel Prize in 1992, argues that polygamy under certain circumstances can be justified rationally, because women's value will increase the market when men can have more than one woman. Marriage is analyzed in this manner by using the implicit calculations of economic gain. Becker even believes that there must be an economic explanation for the Nazi persecutions of the Jews because this gave Nazi Germans better social possibilities when the Jews were deprived of their positions in society. Becker believes so much in a selfish rationale behind social behavior, that he explains altruism as a form of selfishness from the so-called "rotten kid theorem," in which the child, and more generally the human individual, realizes that the altruistic act in the long term will create the greatest economic benefit, and therefore acts altruistically for pure economic motives. One can say that the Chicago school continues Protestant ethics and the notion of a rational economy, while giving up the idea of the calling and vocation of the individual (Nelson 2001: 67; Rendtorff 2013b, 2013c). The Chicago school thus expresses the crisis of the modern economy, because by virtue of its completed rationalism it is in fundamental conflict with Protestant ethics, since it considers utility and value maximization to be the only absolute values. Values like efficiency and economic progress have taken the place of respect for the divine commandments, just as the notion of sinful man can be generalized from a secular perspective. Accordingly, the secularized Chicago school keeps the Calvinist view of human nature without retaining the belief in revelation and in the divine.

Economic existentialism

Following the description of the relationship between capitalism and Protestantism, modern economic thinking, inspired by the concept of neoclassical economics is in the ethical sense defined as a kind of existentialist thought (Arnsperger 2001; Rendtorff 2014a). The driving force of society is considered as the battle of the scarcity of resources, and every social phenomenon can in fact be explained on the basis of this relationship. According to the economist, it is self-deception to give things a meaning other than the one which is provided by a purely economic description of the world as a result of the struggle for resources and the costs associated with specific social actions. This is not far from an existentialist thinker such as the French philosopher Jean-Paul Sartre, who emphasized that the real world is an illusion and that behind this world is just pure solid materiality, to which people give meaning and existential significance. For Sartre, the relation between human beings is also a struggle and conflict, and the driving force of history is scarcity.

Christian Arnsperger has proposed an existentialist interpretation of capitalism in his books *Critique of Capitalist Existence: For an Existentialist Ethics of the Economy* (2005) and *Ethics of Post-Capitalism: For an Existentialist Aktivism* (2009). These books can be considered as the basis for an existentialist approach to economics (Rendtorff 2014a). This approach searches for authentic existence in the context of the critique of alienation of contemporary society. The existentialist approach focuses on the importance of meaning to understand social existence and the role of capitalism in economics. Arnsperger proposes existentialist philosophy as a kind of social therapeutics of capitalist economics. Inspired by Kierkegaard, Heidegger, and Sartre, existentialism analyzes the tension between authenticity and inauthenticity in the economic system. To exist is to understand the finitude, contingency, and morality of life. Here, we find a close relation between economics and existentialism, since economics studies scarcity and the satisfaction of unlimited needs. In this sense, economics deals with the authentic realization of human finitude.

Here we find a surprising similarity between economics and existentialism, since economists are fundamentally obsessed by moving beyond appearance to the pure material fact of existence. Economists can be seen as agents who search for authentic economic existence facing the true fact of our economic life, based on material calculation of utility and efficiency. In this sense, economics can be considered as an economy of sublimation where the existentialist approach to economics tries to unmask the existentialist authenticity of human existence. *Homo economicus* from the existentialist perspective is an expression of our naked existence and it enables an understanding of the alienation and narcissism of the individual in relation to the authentic existence facing death and finitude. In this way, *homo economicus* can be considered as the material existence of human beings based on the nothingness of purity combined with the desire for the infinite that according to existentialism characterizes human life.

However, at the same time we face a need to reinvent our economic existence. Authenticity in economics means facing the real materiality of life while overcoming this meaninglessness in the search for meaning and recognition of the individual to overcome anguish and nothingness. By revealing our pure material existence, economics provides us with the basis for searching for another community-oriented, non-instrumental authentic economic existence (Rendtorff 2014a). Arnsperger argues that we need to overcome the alienations and sublimations of capitalist economics in order to develop a new authentic and democratic reciprocity between human beings as the basis for a life in an economic community respecting human finitude and endless desire.

Toward new legitimation forms

We can consider a company's search for new values as a part of an attempt to get beyond the restricted economic understanding of the company's ethics (Chakraborty 2001) Advertising man Jesper Kunde's book *Corporate Religion* (2000) can be read as an attempt to challenge the loss of values in the rational understanding of the economy (see also Rendtorff 2013d). The book claims that clearly focused company values are a condition for survival in today's value fragmentation.

Both employees and customers must again be tied emotionally to the company if it is to have a chance for survival in international competition. The company argues for a return to a "religion-based company" that not only bases its values on rational and economic bottom line considerations, but which also founds strategy and management holistically in the company's qualitative and emotional values. According to this view, "religion," understood as a shared vision, ideals, and ideology, is needed to create a well-functioning modern enterprise. In a series of case studies of companies such as Microsoft, Coca-Cola, Nike, Walt Disney, and Body Shop, Kunde explains how these companies can be said to operate by a concept of "corporate" and "brand religion," where the company is bound together with strong common values, while consumers and customers have an emotional relationship with the company's products.

The classic example is the American motorcycle manufacturer Harley-Davidson, which as a company has understood the need to cultivate intangible values. Although their motorcycle products are not necessarily better than other products, the Harley-Davidson is considered by the general public to be more than a simple motorcycle. The motorcycle represents rather a way of life – the key to freedom and the American dream. At a time when the company was about to go bankrupt, Harley-Davidson proposed a new strategy where they cultivated "brand value" as a kind of religious image of the product. The company organized among others motorcycle rallies for its customers – or should we say disciples.

Jesper Kunde mentions interchangeably numerous examples of companies that by cultivating intangible assets have improved their products' emotional importance to consumers and they have also intensified employees' motivation. The company will link consumers religiously to the company's culture and brand by making its product express attitudes and values. Accordingly, the company organizes "events" and will ensure consumer loyalty by using slogans that sell the product as a lifestyle through the organization's image. The ideological concept of "corporate religion" is based on a number of simple principles that from the top is distributed to the entire company, a message which Kunde compares with the Bible (Kunde 2000; Rendtorff 2013d). In the struggle to establish an emotional engagement in the company the simple and universal formulation of strong values is elemental to give the vision explosive force. He also stresses that a charismatic, forceful leadership is a condition for realizing values. The leader must appear as a symbol and a unifying personality of the company.

Cynical approaches to business ethics and corporate social responsibility

These approaches may be viewed as a critical analysis that shares existentialism's demystifying criticism of the religious approach to ethics and CSR. These approaches are inspired by continental philosophy (Painter-Morland and Ten Bos 2011; Rendtorff 2014a). The cynical analysis challenges any kind of normativity in business ethics, and this approach looks at the company from a distanced social science analytical horizon. Corporate ethics and responsibility are considered media-determined fashion phenomena and a powerful instrument that hides the corporations' real interest, to earn money and gain profit. As in institutional theory, corporate ethics and responsibility are analyzed as an expression of the functional efforts of organizations to adapt to society's expectations.

The discourse analysis approach (Jørgensen and Philips 1999) emphasizes that social responsibility is constructed as a discourse that legitimizes companies in relation to their environment. Socially responsible companies are at the same time economic and community oriented. According to discourse analysis you can describe corporate ethics and social responsibility as a social construct, i.e. an articulation of the company's brand and values in a particular ideological way. Discourse is the result of societal contradictions and conflicts in which different actors seek power over each other. The discursive field consists of liquid structures of meaning that by virtue of the power relationships create discourses. The discourse about the social responsibility of the firm expresses a struggle to give the community the power of companies, or an effort to legitimize corporate profit maximization in society.

The system-theoretical approach to CSR considers the company as a social system which complies with certain economic codes where profit and competition are the fundamental media of control. This approach is inspired by the sociologist Niklas Luhmann. From the perspective of the system theory approach, perceived social responsibility as a measure of the company attempts to adapt to society's public as an interface between political, economic, and social systems (Holmström 2004). Gaining public acceptance is important because it determines the limits and opportunities for corporate meaningful actions. The system theoretical approach also emphasizes that business ethics and CSR function as a marker by which the business corporation is able to adapt to its environment, avoiding bankruptcy and the risk of loss of legitimacy. The discourse-analytical and system-theoretical approaches are useful for dealing with the implicit suppression of religious activities in the business corporation and to understand the staging of social responsibility as part of the organization's profit maximization and efforts to survive with legitimacy in society, but they cannot cope with the strategic questions about well-founded ethical action, and therefore fail, for their methodical force is also their own blind spot, namely, they are completely distanced from the phenomenon they are describing.

Spirituality and the enchanted company

The cynical attitude to CSR can be seen as a reaction to a spiritual interpretation of business ethics as a kind of religion of the company. It is sometimes the case that otherwise rational economic-minded managers in the company suddenly need a spiritual dimension of existence and therefore turn to religious or Eastern mysticism, which they will realize through the company's "Corporate Karma" or "Corporate Bible." An illustration of such an endeavor to go back to mystify the employment relationship in a criticism of the goal rational and utilitarian mindset that characterizes Protestant ethics may be derived from the Danish author Martin Fuglsang's book *To Be at the Limit* (1998). This work is an analysis of a young biotech entrepreneur's self-understanding and activities as a researcher and innovator. It is characteristic of Fuglsang's analysis that it is characterized by a deep desire to rediscover poetics and the passion of human life in business.

Fuglsang looks for mythic, poetic, and almost religious elements of the work, and his analysis can therefore be regarded as a radical departure from the strict moderation of the Protestant ethics. Fuglsang's new mystery corresponds very well to the need for a new spiritualization of life that characterizes many business leaders. They seek symbols and holy places in their daily work, and they cannot stand the Protestant ethic and want to rediscover the irrational and supernatural. They are attracted by Eastern mysticism or astrology as a means to provide the company with a new spirituality (Chakraborty and Chakraborty 2008). Different types of consultants are therefore invited to help them make daily routines more religiously meaningful and significant in the company. The new mystery acts as a dynamic catalyst to rediscover the lost spiritual sense in dull and monotonous daily lives. This quest for spiritual leadership is often combined with a belief in a deep cohesion between man and nature, an ecological consciousness in which man is integrated into the cosmos through mystery (Beyer 2006: 53; Bubna-Litic 2009).

We can see the emergence of the ethical and political corporation as a kind of attempt to overcome the secular work ethic in Protestant ethics. Normally, one does not consider a political activity as a religious entity, but rather views it as a necessary response to the complexity of modern society, which requires that the company is socially responsible and involves all stakeholders in the formulation of strategy and values. In some cases, these efforts have an almost religious content, which is not far from being "corporate religion" when CSR is launched as part of the company's image and product marketing with a powerful emotional content.

Jesper Kunde mentions cosmetics manufacturer Body Shop as a company that has managed to give its products both a political and a religious content. This company not only sells cosmetics, but is a knowledge-based company, which through its products also conveys environmental awareness and lifestyle to consumers (Kunde 2000; Rendtorff 2013d). Body Shop has with its concept of "caring cosmetics" given cosmetics a specific "brand value" for customers who use products to signal their basic political attitudes. Body Shop can be said to have made environmental awareness and the green profile a religion, if we understand religion as a set of strong emotional values that bind consumers and other stakeholders close to the company. The trend is sometimes toward that the political activity must fill the void left by Protestant ethics and take care of the absence of a religious values-driven identity of the company. This is illustrated by the unreflective way in which some companies are working to launch human rights as central external and internal priorities of business goals.

The political-religious corporation places itself morally in society in the frontline of ethical innovation. It captures the key trends, and thus it can help to change society. Interestingly enough, this does not need to be in conflict with Protestant ethics, but can be understood in light of Weber's thinking. The point is not only the development of Protestant ethics, but to a much larger degree, that the company, not only economically but also culturally and with regard to its basic values, is taking a leading role in social development.

The values-driven company thus expresses the radicalization of Weber's point about the relationship between economics and ethics. From this perspective, the political corporation is just a good example of the current development of society. We live in a time where we face a fundamental remoralization where we all have to be politically correct, and this affects also companies who have understood that ethics and soft skills are a condition for survival in the global market.

I would therefore suggest an interpretation of the ethical and political corporation, based on republican business ethics (Ulrich 1998: 289 et seq.). This approach can be said to represent a community-driven foundation for corporate legitimacy that represents an alternative to the Protestant traditional, rational, and mythological-charismatic legitimation forms. In republican business ethics the ethical motivation is founded not on personal self-interest in salvation, but on the feeling of an obligation to the community and to serve the common good. As a good corporate citizen, the company strives to live up to societal demands for political and social justice. It is introducing values that actively contribute to improving the social and political conditions of citizens in society.

Legitimate economic activity is understood as a contribution to a just society (Ulrich 1998: 235). As mentioned, in such a political corporation it is important to highlight the triple bottom line, environmental sustainability, security of the employee's right to personal development in creative work, and respect for individual rights.

Importantly – as opposed to the "corporate religion" concept – is that these values are justified reflexive-rationally based on the company's self-understanding as an active corporate citizen, participating in an ethical and political discussion process based on deliberations in a critical public sphere. Such an identification model does not exclude the religious elements that are to be subsumed within republicanism. The recognition of the right of the individual to religious freedom is a central element in republican business ethics, which implies respect for the individual's right to his private conception of the good life. Business ethics and CSR are therefore from this perspective primarily justified by the affiliation of business with a democratic political public sphere where all members shall endeavor to respect the community (Table 15.1). The ethical principles of respect for stakeholder's autonomy, dignity, integrity, and vulnerability are important features of the company's values and professional ethics (Crowther 2006: 31).

Values in the political corporation express a new kind of management discourse that overcomes a pure hierarchical decision model based on the manager's absolute sovereignty. Political communication about values must create meaning and context in the political message, which means that it also can improve the organization's legitimacy in the community. Ethics should not be merely cosmetic window dressing, but a genuine and integral part of the company's business strategy. This is a condition that companies can achieve real social acceptance and economic sustainability in the longer term.

This criticism of any form of corporate religion is against the use of values-driven management and ethics to manipulate and unify employees. Focus on CSR and corporate

Table 15.1 Dynamic CSR: development levels of corporate social responsibility

Level of development	*Dominant traits*	*Typical activity*	*Examples*
1	Window dressing Reputation management	Restructuring of the company reporting	Changed usage of words in relation to CSR language
2	Cost containment (economizing)	Restructuring of the business process	Energy efficiency programs
3	Engagement of stakeholders	Development of the balanced scorecard (balanced metering value) (in various fields, e.g. finance, customer satisfaction, business processes, learning)	Customer and employee satisfaction survey
4	Measurement and reporting	Sophisticated measurement mechanisms	CSR reports
5	Sustainability	Definition of sustainability Redefinition of business processes	Reporting on sustainability
6	Transparency	Need for responsibility from suppliers, i.e. supply chain management	Human rights, child labor
7	Credibility	Reconfiguration of the value chain	Restacking activities in relation to developing countries

governance aims precisely at creating a space for a critical democracy within the company, where employees and other stakeholders are honestly involved and open in the decision-making processes. There does not have to be a contradiction between strategic management and such an approach to good corporate citizenship, if business ethics is integrated in a comprehensive strategic framework that combines economic considerations with stakeholder management and strategic planning.

16 Cosmopolitan business ethics as global corporate citizenship

In this chapter we can summarize the international dimension of cosmopolitan business ethics. An important aspect of this is the idea of republican business ethics defined as involvement of corporations for the common good, *res publica*, expressed in the concept of corporate citizenship with integrity and responsibility (Rendtorff 2009: 425–461). The need for a universal regime of business ethics and human rights is presented and we also promote the concept of corporate citizenship as an important development of integrity and responsibility in international business. Corporate citizenship can be defined here as cosmopolitan corporate citizenship aiming at developing a world ethos of common cosmopolitan ethical principles and norms of the international community based on human rights and business ethics. With this we move toward a concept of global corporate citizenship (Scherer and Palazzo 2008; Rendtorff 2009).

Cosmopolitan business ethics and civil society

In the article "Governing the globe" the political theorist Michael Walzer (2004: 186) presents a framework for understanding the future constitutional structures of world society. He draws a line of continuum from total anarchy to a global state. The issue is what kind of constitutional structure that would be most suitable for world society and in this context we can also ask what the role of corporations in markets and civil society would be.

From the left side called UNITY (Table 16.1), Walzer mentions global state, multinational empire, and federation, and from the right side called DIVISION he defines the third degree, second degree, and first degree of global pluralism, and finally world anarchy. In contrast to the government of strong empire and close to a weak federation, third degree of pluralism is a condition of the international community, where states build up international institutions without creating a supranational government.

Walzer's model is useful for understanding the framework of multinational corporate activities in the world community. The problem is how we should determine the right conditions of government of the world community and what relations government will have with non-state actors like corporations. In fact, dealing with business ethics of

Table 16.1 Levels of interdependence: a continuum of international relations

From the left side: UNITY					*From the right side: DIVISION*	
Global state	Multinational empire	Federation	3rd degree	2nd degree	1st degree of global pluralism	Anarchy

corporations we can say that they contribute to the formation of cosmopolitan political structures based on interactions between sovereign states and strong civil society actors like corporations and other organizations. This situation implies a position somewhere in the middle of Walzer's model, between federation and third degree of pluralism. Corporations function as non-state actors in the international community that contribute to the formation of global structures of decision-making built on a variety of social and political institutions.

The challenge of cosmopolitan business ethics is the requirement to develop ethical norms and institutional foundations of these norms that can help and guide companies in international business. In this sense there is a close connection between CSR and human rights in business (Sullyvan 2003).

From the perspective of international institutional theory of regime-building (Powell and DiMaggio 1991) as a way to overcome the concept of international relations as a power game of actors who are in a quasi-state of nature, we can point to the potential possibilities of business to build and maintain international institutional bonds. Recent studies in international regime theory point to the fact that international interaction not only takes place at the level of high politics among states but indeed also at the level of commerce, increasing selling and buying of goods among members of civil society.

Our view of international relations from the perspective of cosmopolitan business ethics cannot but endorse the emphasis of the positive impact of international business relations on integration of world affairs. An enlightened cosmopolitanism based on the philosophy of Immanuel Kant argues for world peace and international cooperation as the aim of world history (Bowie 1999a: 14). As Francis Fukuyama (1992) has emphasized, liberal society at the end of history is about business relations and cooperative recognition among civil societies. Capitalist economies have had tremendous influence on modernization and democratization of the world. With Kant we can try to formulate a minimum morality for international affairs, which could be used to outlaw unethical practices that cannot be submitted to the test of universal validity of the categorical imperative.

Sometimes such an unreflective universalization of Western values ends up in a kind of a naive moralist thinking, believing in the possibility of a universal morality for corporations acting in different countries. This point of view quickly meets the reality of a global and multicultural way of life in many different countries, which have very different concepts of ethics and morals. What is important for the idea of republican business ethics is a situated view of the possibility of universalization as a critical hermeneutics taking into account the integrity and particularity of national culture (Rendtorff 2014a).

The idea of organizational integrity based on self-imposed norms may not be very simple. What is important in De George's analysis is that "integrity matters" and that "integrity really makes a difference." To act with integrity means that you cannot compromise on your fundamental principles and values (Desjardin and McCall 2000: 495; Brown 2005). Therefore if the firm is committed to human rights, it cannot do business with countries or partners who commit violations of fundamental human rights, because this would be inconsistent with regard to basic ethical principles. From the point of view of republican business ethics we can say that the self-imposed norms of the firm include the respect for basic ethical principles of autonomy, dignity, integrity, and vulnerability of human persons. Moreover, the ethics of self-imposed norms requires constant and independent exercise of judgment in order to establish basic values of interaction in international business. Thus, corporations need to formulate guidelines and ethical codes of conduct to compete with integrity in international business.

Human rights and universal ethical guidelines for multinational corporations

In fact, we can analyze an element of strong regime-building in international relations as a basis for promotion of such guidelines for multinational corporations. In some cases it may even be argued that the process of formulating guidelines and codes of conduct for business goes beyond or lies at the forefront of what it has been possible to achieve at the level of national regulations, because these are still very dependent on the cultural frameworks of tradition and culture of the nation states.

Applying Richard W. Scott's definition of institutions to international guidelines we may consider these guidelines as contributing to the shaping of international institutions in so far as an institution is conceived as a set of "cognitive, normative and regulative structures and activities that provide stability and meaning of social behavior" (1995: 33). But the emergence of international regimes may even have economic interpretations, because they may contribute to reducing transaction costs with regard to public criticism of dubious ethical behavior of international corporations.

In this context, cosmopolitan business ethics implies defending the idea of the emergence of an international human rights regime as the foundation of the minimum norms to guide the action of multinational corporations. This is the fundamental meaning of the power of human rights in business and economics (Rendtorff 2011a). This human rights regime can be said to have emerged out of the international declarations and conventions on human rights (Nickel 1987). The 1948 Declaration of Human Rights has laid the basis for the later conventions on political and social rights. Also declarations on cultural rights and on the protection of the human genome in technological development can be mentioned. These conventions have been adopted by most countries in the world, and human rights function as a reference for discussion and improvement even for states that do not fulfill their international obligations with regard to the protection of human rights.

Some of these international conventions and declarations have direct impact on corporations, for example when they concern work conditions and protection of children, or deal with the freedom of assembly. But we can also mention specific codes of conduct and regulations of soft law concerning multinational corporations directly. The International Labour Organization (ILO) has worked with formulating a number of codes of conduct for workplaces all over the globe. The World Health Organization (WHO) has formulated similar recommendations within controversial health issues, for example on pharmaceutical companies and their distribution of drugs or marketing of controversial products (Donaldson 1989: 164). Moreover, we can mention guidelines and regulations from the World Trade Organization and the World Bank, the OECD guidelines for multinational corporations and not least the Global Compact principles from the United Nations' summit on world economic affairs in 1999. The Global Compact has really been an important strategic policy initiative to support the universal principles of human rights in the context of international business (Rasche and Kell 2010). All these organizations contribute with their guidelines to creating soft law regimes of common values and norms of cooperation of international business organizations.

It is in this context that we should consider the Global Reporting Initiative, which is an accounting and certification instrument ensuring sustainability and human rights on the basis of UN standards. Moreover, the SA8000 Standard is also directed toward documentation of whether the corporation complies with international norms for protection of human rights. The important work of the United Nations Human Rights Commission has implied a proposal for principles for the responsibility of corporations for human rights. This resulted in the establishment of the UN guiding principles for business and human rights. These norms represent an important initiative to formulate internationally binding norms for international corporate citizenship that combines human rights and business citizenship (Ruggie 2013; Buhmann 2014). They have to go through the system of negotiation of the UN and all stakeholders, investors, public authorities, unions, and NGOs are included in the debate on these norms. So we can talk about an international binding human rights regime for business corporations (Ruggie 2013).

Norman Bowie argues on the basis of Immanuel Kant's philosophy that moral obligations of multinational corporations in the international community can be justified. Indeed, multinationals can help to promote democracy and freedom when they follow the morality of Kantian capitalism, which implies a universal morality of the market (Bowie 1988, 1999a; Arnold and Harris 2012).

Bowie argues that cultural relativism is incoherent. Cultural relativism ends in individual relativism and there is no argument against realism and free-rider opportunism in international relations. Hence, the universalist position seems preferable, because it helps in formulating stable norms to guide multinational corporations. And this position is more closely connected to the reality of international relations, in which countries are boycotted by corporations because of human rights violations or racist policies. In the case that we accept the universal position we cannot deny that multinational corporations have obligations in international politics. These obligations would imply that they should respect the minimal moral rules of morality of the countries in which they operate. In cases where there may be rules with universal justification, which although not practiced internationally, but in the given countries, then the corporations also would have to promote and respect such rules. Moreover, when the foreign countries follow moral principles that cannot be universally justified, multinational corporations should stand to their integrity and refuse to apply these rules.

In so far as they accept the market morality of capitalist society, multinational corporations may, as we emphasized in relation to regime-building, even have an active role to play in promoting universal norms for the international community. We can emphasize that corporations already contribute to building this morality by following the good customs and the laws of healthy markets implying reliability in contracts, promise-keeping, truth-telling, and establishment of reciprocity and mutual trust relations among business partners. When multinationals follow and promote such rules of markets and when they keep the norms of local cultures, which are universally justified, they are helping to construct international regimes of economic behavior that may help to promote democratic attitudes in different parts of the world.

From the perspective of Kantian morality, systematic free-rider opportunism would be contrary to this morality of the market, which is implied in the capitalist economic attitude considering freedom to buy and sell goods in the market as essential for economic prosperity. And the full consequence of this approach would be necessary respect for human rights as a precondition for economic freedom, because racism, discrimination, or deprivation of liberty simply is inefficient and represents a hindrance for development of free economic markets.

Therefore, principles of human rights, codes of conduct, and values-driven management for multinationals in the international community may both help to stabilize, shape, and form the activities of the corporation, while at the same time representing an active contribution to the promotion of democratic values in the cultures of the countries in which they operate. However, there is still the problem of defining exactly which norms and values are truly universal and not only mistaken reflections of Western ethnocentrism. Therefore, the task of developing codes and norms of conduct at the international level is a very subtle and time-consuming process. We need global values but the process of value creation has to take careful account of the plurality of values in the international community.

In this context we may refer to John Rawls' discussion of the possible agreements in international relations in his work *The Law of Peoples* (1999) as a reply to international regime theory. His theory of the law of peoples can be considered as an effort to find a common point of view besides the comprehensive doctrines, which characterizes different local cultures in the international community (Rawls 1999). Rawls interprets the law of peoples as a result of a double process of constituting a social contract. Ideally, a democratic republic is the result of rational deliberation among free individuals who choose to live in a democracy. Rawls' concept of the original position is considered by him to be a hypothetical situation of interpretation of a social contract. Moreover, after a democratic regime is constituted with the social contract it chooses to form an international community with others and hypothetically it enters a second or similar situation of a social contract which becomes the foundation of the law of peoples between states. The law of peoples is founded on an original contract between states and on use of free public reason (Rawls 1999: 56). The idea of a universal law between states and of protection of the humanity of world citizens is realistic because it is built on democratic principles and because it recognizes pluralism and the impossibility of a world state. The idea of the law of peoples is built on agreements between different state with democratic constitutions and overlapping consensus. The principle of toleration of difference and pluralism seems to be important in such a "realistic utopia."

Corporate citizenship as global cosmopolitan citizenship

With his concept of the law of peoples, Rawls gives us the foundation of cosmopolitan citizenship in international society. However, the question remains whether corporations can be citizens. With the many important international guidelines we can perceive the framework for the concept of global corporate citizenship in international relations (Scherer and Palazzo 2008). Jeanne M. Logsdon and Donna J. Wood argue that global business citizenship implies that the libertarian free market thinking is replaced by a sort of communitarian approach based on the promotion of citizenship in different countries. However, with the concept of global citizenship they also emphasize that we need to go beyond the nation state in order to establish a firm basis for global business ethics (Logsdon and Wood 2002). With this article the authors want to redefine CSR and values-driven management in terms of corporate citizenship. Here, global cosmopolitan citizenship is the culmination of moving on the stages of corporate citizenship (Mirvis and Googins 2006). The authors continue with the discussion whether the rights and duties of individual citizens can be used as a useful concept for understanding the role of corporations in society.

While the corporation at the national level emerges as a responsible actor that is committed and engaged in community, corporate citizenship at the international level means that the organization is committed to hypernorms while recognizing the free moral space of specific cultures (Logsdon and Wood 2002: 156). When we consider the corporation as a universal citizen, a member of the international community, we acknowledge that corporations are entitled to work for their stakeholders and contribute to the positive development of international community.

We may therefore argue that this concept of global business citizenship encloses both the concept of respect for human rights and the concept of corporate social responsibility. The idea of citizenship at the international level is based on the idea of the morally responsible corporation which is the foundation for policies on CSR. To argue for good corporate citizenship at the international level is to focus the notion of CSR on a specific conception of the corporation and its obligations toward the international community. In international business self-regulation of corporations from the point of view of corporate citizenship is the solution to the definition of the corporation in society. It is important to notice that the obligations of business to society are based on this adaptation of the concept of global corporate citizenship.

We may argue that the defense of human rights is very important for development of citizenship at the international level. Human rights may be considered as a level of foundation of universal ethical principles. Focus on human rights implies that the good society protects basic rights of individuals and it finds the right balance between protection of those rights and development of welfare policies for community. As good corporate citizens, corporations comply with the Universal Declaration of Human Rights and they work to promote business ethics on that foundation. We can say that the corporation takes part in a macro-social contract, where they follow universal ethical principles (Logsdon and Wood 2002: 170). However, it is also important to recognize the cross-cultural variations that are permitted within consistent local norms and a free moral space as long as they do not violate the hypernorms of macro-social contracts. From the strategic perspective this means that corporations should actively engage for the protection of the norms of macro-social contracts.

However, at the same time, moral free space gives the corporation the possibility to try to respect local cultural values as long as they are not inconsistent with hypernorms. When dealing with principles of business ethics, human rights, and CSR at the global level, we can propose the basic ethics principles as the foundation for the required protection of human beings in international business. I would argue that the principles of respect for human autonomy, dignity, integrity, and vulnerability constitute what Klaus M. Leisinger calls a required *minima moralia* for multinational corporations. From this point of view respect for human dignity is the fundamental responsibility of business when it operates on the global scale (Leisinger 1999: 330).

This respect for human dignity is expressed in the concern for fundamental human needs as the foundation for universal human rights. With Hans Küng, as mentioned earlier, we can make respect for the "golden rule" express this concern for a fundamental ethics of the international community (Küng 1990). Küng has taken the initiative to formulate an ethics for the world community, the so-called *Projekt Weltethos*, an ethos of the world where universal moral norms are expressed as the foundation of international transactions. In this ethos of the world we can argue that it is essential to protect the basic ethical principles of autonomy, dignity, integrity, and vulnerability within the framework of the vision of the good life with and for others in just institutions.

In terms of political philosophy of the international community we can place this vision of corporations as good citizens of the international peace in the light of Immanuel Kant's search for perpetual peace in the international community. In contrast to the argument that it is impossible to find good ways of handling the anonymous structures of power in globalization, the vision of global corporate citizenship imagines the corporation as a contributor to the support of democracy and global sovereign states (Scherer and Palazzo 2008; Scherer, Palazzo, and Matten 2014). Kant conceived perpetual peace and teleology of the international community in "*Zum Ewigen Frieden*" (1795 (1983)) as a development toward a global rule of law in international relations with respect for the rational interdependence of states. The Kantian concept of republicanism implies protection of democratic representative government of sovereign states in the international community. We may argue that corporations contribute to this vision of a cosmopolitan condition by the development of codes of conduct for business ethics and values-driven management of good citizenship in the international community (Fischer, Lovell, and Valero-Silva 2013). The individual citizen, but also the corporation, must be a world citizen, and the state must, in order to establish a universal legal community, collaborate with other states and create international and cosmopolitan institutions. This is the final aim of the law of cosmopolitan citizenship (Kemp 2011), which is the peaceful enlightenment and development of culture and art of humanity by the universalization of particular principles of people's sovereignty.

With this cosmopolitan approach in this book we have argued that the corporation can contribute as a world citizen to solve the important problems of modernity. As actors at the global level in a time of interstate interdependence with regard to world ecological, economic, and political problems, it is a challenge of the corporation to contribute to build up an international community of virtue and protection of basic rights. We can define this vision of universal corporate citizenship as the world ethos of business ethics. Corporations shall not only protect universal human rights but they shall also give those rights meaning in relation to the particular cultures in the countries where they operate. By protecting universal rights that are dependent on the charter and declarations of the United Nations as well as the UN sustainability goals, corporations can act for good international relations that go beyond the interests of particular communities of republics and nations. By doing this, corporations can, when they really want to appear as good citizens, help to build a world community that implies universalization of procedural virtues of liberal society. Corporations can at the same time be cosmopolitan and situated in particular societies in the sense that they foster universal principles while making those principles work in concrete practice.

17 Decision-making model for cosmopolitan business ethics

In this book, we have analyzed different elements of an ethical decision model for business ethics that can be used to make informed choices in relation to specific cases of ethics in companies. We shall now extend this to ethical action (Ladkin 2015; Rendtorff 2015b). The ethical decision-making model is crucial to linking between the ethical horizon of meaning and values that first arise, the ethical theories, fundamental ethical frameworks, ethical principles and ethical guidelines, and the specific ethical dilemmas faced by the individual decision-makers and organizations (Crane and Matten 2016). Working with an ethical decision model is essential in order to evaluate and assess the specific ethical dilemmas and ethical issues in private businesses and public organizations.

Dimensions of a model for decision-making

Decision models and their related decision-making processes include the following five basic steps toward an informed ethical decision:

1 Phenomenological and critical hermeneutical analysis of meaningful context of a particular situation
2 Analysis of the ethical dilemma of the situation in the light of the various ethical theories
3 Analysis of the ethical dilemma in light of the ethical principles
4 Use of the ethical guidelines for compliance and business ethics for understanding the dilemma
5 Decision and action instructions, including evaluation and discussion of the consequences of the decision.

These five steps emphasize following fundamental steps of decision-making:

1 Identification of ethically relevant themes and issues
2 Development of alternative approaches
3 Assessment of short-term and long-term advantages and disadvantages of each of the procedures in relation to all involved or who may be affected
4 Selection process after thorough assessment based on values, principles, and guidelines
5 Action – the obligation to take responsibility for the consequences of the action
6 Evaluation of the results of the method.

In relation to the settlement of this decision process, it is important that the business managers and decision-makers during the evaluation should address any negative consequences and eventually modify their decision. This is especially necessary if it turns out that there are ethical issues that are not resolved.

If we are to make such a detailed description of the ethical decision-making model in relation to a particular business ethics case, we propose that it should contain the following analytical steps:

1. Preparation of the case and case content and problems, including phenomenological and hermeneutical analysis
2. Analysis of the ethical sense context (values and narratives)
3. Description of the core of the ethical dilemma or problem
4. Preparation of the basic ethical framework
5. Analysis of the ethical theories in relation to the concrete context
6. Analysis of ethical principles in relation to the dilemmas and problems
7. Review of the case in relation to the ethical guidelines
8. Proposal of options and possibilities for action in relation to ethical dilemmas and ethical issues
9. Proposition of evaluation opportunities for action and evaluation of success criteria in relation to decision and action.

This model expands on individual aspects of the various dimensions of the ethical decision-making, and elaborates some of the dimensions of the proposed five-step model that coincide in one step. The problem is whether or not it is excessive, and we can argue that we maintain a smaller but more useful model.

Jørgen Husted has proposed a so-called ethical wheel (Figure 17.1), where he integrates ethics of duty and virtue in an ethical decision-making model for professions in

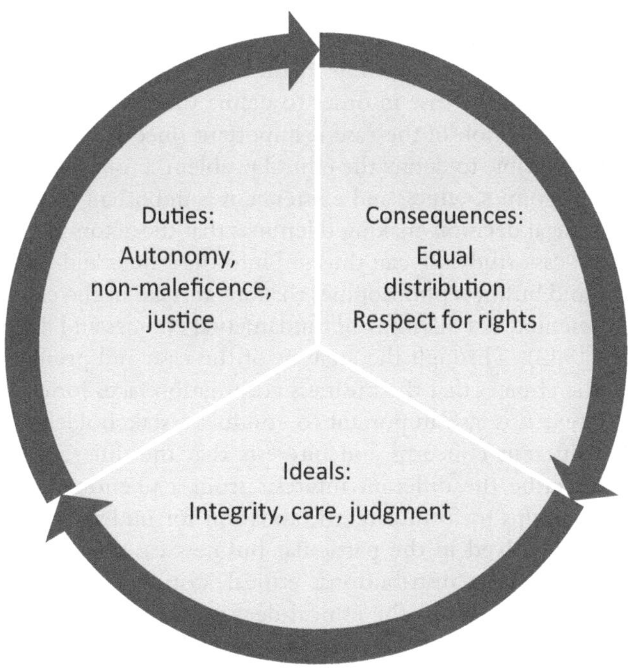

Figure 17.1 Ethical wheel of obligations.

the form of an ethical circle that rolls between duties, ideals, and consequences as the basis for a considered and informed decision (Husted 2009: 186-187). To integrate the ethical considerations of ethical wheels must mean that the different ethical concerns basically are all very important, but they must be in the right balance with each other in the actual decision. The wheel can roll from one ethical concern to another. To get hold of the wheel, one can operate with a resolution model that includes the following aspects: (1) identification; (2) ethical analysis; (3) balance; (4) consultations; (5) decision (Husted 2009: 189–191).

This is a simple model that is quite useful for concrete decisions. But it is not as precise as the five-step model, which we prefer, because it involves a more holistic involvement of interpretation, ethical theories, ethical principles, and practical considerations of relevant facts. However, this must be deepened if the five-step model is to be fully operational, as we will now clarify.

Phenomenological and critical hermeneutical analysis

The first step in the ethical decision-making process is a narrative reconstruction and presentation of the ethical problem of dilemma present in the case. The normative understanding of the situation in its totality is the perspective of the different philosophies of cosmopolitan business ethics. On this foundation, the phenomenology and critical hermeneutics of the case imply a critical reconstruction of the case in relation to stakeholders, implied actors, and those values that play a role in the case. At the basis of this reconstruction of the case, the ethical dilemma or problem is presented as the basis for decision-making. This description takes place from the perspective of the horizon of meaning that is the basis for the ethical problem or dilemma of the business case.

From the hermeneutic perspective, the meaning of the business ethics problem is interpreted in a hermeneutic circle of understanding between the totality and the parts, as well as between the individual and the universal in the specific context (Gadamer 1960). Such a hermeneutical approach to decision-making in the case implies interpretation and understanding of the meaning of the case in order to define the ethical problem or dilemma. Such a narrative reconstruction of the case is important since it already lies in the interpretation that makes it possible to define the ethical problem. From the perspective of the relation between economics, ethics, and existence it is important to focus on the existential aspects of the ethical decision-making dilemmas that the actors are facing.

With the description of the case study we can thus get into the values and ideas and the business ethics dilemmas and business philosophies that are at stake in the case. The business ethics case can be presented as a dilemma of fundamental choices and decisions about good and evil (Sartre 1943). Through the analysis of the case and presentation of the dilemma, we can see the choices that the business corporation faces for concrete decision-making. In this context it is also important to conduct a stakeholder analysis (Freeman 1984: 46) of the different concerns and interests that the different parties of the case are facing. To describe the different interests from a phenomenological and hermeneutical perspective helps to formulate a foundation for understanding the ethical dimensions and values involved in the particular business case. This involves different understanding of values, role distributions, ethical attitudes, and codes of conduct of the individual players. With this the ethical decision-making starts with a presentation of the stakeholders, values, and facts of the particular case for decision-making in the corporation.

Analysis from the perspective of the different ethical theories

The second step in the ethical decision-making process is an analysis of the ethical problems or dilemmas in relation to the relevant stakeholders in the light of the different ethical theories in relation to business and organizations. We have mentioned virtue ethics, duty ethics, utilitarianism, conversation ethics, and the different concepts of philosophy of management, and we have already formulated the main basis for the ethical analysis in the fundamental theories of business ethics and ethical economy. Concepts from these ethical theories can now be used at this level to analyze the ethical dilemma in the specific business case. Here one can either analyze the ethical problem or dilemma as a conflict between the various ethical theories, or one can see the ethical theories and terms as ranked on different levels, so that they each come with inputs for the solution of the specific ethical dilemma. Whether it is possible with such a mixture of ethics, or whether the ethical theories are mutually exclusive, depends on the specific ethical problem or dilemma in the private business or public institution.

The ethical theories focus fundamentally on different ethical considerations, and this affects the concerns that they represent in relation to the specific cases. Virtue ethics emphasizes an extension of Aristotle, in which the aim of the good ethical decision must be to promote the interests of luck or "the good life." The good life is to live an active life in accordance with basic virtues and the ethical tradition that is appreciated as a part of a basic philosophy of management. Virtue ethics focuses on the concern for the good life of the stakeholders and seeks a decision that promotes the good life. The ethics of duty follows as a continuation of Immanuel Kant that the aim of the good ethical decision is to respect the universal moral law, ethical duty, justice, and respect for fundamental human rights. Duty ethics emphasizes that all fixed norms and universal moral rules are complied with by the actors in the case, and that all are treated in a fair, just, and equitable manner.

The ethics of utility, or consequentialism, is an extension of the emphasis of Bentham and Mill on the concern for the good consequences of the decisions. The good act is the act that brings the best outcome and the greatest good for the greatest number. This approach considers the dilemma in the case pragmatically, and aims to prevent pain and suffering by ensuring the most effective and useful actions with the best consequences.

Procedural conversation ethics, inspired by Habermas, is concerned with the fact that the ethical decisions are made through a democratic process and procedure, where all the good arguments are examined, and this involves a domination-free dialogue situation where the weaker parties in the case history have their say and have their views taken into account in relation to solving the ethical problem or dilemma.

At this level it is the task to review the ethical case in the light of these various ethical theories. We can analyze the case as an ethical dilemma between two ethical theories, such as duty ethics versus utilitarianism, or duty versus the consequences, but it may also be that the theories on their respective levels help to illuminate the problem or dilemma in the case, so that they relate to different terms at different levels and in relation to the case may be combined and point in the same direction relative to the understanding of the problem or dilemma.

Analysis from the perspective of the ethical principles

At this level we analyze the case in the light of the basic ethical principles, i.e. autonomy, dignity, integrity, and vulnerability (Rendtorff and Kemp 2000; Rendtorff 2015b). These principles must here be related to the parties involved, i.e. the business manager must analyze the role of ethical principles in decision-making.

We can briefly recall the definition of the basic ethical principles. Autonomy is considered as a principle of the self-legislation of rational human beings taking part in the same life-world. Autonomy refers to the republican vision of "the good life with and for others in just institutions" (Ricoeur 1990: 202). Human dignity can at the same time be defined as intrinsic value of the human being and intersubjective concern for each human being in society. Accordingly, it expresses the intrinsic worth and fundamental equality of all human beings. Integrity refers both to a totality of life and coherence that must not be touched and to a virtue of uncorrupted character, expressing uprightness, honesty, and good character. It is also a legal and organizational notion referring to the wholeness and ethical coherence of an organization or institution. Vulnerability expresses the vulnerability of the human condition and vulnerability is the foundation of ethics reminding us of the fragility of life, human beings, and nature (Rendtorff and Kemp 2000; Rendtorff 2015b).

From these definitions of the ethical principles, the task is to apply them to the analysis of the business case not only in terms of individual players, but also in relation to the business in the market as a whole. The specific meaning of the principles depends on case content. It is clear that one can pick out the principles that best fit the analysis of the business case.

Analysis with values, codes of conduct, and compliance programs

The analysis of cases in the light of the ethical principles in codes of ethics and compliance, as well as values and mission statements, goes a step further and looks at the case in the light of the specific ethical guidelines for business corporations. Here the emphasis is on how the principles of ethics and compliance as formed in codes of conduct and values-driven management are important in relation to the business corporation's handling of the ethical problem or dilemma in the case. At this level the manager and business corporation include values, codes of conduct, and compliance programs as a basis for concrete decision-making in relation to business cases.

Decisions, decision-making, and evaluation

Ethical decision-making, as mentioned, is described as an activity for good judgment, based on ethical awareness and ability to act well (Rendtorff 2015b). Immanuel Kant defined judgment as the ability "to put oneself in the other's place," and that is what happens when we apply decision-making in the process of four steps before the final action and evaluation. Decision and action instructions, including evaluation and discussion of the consequences of the decision, can be regarded as a final summary and evaluation of the ethical decision-making.

The phenomenological and narrative reconstruction of the ethical business case defines the basis for applying the ethical theories and ethical principles in relation to the case. Here we gather background information and the case clarifies the ethical values that are at stake in the business case. The task is then to involve the ethical theories, i.e. virtue ethics, ethics of duty, utilitarianism, and conversation ethics in relation to the actors and stakeholders who are involved in the case, for example, customers, employees, managers, board members, consumers, general public, journalists, and actors in society in general. The analysis may also touch on whether there is a conflict between the ethical theories, or whether they point to the same decision. This involves the ethical principles of respect for autonomy, dignity, integrity, and vulnerability. These principles should be related to the various actors and stakeholders in the business case as a whole. Finally, we need to include codes of ethics and compliance and mission and vision statements as they are presented in codes of conduct and ethics programs of the organization.

On this basis we can formulate a decision or judgment that integrates the various considerations in relation to the specific decision and decision-making process about the right judgment in the specific case. Fundamentally, decision and action include a unique existential decision in which individual managers and leaders who are responsible independent and accountable must make a decision that can be justified by the ethical theories and principles, including mission and vision statements. But while the decision finds its basis in ethical theory, we now face the transition from theory to practice, where it is the individual manager who must make the decision between right and wrong, based on the consideration of what kind of ethics is relevant for making a just and good decision.

Decision and action will, however, get their meaning through the ethical justification. The decision as such can be justified by the individual decision-maker, as formulated in the particular case of ethics. In addition the justification comes from the analysis of the ethical theories, ethical principles, and ethical guidelines. These are integrated into a unity, thus constituting a rational justification for the decision and solution, which in turn is evaluated in the light of the ethical theories and principles.

The evaluation is again based on the interpretation of the particularity of the case, ethical theories, and ethical principles, in relation to the ethical guidelines for values, compliance, and codes of conduct. The goal of the evaluation is to assess whether the result of the decision and action was in accordance with what was the target of the action. At the same time the evaluation improves the involved persons' abilities to make ethically sound and reasoned decisions. Here there is a basis for more ethical awareness and informed ethical decisions in business in the future.

18 Strategy for cosmopolitan business ethics

We have been dealing with most aspects of business ethics and it is appropriate to sum up with a list and a vision for a business strategy that can integrate corporate social responsibility, ethics, and values-driven management in the company's general development. To propose a strategy for cosmopolitan business ethics is an attempt to manage business ethics right with straight talk (Treviño and Nelson 2014). This strategy must be based on ethical principles and values as a basis for ethical business management. It is a strategy for responsibility, ethics, and legitimacy of corporations (Rendtorff 2009). The basis of the strategy is that business ethics and CSR help to create a better and more sustainable company, and not least to enhance corporate social legitimacy in the general public in the national and international community.

The basis of the company's strategy for ethics

- *Focus.* The company must have a focused strategy to integrate ethics, values, and social responsibility at the heart of company management and culture.
- *Reassessment.* The company should rethink its previous strategy in the light of a comprehensive review of the company's activities seen in the context of business ethics theory and practice (Rendtorff 2009: 461–485).
- *Sustainability.* The strategy must be built on a close relationship between values, organization, and management. A strategy that is oriented toward sustainability should integrate values in the description of the organization's purpose.
- *Integrative business ethics.* The strategy must aim at integrating the various models of business ethics and organizational theory as a coherent whole for developing the company's good citizenship.
- *Strengthening the ethical principles of the organization.* The strategy must focus on fairness, thus strengthening the ethical principles of respect for autonomy, dignity, integrity, and vulnerability in organizational ethics. These principles can be further seen in the light of concepts such as justice and fairness.
- *Development of institutional responsibility.* The concept of responsibility in the institutional sense must be central to a business ethics strategy. This understanding of responsibility is based on the shift from shareholder to stakeholder responsibility and a formulation of procedures for the company's internal decision-making structure.
- *Proactive strategy for compliance.* The company must work for enlightened and reflexive self-regulation by following legal regulation and judicial procedures. Strategies for compliance must be built around the notion of institutional responsibility and ethics as more than image and window dressing.

- *Dynamic tension between ethics and law.* Strategic business management must integrate values and compliance, so that ethics and corporate governance are based not only on what is legal but also on making an extra effort beyond what is legally required.
- *Ethics at the heart of the company's culture.* The idea is to make ethics and ethical values fundamental to the company's culture. The requirements for this are: (1) Identify ethical problems. (2) Make ethics a core value. (3) Management must work with ethical goals and visions. (4) Debate on ethical issues must be taken seriously, and the company must be aware of the dilemmas and potential conflicts of interest. (5) Employees should be engaged in ethics. There must be continuous evaluation and renewal of the company's ethical goals and visions.
- *Integrity as the basis for the company's strategy.* The aim of company strategy is to have integrity at the organizational level, but also as the focus of individual behavior. Integrity is defined as a virtue for good and consistent behavior as the basis for the good corporate citizenship found in the organization's culture, history, and values.
- *Awareness of problems with values-driven management.* A focus on ethics and responsibility in the company's strategy should be critical of possible alienation and instrumentalization of ethics in business. This is to avoid the "soft values" becoming "hard values" that simply promote purely economic interests without touching the substance of the company's ethical problems.
- *The individual and the institution.* In the institutional approach to corporate ethics and responsibility, it is important that we do not forget the importance of individual responsibility. Strategies, missions, visions, and codes of conduct should never wipe out personal responsibility and the need for good education in the ethical judgment of the institution's executives and employees.

Social responsibility as a practical strategy

The Danish Business Authority, in a project supported by the European Social and Labour Market Authority in collaboration with the Ministry of Economic and Business Affairs, has compiled practical information and training materials on corporate social responsibility that specifically define a number of practical and strategic initiatives for small and medium-sized companies working with CSR (Rendtorff 2009). The project led to the publication *People and Profit: A Practical Guide to Corporate Social Responsibility* (2006). This work has been continued in several projects and publications, e.g. *From Principle to Practice: Strategic CSR in Small and Medium Enterprises. A manual for SMEs focusing on making their CSR effort more systematic and strategic* (2014). This material is a good illustration of the public authorities' commitment to encouraging CSR. At the same time it shows a number of specific strategic activities that can be undertaken when working with CSR.

Overall, the material highlights that CSR should be used strategically to improve the company's bottom line and competitive advantage through a CSR-based practical approach to business management, vision, and values. This involves dialogue and communication with the company's stakeholders (Danish Business Authority 2006: 11, 2014). Activities based on dialogue with stakeholders include asset selection and making proactive contact. It also highlights that one can talk about CSR innovation, i.e. integration of CSR in relation to the company's innovative processes. In addition to these main activities we can also mention activities in relation to employees, customers, the environment, society, and suppliers as focal points for internal and external strategic CSR. Employees represent here an important stakeholder, and strategic CSR concerns in this regard improvement of occupational health, physical and mental impact of the work environment, retention of seniors, diversity in the company, and all in all, key health and safety problems (Danish Business Authority 2006: 37f.)

Strategic customer activities are defined as dialogue with customers about their expectations, but also concern being conscious of product liability, for example through labeling of products, as happens with environmental labels like the swan, the EU's eco-label and the flower label, which is the Nordic eco-label (Danish Business Authority 2006: 79f.). By living up to the demands of environmental labels, businesses can signal credibility and social responsibility to customers, which can increase the long-term sustainability of the company.

Supplier activities include direct intensive communication concerning CSR with suppliers. The business can operate with a schedule for clarification of the suppliers' handling of forced labor, child labor, non-discrimination, freedom of association, occupational health, employment, disease prevention and access to health products, corruption and bribery, and the environment (Danish Business Authority 2006: 99, 2014). Suppliers' attention is also drawn to international regulations such as the Global Compact principles. Social activities include the company's community involvement. This can be done with community support in the form of sponsorship, cultural events or sporting events, support for charity, assistance to education through the creation of apprenticeships, employment of trainees, etc. (Danish Business Authority 2006: 113, 2014).

Strategic environmental activities include working with environmental management as an integral element of the company's products and services. Examples of strategic environmental activities are good housekeeping by saving energy and water consumption; requirements to suppliers, e.g. of raw materials, to use cleaner and less-polluting technologies or to use organic materials; and design of products (Danish Business Authority 2006: 125, 2014). Such a practical guide to corporate social responsibility witnesses how CSR is becoming a tool that naturally emerges as one of the company's key instruments to improve and ensure sustainability. Social responsibility no longer expresses an abstract philosophical discussion (talk the talk) but in many companies it is considered a part of practical daily life (walk the talk!).

Corporate governance and stakeholder management

- *Corporate governance and sustainability.* The company's strategy for corporate governance should be founded on the triple bottom line. Organizations should commit themselves to live up to environmental, social, and economic sustainability requirements (Rendtorff 2009). The triple bottom line is also central to the company's strategy for values-driven management.
- *Corporate governance and international rules.* The company should actively seek to live up to international agreements as expressed in the World Commission's (1987) Brundtland Report, *Our Common Future: Sustainable Development in International Politics*, the UN Development Goals for Sustainability, the Universal Human Rights Declaration, the Global Compact principles, Sullivan principles and Caux Round Table Principles, etc.
- *Transparent framework for corporate governance.* The company's strategy should be based on an ethical understanding of corporate governance with high integrity and transparency, for example by developing clear principles for corporate governance combined with social responsibility, so shareholders and the other stakeholders can get in-depth insight into the company management and other activities.

- *A vision of good corporate governance.* It is important that the corporation develops a vision of what values should be central to the future, such as integrity, credibility, transparency, commitment to stakeholders, and the company's good citizenship.
- *Corporate governance and social responsibility.* Corporate social responsibility must, like stakeholder responsibility, be regarded as an integral part of corporate governance. Work on social responsibility integrates human rights and international labor standards. Social responsibility in corporate governance implies integration of stakeholder management and of the company's strategy and management.
- *Environmental responsibility and corporate governance.* Environmental liability, as an integral part of corporate governance involves a sustainable strategy, integrating economic and ecological concerns in the company's social context. Technology should be ecologically effective, which is why life-cycle analysis should be integrated into the company's strategy.
- *Corporate governance as stakeholder management.* Stakeholder management is the general framework for good corporate governance. Stakeholder management is based on communicative dialogue with stakeholders, broadly defined as "those who affect and are affected by the organization." Stakeholder management must be oriented toward the common good (including civil society stakeholders).
- *Open vision of stakeholder management.* Stakeholder management must be used to improve the company's self-reflection in a sustained and open decision-making process which involves all relevant stakeholders. The company should not place itself at the center of the stakeholder diagram but should emerge as one among other players that contribute to good corporate citizenship in society as a whole.
- *Basic principles of stakeholder management.* Stakeholder management must follow Freeman's basic stakeholder principles (2004; Freeman and Velamuri 2008): (1) Stakeholder interests converge over time. (2) Stakeholders are real people with names, faces, and children. People are complex. (3) We need solutions that satisfy multiple interests simultaneously. (4) We need intensive communication and dialogue with our stakeholders. (5) We should follow a voluntarist philosophy and manage our stakeholder relationships themselves rather than involve third parties such as governments. (6) It is necessary to generalize marketing approaches. (7) Everything we do serves our stakeholders. We never exchange one of our stakeholders' interests in favor of someone else's interest. (8) We are negotiating with primary and secondary stakeholders. (9) We will continually monitor and redesign processes to serve our stakeholders better. (10) We work to meet our commitments to our stakeholders. We work to meet our dreams.
- *Stakeholder responsibility and the common good.* The company is governed from the perspective of the notion that stakeholder responsibility in corporate governance with the French philosopher Paul Ricoeur's words aims toward "the good life with and for others in just institutions" (Ricoeur 1990: 202). Corporate citizenship is not only about survival and self-interest, but also about the company's contribution to the common good of society.
- *Stakeholder management and justice.* A universalist and republican corporate governance approach emphasizes fairness and reasonableness in organizations as key justice principles of a stakeholder economy. Here we highlight the philosopher John Rawls' principles of political freedom and respect for the weakest in society.
- *Stakeholder management and judgment.* Judgment should be recognized as a fundamental principle of corporate governance and stakeholder management. Sustainability, justice, and ethics are abstract visions, which make sense only in specific situations of use that require judgment (Table 18.1).

Table 18.1 Strategic relationship between ethics, values, and social responsibility

Ethical strategy formulation	*The company's strategy*	*Ethical principles*	*Implementation process*	*Evaluation and development*	*Values and social responsibility*
Ethics Committee/ Ethics Officer	Mission vision	Business ethics values	Ethics vision formulation	Process with values	Respect for the environment
Ethical leadership principles	Fundamental ethical view	Stakeholder ethics	Implementation strategy	Value formulation	The triple bottom line
Ethical code	Stakeholder management	Human resource management and ethics	Ethical, social and environmental accounting	Value development	Social and legal principles
Integrity	Communication	Individual ethics	Societal acceptance and legitimacy formation	Change logic of value development	Philanthropic conditions

Basic ethical principles in values-driven management

- *Stakeholder management as values-driven management.* An ethical strategy for corporate governance and stakeholder management implies values-driven management. The basic ethical principles about the consideration of autonomy and respect for rights, the principle of dignity and respect for people, the principle of integrity and respect for the identity and life context, the principle of vulnerability and respect for human frailty, as well as fairness and reasonableness in the light of discernment, are here fundamental to values-driven management (Rendtorff 2009).
- *Values-driven leadership and integrity.* Values-driven management is based on an integrity strategy. Lynn Sharp Paine expresses this with the three P's: Purpose, Principle, and People (Paine 2003). On this basis, an integrity-based strategy seeks to establish ethical coherence in the organization.
- *Standards for values-driven management.* Organizational development should be based on the company's core values. In this context we can include integrity, trustworthiness, responsibility, fairness, transparency, citizenship, compliance, and honesty as elements of the company's code of values-driven management.
- *Tension between compliance and values.* A good program for values-driven management should recognize the difference between compliance and values. While compliance programs based on respect for the law concern values of intrinsic motivation, programs of values-driven management focus on individual responsibility in the framework of the law and in relation to the company's obligations to society.
- *Important steps for values-driven management.* Values-driven management should influence the company's institutional structure. With Michael Hoffman, we can here emphasize ten key steps for values-driven management (Hoffman and Schwartz 2001; Rendtorff 2009): (1) self-assessment; (2) top management commitment; (3) codes of business conduct; (4) ethics communications; (5) training; (6) help resources; (7) ownership of the organization; (8) interconnecting response and enforcement; (9) accounting and measurements; (10) revision and improvement.

- *The implementation of ethics programs.* Depending on the size of the company, it should follow the recommendations of the US Federal Sentencing Guidelines: (1) establishing standards and procedures; (2) assigning the overall responsibility; (3) delegation of discretion and authority; (4) communication of standards and procedures, working for employee inclusion (employee compliance); (5) monitoring, auditing and disclosure; (6) enforcementand discipline; (7) organizational response to ethics violations.
- *Values and collective identity.* Values and ethics are considered the key for the common good of the organization. They create a reflexive self-awareness that promotes the organizational learning process. It is also important to give attention to respect for individual rights and values as part of the organization's collective identity.
- *Values and international business ethics.* The Global Compact principles and Caux Principles are in this context fundamental for the development of values-driven management in international business ethics. The Caux Principles include the following: (1) corporate responsibility: from shareholders to stakeholders; (2) the economic and social impact on the companies: toward innovation, justice, and the cosmopolitan world community; (3) the company's behavior: in addition to respect of the law, toward a spirit of trust; (4) respect for rules: in addition to trading, toward cooperation; (5) support for multilateral trade: beyond isolation, toward the world community; (6) respect for the environment: in addition to protection, toward enforcement; (7) avoiding illegal operations: in addition to profit, toward peace (Enderle 1999: 143-155). Such principles are important for special application within the different areas of the business economy.
- *Values-driven management in the interests of employees.* Since employees are among the key stakeholders, it is important that values-driven management is used for communication between employer and employees to ensure rights and employee motivation, to create wellbeing and confidence at work, and to contribute to democratization of decision-making processes.
- *Judgment and values-driven management.* It is important that values-driven management is not reduced to a matter of applying rules but also is used as a basis for understanding the context of specific decisions. Therefore, the values must be applied by using good judgment and the manager's capacity for moral thinking is the basis for concrete decisions.
- *Judgment as a decision-making model for values-driven management.* This implies that the company defines good judgment as the basis for innovation and strategy. Ethical issues are integrated into the strategic decision-making of the company so that business ethics, professional ethics, environmental ethics, organizational ethics, and ethics in relation to the company's different stakeholders will guide the strategic development process in the company. This combines values-driven management with stakeholder management.
- *Critical judgment and specific ethical questions.* Concrete decisions in the context of values-driven management should be considered as context-sensitive and include concrete and situational ethics issues. A model for critical ethical judgment includes in this context investigation of: (1) information about the case; (2) the affected partners; (3) relevant principles and values of the company; (4) the decision and its implementation.

Table 18.2 illustrates the close relationship between ethics, values, and social responsibility in relation to strategic business development.

Table 18.2 Strategy and management with ethics and values

Application of SWOT analysis	*Application of CSR and values-driven management*	*Application of business ethics analysis*	*Development of strategy*	*Implementation of strategy*
Strategic analysis of the business	Perspective for ethics	Ethics as a tool for strategic analysis	Competitiveness and ethics	Evaluation of mission and vision
Threats and opportunities in the outside world	Social responsibility and CSR as perspectives	Mission – possibilities and limits	Corporate governance and ethics	Organizational development according to values
Strengths and weaknesses in the organization	Values-driven management and stakeholder analysis	Vision as a limit and possibility of further organizational development	Ethics integrated into the strategy of the organization	Integration of strategy into the company's practical reality
Evaluation of structures	Legitimacy analysis	Ethics in practice	Strategy evaluation	Evaluation of strategy in reality

Bibliography

Adams, Guy B. and Danny L. Balfour (2009). *Unmasking Administrative Evil*, 3rd edition. Armonk, NY/London: M.E. Sharpe.

Althammer, Jörg (2000). *Ökonomische Theorie der Familienpolitik: theoretische und empirische Befunde zu ausgewählten Problemen staatlicher Familienpolitik* [Economic Theory of Family Policy: Theoretical and empirical findings in relation to selected problems of state family policy]. Heidelberg: Physica.

Andersen, Kirstine (2005). *Kierkegaard og ledelse* [Kierkegaard and Management]. Copenhagen: Frydenlund.

Andersen, Niels Åkerstrøm and Asmund W. Born (2001). *Kærlighed og Omstilling – Italesættelsen af den offentligt Ansatte* [Love and Conversion. Discursive Invention of the Public Employee]. Copenhagen: Nyt fra samfundsvidenskaberne.

Apel, Karl-Otto (1994). *Die Transformation der Philosophie* [The Transformation of Philosophy]. Frankfurt am Main: Suhrkamp Verlag.

Aras, Güler and David Crowther (eds) (2009). *Global Perspectives on Corporate Governance and CSR,* Corporate Social Responsibility Series. Farnham: Gower.

Arendt, Hannah (1964). *Eichmann in Jerusalem. A Report on the Banality of Evil.* New York: Penguin Books.

Argandoña, Antonio (1998). "The stakeholder theory and the common good," *Journal of Business Ethics,* 17: 1093–1102.

Aristotle (1999). *Nicomachean Ethics*, trans. T.H. Irwin, Introduction. Indianapolis: Hackett Publishing Company.

Arnold, Dennis G. and Jared D. Harris (eds) (2012). *Kantian Business Ethics. Critical Perspectives.* Cheltenham/Northampton, MA: Edward Elgar.

Arnsperger, Christian (2001). "Entre impartialité, horizon de sens, et précarité existentielle. Les fondements de l'éthique économique et sociale" [Between impartiality, horizon of meaning and existential precarity. the foundations of economic and social ethics], in Christian Arnsperger, Cathrine Larrère, and Jean Ladrière, *Trois essais sur l'éthique économique et sociale* [Three Essays on Economic and Social Ethics]. Paris: INRA Éditions.

Arnsperger, Christian (2005). *Critique de l'existence capitaliste: pour une éthique existentialiste de l'économie* [Critique of Capitalist Existence. For an Existentialist Ethics of the Economy]. Paris: Éditions du Cerf.

Arnsperger, Christian (2009). *Éthique de l'existence post-capitalisme: pour un militarisme existentiel* [Ethics of Post-Capitalism. For an Existentialist Activism]. Paris: Éditions du Cerf.

Assländer, Michael (ed.) (2011). *Handbuch Wirtschaftsethik* [Handbook of Business Ethics]. Stuttgart/Weimar: Verlag J.B. Metzler.

Badaracco, Joseph L., Jr. (1997). *Defining Moments. When Managers Must Choose Between Right and Right.* Boston: Harvard Business School Press.

Bak, Christian (1996). *Det etiske regnskab* [The Ethical Accounting Report]. Copenhagen: Handelshøjskolens forlag.

Bakan, Joel (2004). *The Corporation: The Pathological Pursuit of Profit and Power.* London: Constable.

Ballet, Jérôme and Françoise de Bry (2001). *L'éthique de l'entreprise* [The Ethics of the Firm]. Paris: Éditions du Seuil.

Baruchello, Giorgio, Jacob Dahl Rendtorff, and Asger Sørensen (2016). *Ethics, Democracy and Markets. Nordic Perspectives on World Problems.* Helsinki: NSU Press.

Bauman, Zygmunt (1999). *Globalization: The Human Consequences.* New York: Columbia University Press.

Beck, Ulrich (2000). "Living your own life in a runaway world: individualism, globalisation and politics," in Will Hutton and Anthony Giddens (eds), *Global Capitalism.* New York: The New Press.

Beck, Ulrich (2002). *Macht und Gegenmacht im globalen Zeitalter. Neue weltpolitische Ökonomie* [Power and Contra Power in the Global Age. New world political economy]. Frankfurt am Main: Edition Zweite Moderne, Suhrkamp.

Beck, Ulrich (2006). *Qu'est-ce que le cosmopolitisme?* [What is Cosmopolitanism?]. Paris: Éditions Aubier.

Bentham, Jeremy ([1788] 1988). *The Principles of Morals and Legislation.* New York: Prometheus Books.

Bertram, Christopher (1997). "The need for basic income: an interview with Philippe Van Parijs" conducted by Christopher Bertram (*Imprints* Vol. 1, March). Online: http://eis.bris.ac.uk/~plcdib/imprints/vanparijsinterview.html

Beschorner, T. and T. Hajduk (2014). "'Der ehrbare Kaufmann' und 'Creating Shared Value': Eine Kritik im Lichte der aktuellen CSR-Diskussion" ["The Honest Business Man" and "Creating Shared Value": A critique in the light of the actual CSR discussion], in A. Schneider and R. Schmidpeter (eds), *Corporate Social Responsibility: Verantwortungsvolle Unternehmensführung in Theorie und Praxis* [Corporate Social Responsibility: Responsible business management in theory and practice]. Berlin/Heidelberg: Springer Gabler, 269–280.

Beyer, Peter (2006). *Værdibaseret ledelse. Den ældste vin på nye flasker.* [Values-based Management. The oldest Wine in New Bottles]. 2nd edition. Copenhagen: Forlaget Thomson.

Bidault, Jacques, Francis Bidault, Pierre-Yves Gomez, and Gilles Marion (eds) (1997). *Trust, the Firm and Society.* London: Macmillan.

Bidet, Jacques (2016). *Le néoliberalisme. Un autre grand récit* [The Neoliberalism. Another Great Story]. Paris: Les Prairies ordinaires.

Bird, Frederick Bruce (1996). *The Muted Conscience. Moral Silence and the Practice of Ethics in Business.* West Port, CT/London: Quorum Books.

Blowfield, Michael and Alan Murray (2011): *Corporate Responsibility*, 2nd edition. Oxford: Oxford University Press.

Boatright, John R. (1996). "Business ethics and the theory of the firm," *American Business Law Journal*, 34(2).

Boatright, John R. (1999a). "Does business ethics rest on a mistake?" (Presidential Address to the Society for Business Ethics, 1998), *Business Ethics Quarterly,* 9(4): 583–591.

Boatright, John R. (1999b). *Ethics in Finance (Foundations of Business Ethics).* Oxford: Basil Blackwell Publishers.

Boatright, John R. (2003). *Ethics and the Conduct of Business,* 3rd edition. Upper Saddle River, NJ: Prentice Hall.

Boltanski, Luc and Eve Chiapello (1995). *Le nouvel esprit du capitalisme* [The New Spirit of Capitalism]. Paris: Gallimard.

Bonnafous-Boucher, Maria and Jacob Dahl Rendtorff (2014). *La théorie des parties prenantes* [Stakeholder Theory]. Paris: Editions La Découverte (La Collection Repères, Vol. 627).

Bonnafous-Boucher, Maria and Jacob Dahl Rendtorff (2016). *Stakeholder Theory: A Model for Strategic Management* (Springer Briefs in Ethics). New York: Springer Science+Business Media B.V.

Bordum, Anders and Jacob Holm Hansen (2005). *Strategisk ledelseskommunikation. Erhvervslivets ledelse med visioner, missioner og værdier.* [Strategic Management Communication. Business' Leadership with Visions, Missions and Values]. Copenhagen: Jurist- og Økonomforbundets Forlag.

Bosch-Badia, Maria Teresa, Joan Montllor-Serrats, and Maria Antonia Tarrazon (2013). "Corporate social responsibility from Friedman to Porter and Kramer," *Theoretical Economics Letters*, 3: 11–15.

Bovbjerg, Kirsten Marie (2001). *Følsomhedens Etik: Tilpasning af personligheden i New Age og moderne management* [The Ethics of Sensitivity: Appropriation of Personality in New Age and Modern Management]. Århus: Hovedland.

Bowie, Norman (1988). "The moral obligations of multinational corporations," in Steven Luper-Foy (ed.), *Problems of International Justice*. Boulder, CO: Westview Press.

Bowie, Norman (1999a). "A Kantian approach to business ethics," in Robert E. Frederick (ed.), *A Companion to Business Ethics* (Blackwell Companions to Philosophy). Oxford: Blackwell Publishing.

Bowie, Norman E. (1999b). *Business Ethics. A Kantian Perspective*. Oxford: Basil Blackwell.

Boyer, André (ed.) (2001). *L'impossible éthique des enterprises* [The Impossible Ethics of Businesses]. Paris: Éditions d'organisations.

Brenkert, George G. (2008). *Marketing Ethics*. Oxford: Basil Blackwell.

Brink, Alexander (2007). "Corporate Governance, Kapital und Ethik. Eine institutionenökonomische Kapitaltheorie impliziter Verträge" [Corporate governance, capital and ethics. An institutional economic capital theory of implicit contracts], in Birger Priddat (ed.), *Moral als Indikator und Kontext von Ökonomie* [Morality as Indicator and Context of the Economy]. Marburg: Metropolis.

Brown, Garrett Wallace and David Held (2010). *The Cosmopolitan Reader*. Cambridge: Polity Press.

Brown, Marvin T. (2005). *Corporate Integrity. Rethinking Organizational Ethics and Leadership*. Cambridge: Cambridge University Press.

Bruin, Boudewijn de (2015). *Ethics and the Financial Crisis. Why Incompetence is Worse than Greed*. Cambridge: Cambridge University Press.

Bubna-Litic, David (2009). *Spirituality and Corporate Social Responsibility. Interpenetrating Worlds*. Corporate Social Responsibility Series. Farnham: Gower Publishing.

Buhmann, Karin (2006). "Risikostyring igennem retlige standarder i CSR-værktøjer" [Risk management through legal standards in CSR instruments], in Helene Tølbøll Djursø and Peter Neergaard (eds), *Social ansvarlighed. Fra idealisme til forretningsprincip* [Social Responsibility. From Idealism to Business Principle]. Copenhagen: Academica.

Buhmann, Karin (2014). *Normative Discourses and Public–Private Regulatory Strategies for Construction of CSR Normativity. Towards a Method for Above National Public-Private Regulation of Business Social Responsibilities*. Copenhagen: Multivers Academic.

Buhmann, Karin and Jacob Dahl Rendtorff (2005). *Virksomheders ledelse og sociale ansvar* [Business Leadership and Social Responsibility]. Copenhagen: DJØFs forlag.

Caillé, André (2000). *Éthique et économie. L'impossible (re)marriage?* [Ethics and Economics. Impossible (Re)Marriage?]. Paris: La Découverte/Revue du Mauss.

Campbell, John L. (2006). "Institutional analysis and the paradox of corporate social responsibility," *American Behavioral Scientist*, 49: 925–938.

Cannon, Tom (2012). *Corporate Responsibility. Governance, Compliance and Ethics in a Sustainable Environment*. Harlow: Pearson Education.

Capron, Michel and Françoise Quairel-Lanoizelée (2004). *Mythes et réalités de l'entreprise responsable. Acteurs, enjeux, stratégies* [Myths and Realities of the Responsible Business. Players, Stakes, Strategies]. Paris: La Decouverte.

Carroll, Archie B. (1979). "A three dimensional model of corporate social performance," *Academy of Management Review*, 4: 497–505.

Carroll, Archie B. (1993a). "Corporate social responsibility. Evolution of a definitional construct," *Business & Society*, 38(3): 268–295.

Carroll, Archie B. (1993b). *Business and Society: Ethics and Stakeholder Management*. Cincinnati, OH: South-Western Publishing.

Carroll, Archie B. (2009). *Business Ethics. Brief Readings on Vital Topics*. London: Routledge.

Castells, Manuel (1996). *The Rise of Network Society, The Information Age, Economics, Society and Culture*, Vol. I. Oxford: Blackwell Publishers.

Caux Principles for Business, Caux Round Table, Haque (1994). Reprinted in Georges Enderle (ed.) (1999). *International Business Ethics. Challenges and Approaches*. London: Notre Dame University Press.

Chakraborty, S.K. (2001). *The Management and Ethics Omnibus. Management by Values. Ethics in Management. Values and Ethics for Organizations*. Oxford: Oxford University Press.

Chakraborty, S.K. and Debangshu Chakraborty (2008). *Spirituality in Management. Means or Ends*. Oxford: Oxford University Press.

Christensen, Lars Thøger, Mette Morsing, and Ole Thyssen (2013). "CSR as aspirational talk," *Organization*, 20(3): 372–393.

Ciulla, Joanne B. (2000). *The Working Life, The Promise and Betrayal of Modern Work*. New York: Three Rivers Press.

Coase, R.H. (1937). "The nature of the firm," *Economica*, 4: 386–405.

Coff, Christian (2005). *Smag for etik. På sporet af fødevareetikken* [Taste for Ethics. In Search of Food Ethics]. Copenhagen: Museum Tusculanums Forlag.

Colby, Anne, Thomas Ehrlich, William M. Sullivan, and Jonathan R. Dolle (2011). *Rethinking Undergraduate Education: Liberal Learning for the Profession*. The Carnegie Foundation for the Advancement of Teaching. San Francisco: Jossey-Bass.

Copenhagen Centre (1998–). *Local Partnerships in Europe. Reports from 1998...* Copenhagen: Copenhagen Centre.

Crane, Andrew and Dirk Matten (2004). *Business Ethics. A European Perspective*. Oxford: Oxford University Press (2nd edition 2007, 3rd edition 2010).

Crane, Andrew and Dirk Matten (2016). *Business Ethics*. Oxford: Oxford University Press (4th edition 2016).

Crane, Andrew, Dirk Matten, and Jeremy Moon (2008). *Corporations and Citizenship*. Cambridge: Cambridge University Press.

Crane, Andrew, Dirk Matten, and Laura Spence (eds) (2008). *Corporate Social Responsibility. Readings and Cases in a Global Context*. London/New York: Routledge.

Crane, Andrew, Guido Palazzo, Laura J. Spence, and Dirk Matten (2014). "Contesting the value of creating shared value," *California Management Review*, 56(2): 130–153.

Crowther, David (2004). *Managing Finance. A Socially Responsible Approach*. London: Elsevier Butterworth-Heinemann.

Crowther, David (2006). "Standards of corporate social responsibility, covergence within the European Union," in Duro Njavro and Kristijan Krkac (eds), *Business Ethics and Corporate Social Responsibility. International Conference Papers*. Jordanovac, Zagreb, Croatia: Zagreb School of Economics and Management.

Cuilla, Johanne B., Clancy Martin, and Robert C. Solomon (2007). *Honest Work. A Business Ethics Reader*. New York/Oxford: Oxford University Press.

D'Anselmi, Paolo (2011). *Values and Stakeholders in an Era of Social Responsibility. Cut Throat Competition?* New York: Palgrave Macmillan.

Danish Business Authority (2006). (Erhvervs- and Selskabsstyrelsen (2006)). *Overskud med omtanke. Praktisk guide til virksomheders samfundsengagement*. [People and Profit – A practical guide to corporate social responsibility]. Copenhagen: Erhvervs-og Selskabsstyrelsen [Danish Commerce and Companies Agency].

Danish Business Authority (2014). *Manual From Principle to Practice: Strategic CSR in Small and Medium Enterprises. A manual for SMEs focusing on making their CSR effort more systematic and strategic*. Copenhagen: Danish Business Authority.

De George, Richard (1993). *Competing with Integrity in International Business*. New York/Oxford: Oxford University Press.

De George, Richard (1999). "International business ethics," in Robert E. Frederick (ed.), *A Companion to Business Ethics* (Blackwell Companions to Philosophy). Oxford: Blackwell Publishing.

Desjardins, Joseph R. (2014). *An Introduction to Business Ethics*, 5th edition. New York: McGraw Hill.

Desjardins, Joseph R. and John J. McCall (2000). *Contemporary Issues in Business Ethics*, 4th edition. Belmont, CA: Wadsworth.

Devinney, Timothy M., Pat Auger, and Giana M. Eckhardt (2011). *The Myth of the Ethical Consumer*. Cambridge: Cambridge University Press.

Dierksmeier, Claus (2003). Der absolute Grund des Rechts. Karl Christian Friedrich Krause in Auseinandersetzung mit Fichte und Schelling [The absolute Foundation of Law. Karl Christian Friedrich Krause in Discussion with Fichte and Schelling]. Stuttgart-Bad Cannstatt: Fromman-Holzboog.

Dierksmeier, Claus (2010). "The modern corporation and the idea of freedom" (with Michael Pirson), *Philosophy and Management*, 9(3): 5–25.

Dierksmeier, Claus (2011a). "The freedom-responsibility nexus in management philosophy and business ethics," *Journal of Business Ethics*, 1: 1–21.

Dierksmeier, Claus (2011b). "Welche Freiheit?" [Which Freedom?]. *LIBERAL* 4/2011: 9–13.

DiPiazza Jr., Samuel and Robert G. Eccles (2002). *Building Public Trust*. London: John Wiley and Sons.

Djursø, Helene Tølbøll and Peter Neergaard (2006). *Social ansvarlighed: Fra idealisme til forretningsprincip* [Social Responsibility: From Idealism to Business Principle]. Copenhagen: Gyldendal Academica.

Donaldson, Thomas (1989). "Moral minimum for multinationals," *Ethics and International Affairs*, 3(1): 163–182.

Donaldson, Thomas and Lee E. Preston (1995). "The stakeholder theory of the corporation: concepts, evidence and implications," *Academy of Management Review*, 20(1): 65.

Donaldson, Thomas and Thomas W. Dunfee (1999). *Ties that Bind. A Social Contract Approach to Business Ethics*. Boston, MA: Harvard Business School Press.

Driscoll, Dawn-Marie and W. Michael Hoffman (2000). *Ethics Matters. How to Implement Values-Driven Management*. Waltham, MA: Center for Business Ethics, Bentley College.

Elkington, John (1997, 1999). *Cannibals with Forks. The Triple Bottom Line of 21st Century Business*. Oxford: Capstone.

Emmerich-Fritsche, Angelika (2007). *Vom Völkerrecht zum Weltrecht* [From Law of Nations to International Law]. Berlin: Duncker und Humblot.

Enderle, Georges (1999). *International Business Ethics, Challenges and Approaches*. Notre Dame, IN: University of Notre Dame Press.

Enderle, Georges, Karl Homann, Martin Honecker, Walter Kerber, and Horst Steinmann (eds) (1993). *Lexikon der Wirtschaftsethik* [Encyclopedia of Business Ethics]. Freiburg/Basel/Vienna: Herder.

Ertuna, Ibrahum Ozer (2016). *Wealth, Welfare and the Global Free Market. A Social Audit of Capitalist Economics*. Corporate Social Responsibility Series. Farnham: Gower Publishing.

Etchegoyen, Alain (1991). *La valse des ethiques* [The Waltz of the Ethics]. Paris: Le Seuil.

Etzioni, Amitai (1988). *The Moral Dimension. Towards a New Economics*. New York: Collier-Macmillan.

European Commission (2001). Directorate-General for Employment and Social Affairs, Industrial Relations and Industrial Change, Unit EMPL/D.1: *Promoting a European Framework for Corporate Social Responsibility, Green Paper*, July. Luxembourg: Office for Official Publication of the European Communities.

Ferrell, O.C, John Fraedrich, and Linda Ferrell (2005). *Business Ethics, Ethical Decision Making and Cases*. Boston/New York: Houghton Mifflin Company.

Fischer, Collin, Alan Lovell, and Néstor Valero-Silva (2013). *Business Ethics and Values*, 4th edition. Harlow: Pearson Education.

Frederick, William C. (1995). *Values, Nature and Culture in the American Corporation*. New York: Oxford University Press.

Freeman, R. Edward (1984). *Strategic Management. A Stakeholder Approach*. Boston: Pitman Publishing.

Freeman, R. Edward (1994). "The politics of stakeholder theory: some future directions," *Business Ethics Quarterly*, 4(4): 409–422.

Freeman, R. Edward (1998). "The stakeholder corporation," in Laura Pincus Hartman (ed.), *Perspectives in Business Ethics*. Chicago: Irwin McGraw-Hill.

Freeman, R. Edward (2004). "Managing for stakeholders: an argument, ten principles, and eight techniques," Forelæsning ved Copenhagen Business School, November.

Freeman, R. Edward and S. Ramakrishna Velamuri (2008). A new approach to CSR: Company stakeholder responsibility (July 29). Online at SSRN: http://ssrn.com/abstract=1186223 or http://dx.doi.org/10.2139/ssrn.1186223

Freeman, R. Edward, S. Ramakrishna Velamuri, and Brian Moriarty (2006). *Company Stakeholder Responsibility: A New Approach to CSR*. Business Roundtable Institute for Corporate Ethics. Charlottesville, VA: Darden Business School.

Freeman, R. Edward, Jeffrey S. Harrison, Andrew C. Wicks, Bidham L. Parmer, and Simon de Colle (2010). *Stakeholder Theory. The State of the Art*. Cambridge: Cambridge University Press.

French, Peter ([1979] 1991). "The corporation as a moral person," in Larry May and Stacey Hoffman (eds), *Collective Responsibility. Five Decades of Debate in Theoretical and Applied Ethics*. New York: Rowman and Littlefield Publishers.

French, Peter (1984). *Collective and Corporate Responsibility*. New York: Columbia University Press.

Frey, Donald E. (1998). "Individual economic values and self-interest: the problem in Puritan ethics," *Journal of Business Ethics*, October.

Friedman, Milton (1970). "The social responsibility of business is to increase its profits," *New York Times Magazine*, September 13.

Friesen, Hans and Markus Wolf (eds) (2014). *Ökonomische Moral oder moralische Ökonomie. Positionen zu den Grundlagen der Wirtschaftsethik* [Economic Morality or Moral Economy. Positions on the Foundations of Business Ethics]. Munich: Verlag Karl Alber.

Fuglsang, Martin (1998). *At være på grænsen – en moderne fænomenologisk bevægelse* [To Be at the Limit. A modern phenomenological movement]. Copenhagen: Nyt fra Samfundsvidenskaberne.

Fukuyama, Francis (1992). *The End of History and the Last Man*. New York: The Free Press.

Fukuyama, Francis (1995). *Trust. The Social Virtues and the Creation of Prosperity*. New York: The Free Press.

Futtrup, Dorte and John Rydahl (2005). *Management by Bible. Ledetråde til ledelse* [Indices of Leadership]. Copenhagen: Det danske Bibelselskab.

Gadamer, Hans Georg (1960) *Wahrheit und Methode. Grundzüge einer philosophischen Hermeneutik* [Truth and Method]. Tübingen: J.C.B. Mohr.

Garriga, Elisabet and Domènec Melé (2004). "Corporate social responsibility theories: mapping the territory," *Journal of Business Ethics*, 53: 51–71.

Giddens, Anthony (1999). *Runaway World. How Globalization is Reshaping our Lives*. London: Routledge.

Gilbert, Larry (1999). "International business ethics in Western Europe," paper presented at the 1999 International Conference of Academy of Business Administrative Science, Barcelona, Spain.

Goodpaster, Kenneth (1991). "Business ethics and stakeholder analysis," *Business Ethics Quarterly*, 1(1): 53–73.

Goodpaster, Kenneth (2003). "Can a corporation have a conscience?" in *Harvard Business Review on Corporate Responsibility*. Boston, MA: Harvard Business School Press.

Goodpaster, Kenneth (2007). *Conscience and Corporate Culture*, Foundations of Business Ethics. Oxford: Blackwell Publishing.

Goodpaster, Kenneth (ed.) (2012). *Corporate Responsibility. The American Experience*. Cambridge: Cambridge University Press.

Govier, Trudy (1997). *Social Trust and Human Communities*. Montreal: McGill Queens University Press.

Habermas, Jürgen ([1962] 1990). *Strukturwandel der Öffentlichkeit* [Structural Transformation of the Public Space]. Frankfurt am Main: Suhrkamp Verlag.

Habermas, Jürgen (1981). *Theorie des kommunikativen Handelns I–II* [Theory of Communicative Action I–II]. Frankfurt am Main: Suhrkamp Verlag.

Hardis, Jeanet (2004). *Sociale partnerskaber* [Social Partnerships]. Copenhagen: Handelshøjskolens forlag.
Hardt, Michael and Antonio Negri (2001). *Empire.* Cambridge, MA: Harvard University Press.
Hatchuel, Armand, Éric Pezet, Ken Starkey, and Olivier Lenay (eds) (2005). *Gouvernement, organisation et gestion: l'héritage de Michel Foucault* [Government, Organization and Management: The Heritage of Michel Foucault]. Quebec: Presses de l'Université Laval.
Hayek, F.A. ([1973] 1993). *Law, Legislation and Liberty. A New Statement of the Liberal Principles of Justice and Political Economy*, Vols I–III. London: Routledge.
Heidbrink, Ludger (2008). *Verantwortung als marktwirtschaftliches Prinzip. Zum Verhältnis von Moral und Ökonomie* [Responsibility as Principle of Market Society. About the Relation between Morality and Economics] (ed. with Alfred Hirsch). Frankfurt/New York: Campus Verlag.
Held, David (1995). *Democracy and the Global Order. From the Modern State to Cosmopolitan Governance.* Oxford: Polity Press.
Hettinger, Michael (ed.) (2002). *Reform des Sanktionsrechts* [Reform of the Law of Legal Sanctions]. Baden-Baden: Nomos.
Hicks, Donna (2011). *Dignity. Its Essential Role in Resolving Conflict.* New Haven, CT/London: Yale University Press.
Hildebrandt, Steen and Søren Brandi (2005). *Ledelse af forandring. Virksomhedens konkurrencekraft* [Management of Change. The competitive power of business]. Copenhagen: Børsens forlag.
Hodgson, Geoffrey M. (1994). "The return of institutional economics," in Neil J. Smelser and Richard Swedberg (eds), *The Handbook of Economic Sociology.* Princeton, NJ: Princeton University Press.
Hoffman, W. Michael and Mark S. Schwartz (2001). *Business Ethics. Readings and Cases in Corporate Morality,* 4th edition. New York: McGraw Hill.
Hoffman, W. Michael, Robert Frederick, and Edward S. Petry (eds) (1990). *The Corporation, Ethics and the Environment.* Westpoint, CT/London: Quorum Books.
Hoffman, Michael, Judith Brown Kamm, Robert E. Frederick, and Edward S. Petry (eds) (1994). *Emerging Global Business Ethics.* Westpoint, CT: Quorum Books.
Holmström, Susanne (2004). *Grænser for ansvar – den sensitive virksomhed i det refleksive samfund* [Limits of Responsibility – the sensitive business firm in the reflexive society]. Skriftserie, Center for værdier i virksomheder, RUC 5/2004.
Homann, Karl (1993). "Wirtschaftsethik. Die Funktion der Moral in der modernen Wirtschaft" [Business Ethics. The Function of Morality in the Modern Society], in Joseph Wieland (ed.), *Wirtschaftsethik und Theorie der Gesellschaft* [Business Ethics and Theory of Society]. Frankfurt am Main: Suhrkamp, 32–53.
Homann, Karl (2001). "Ökonomik: Fortsetzung der Ethik mit anderen Mitteln" [Economics: continuation of ethics with other means], in Georg Siebeck (ed.), *Artibus ingenuis – Beiträge zu Theologie, Philosophie, Rechtswissenschaft und Wirtschaftswissenschaf* [Contributions to Theology, Philosophy, Legal Science and Business Science]. Tübingen: Mohr Siebeck, 85–110.
Homann, Karl (2002). *Vorteile und Anreize. Zur Grundlegung einer Ethik der Zukunft* [Advantages and Incentives. Towards Foundations of an Ethics of the Future]. Tübingen: Mohr Siebeck.
Homann, Karl (2003). *Anreize und Moral. Gesellschaftstheorie – Ethik – Anwendungen* [Incentives and Morality. Social Theory – Ethics – Applications]. Münster: Lit Verlag.
Homann, Karl and Christoph Lütge (2004). *Einführung in die Wirtschaftsethik* [Introduction to Business Ethics]. Münster: Lit Verlag.
Homann, Karl and Ingo Pies (1994). "Wirtschaftsethik in der Moderne: Zur ökonomischen Theorie der Moral" [Business Ethics in Modernity: Towards Economic Theory of Morality]. *Ethik und Sozialwissenschaften (EUS)* [Ethics and Social Sciences]. 5(1): 3–12.
Homann, Karl and Ingo Pies (2000). "Wirtschaftsethik und Ordnungspolitik – Die Rolle wissenschaftlicher Aufklärung" [Business Ethics and Order Politics. The Role of Scientific Enlightenment], in Helmut Leipold and Ingo Pies (eds), *Ordnungstheorie und Entwicklungsperspektiven* [Order Theory and Development Perspectives]. Series: Schriften zu Ordnungsfragen der Wirtschaft 64. Stuttgart: Der Gruyter Oldenburg, 329–346.
Honneth, Axel (2011). *Das Recht der Freiheit: Grundriß einer demokratischen Sittlichkeit* [The Law of Freedom. Foundations of Democratic Spirit]. Frankfurt am Main: Suhrkamp.

Husted, Jørgen (2009). *Etik og værdier i social arbejde* [Ethics and Values in Social Work]. Copenhagen: Hans Reitzels forlag.

Idowu, Samuel O. (ed.) (2013). *Encyclopedia of Corporate Social Responsibility,* Springer Reference, Vols 1–4. Berlin/Heidelberg: Springer-Verlag.

Idowu, Samuel O., Akubakar S. Kasum, and Asli Yüksel Mermod (eds) (2014). *People, Planet and Profit. Socio-Economic Perspectives of CSR.* Farnham: Gower Publishing.

Ims, Knut J. and Lars Jacob Tynes Pedersen (eds) (2015). *Business and the Greater Good. Rethinking Business Ethics in the Age of Crisis.* Studies in Transatlantic Business Ethics. Cheltenham/ Northampton, MA: Edward Elgar Publishing.

Ishiguro, Kazuo (1989). *The Remains of the Day.* London: Faber and Faber.

Janich, Peter (2002). *Mensch und Natur: Zur Revision eines Verhaltnisses im Blick auf die Wissenschaften* [Human Beings and Nature: For a Revision of This Relationship With a View on the Sciences]. Frankfurt: Franz Steiner Verlag.

Jensen, Frank Dybdahl (1997). *Værdibaseret ledelse – styring mellem regler og visioner* [Values-driven Management: Governance Between Rules and Visions]. Bearbejdet udgave af ph.d-afhandling, Handelshøjskolen i Århus, 1997. København: Jurist- og Økonomforbundets Forlag, 2004.

Jensen, I. (2000). "Public relations and the public sphere in the future," paper presented at the 7th International Public Relations Symposium, Bled. Also published in Mie Femø Nielsen (ed.), *Profil og offentlighed: public relations for viderekomne* [Profile and Publicity: Advanced Public Relations]. Copenhagen: Forlaget Samfundslitteratur.

Jensen, Inger, Jacob Dahl Rendtorff, and John Scheuer (eds) (2013). *The Balanced Company: Organizing for the 21st Century.* Farnham: Gower Publishing.

Jensen, Michael (1976). "A theory of the firm, governance, residual claims and organizational forms," *The Journal of Financial Economics,* 3: 305–360.

Jensen, Rolf (1999). *Dream Society.* Viby: Jyllandspostens erhvervsbøger.

Jensen, Rolf (2013). *The Renaissance Society. How the shift from dream society to the age of individual control will change the way you do business.* New York: McGraw-Hill.

Jeurissen, Ronald (2004). "Institutional conditions of corporate citizenship," *Journal of Business Ethics,* 53: 87–96.

Jonas, Hans (1979). *Das Prinzip Verantwortung* [The Imperative of Responsibility]. Frankfurt am Main: Insel Verlag.

Jones, Thomas M. (1995). "Instrumental stakeholder theory: a synthesis of ethics and economics," *Academy of Management Review,* 20(2): 404–437.

Jørgensen, Marianne Winther and Louise Philips (1999). *Diskursanalyse som teori og metode* [Discourse Analysis as Theory and Method]. Roskilde: Roskilde Universitetsforlag.

Kant, Immanuel ([1785] 1999). *Grundlegung zur Metaphysik der Sitten.* Hamburg: Felix Meiner Verlag. [Groundwork of the Metaphysics of Morals. ed. Mary Gregor. New York: Cambridge University Press, 1998.]

Kant, Immanuel ([1788] 2000). *Kritik af den praktiske fornuft.* Copenhagen: Hans Reitzels forlag. Original title: *Kritik der praktischen Vernunft.* Hamburg: Felix Meiner Verlag. [*Critique of Practical Reason*]. trans. Mary Gregor. New York: Cambridge University Press, 1997.]

Kant, Immanuel ([1790] 1995). *Kritikk av dømmekraften,* trans. Esben Hammer. Original title *Kritik der Urteilskraft,* Hamburg: Felix Meiner Verlag, 1990. [*Critique of Judgment,* trans. Werner S. Pluhar. Indianapolis: Hackett, 1987.]

Kant, Immanuel ([1795]1983). "Zum Ewigen Frieden" [Toward Perpetual Peace: A Philosophical Sketch], in *Werke in Sech Bänden,* Darmstadt: Wissenschaftliche Buchgesellschaft. [Text as in the Suhrkamp edition.]

Kant, Immanuel ([1797] 1983). *Metaphysik der Sitten* in Immanuel Kant. *Werke,* Band IV, Darmstadt: Wissenschaftliche Buchgesellschaft. [*The Metaphysics of Morals,* trans. Mary Gregor. New York: Cambridge University Press, 1996.]

Kaplan, Jeffrey M., Joseph E. Murphy, and Winthrop M. Swenson (1993). *Compliance Programs and the Corporate Sentencing Guidelines, Preventing Criminal and Civil Liability.* New York: West Publishers.

Kaplan, Robert S. and David P. Norton (1996). *The Balanced Scorecard – Translating Strategy into Action*. Boston, MA: Harvard Business School Press.

Kappel, Klemens, Thomas Søbirk Petersen, and Jesper Ryberg (2003). *En god forretning. En bog om virksomhedsetik* [A Good Business Deal. A book about business ethics]. Copenhagen: Nyt Nordisk forlag Arnold Busk.

Kemp, Peter (2005). *Verdensborgeren som pædagogisk ideal* [The Citizen of the World as Pedagogical Ideal]. Copenhagen: Hans Reitzels forlag.

Kemp, Peter (2011). *Citizen of the World: The Cosmopolitan Ideal for the Twenty-First Century*, Contemporary Studies in Philosophy and the Human Sciences. New York: Humanity Books.

Kemp, P., J. Rendtorff, and N.M. Johansen (eds) (2000). *Bioethics and Biolaw*, Vols I–II. Copenhagen: Rhodos International Science and Art Publishers.

Kirkeby, Ole Fogh (1997). *Ledelsesfilosofi – et radikalt normativt perspektiv* [Leadership Philosophy. A radical normative perspective]. Copenhagen: Forlaget Samfundslitteratur.

Kirkeby, Ole Fogh (2000). *Organisationsfilosofi. En studie i liminalitet* [Organization Philosophy. A study in borderlines]. Copenhagen: Forlaget Samfundslitteratur.

Kirkeby, Ole Fogh (2003). *Ledelsesfilosofi* [Management Philosophy]. Copenhagen: Børsens forlag.

Kirkeby, Ole Fogh (2006). *Begivenhedsledelse og handlekraft* [Event and Force of Action]. Copenhagen: Børsens forlag.

Klein, Naomi (2000). *No Logo. Taking Aim at the Brand Bullies*. New York: Picador, Saint Martins Press.

Klein, Naomi (2007). *The Shock Doctrine: The Rise of Disaster Capitalism*. London: Penguin Random House.

Klein, Naomi (2014). *This Changes Everything: Capitalism vs. The Climate*. London: Penguin Random House.

Kleingeld, Pauline (2012). *Kant and Cosmopolitanism: The Philosophical Ideal of World Citizenship*. Cambridge: Cambridge University Press.

Knudsen, Christian (1991). *Økonomisk Metodologi I. Om videnskabsidealer, forklaringstyper og forskningstraditioner* [Economic Methodology I. About scientific Ideals, Explanatory Types and Research Traditions]. Copenhagen: Jurist og Økonomforbundets Forlag.

Knudsen, Christian (1995). *Økonomisk Metodologi II.* [Economic Methodology II]. Copenhagen: Jurist og Økonomforbundets Forlag.

Korton, David C. (1995). *When Corporations Rule the World*. San Francisco: Kumarian Press, Berrett-Koehler Publishers.

Koslowski, Peter (1979). *Zum Verhältnis von Polis und Oikos bei Aristoteles: Politik und Ökonomie bei Aristoteles* [About the Relation between Polis and Oikos by Aristotle: Politics and Economics by Aristotle], 2nd edition, unedited reprint. Straubing/Munich: Donau-Verlag.

Koslowski, Peter (1988a). *Prinzipien der Ethischen Ökonomie. Grundlegung der Wirtschaftsethik* [Principles of Ethical Economy, Issues in Business Ethics]. Tübingen: Mohr Siebeck.

Koslowski, Peter (1988b). *Die postmoderne Kultur* [The Postmodern Culture], 2nd edition. Munich: C.H. Beck.

Koslowski, Peter (ed.) (1995). *The Theory of Ethical Economy in the Historical School, Studies in Economics and Ethics*. Berlin: Springer Verlag.

Koslowski, Peter (ed.) (1998). *The Social Market Economy. Theory and Ethics of the Economic Order, Studies in Economics and Ethics*. Berlin: Springer Verlag.

Koslowski, Peter (2008). *Principles of Ethical Economy, Issues in Business Ethics*. Berlin: Springer Verlag.

Krenchel, Jens Valdemar and Steen Thomsen (2004). *Corporate Governance i Danmark. Om god selskabsledelse i et dansk og internationalt perspektiv* [Corporate Governance in Denmark. About good corporate governance in a Danish and international perspective]. Copenhagen: Dansk Industri.

Kumar, Brij Nino, Margit Osterloh, and Georg Schreyögg (1999). *Unternehmensethik und Transformation des Wettbewerbs. Shareholder Value – Globalisierung – Hyperwttbewerb. Festschrift für Professor Dr. Dr. h. c. Horst Steinmann zum 65. Geburtstag* [Business Management Ethics and Transformation of Competition. Shareholder Value, Globalization, Hyper Competition. Commemorative to Professor Horst Steinmann's 65th Birthday]. Stuttgart: Schäffer-Poeschel Verlag.

Kunde, Jesper (2000). *Corporate Religion*. London: Prentice Hall: Pearson Education.

Küng, Hans (1990). *Projekt Weltethos* [Project World Ethos]. Munich: Piper Verlag.

Küng, Hans (1995). *Weltethos für Weltpolitik und Weltwirtschaft* [World Ethos for World Politics and World Society]. Munich: Piper Verlag.

Küng, Hans (2010). *Anständig Wirtschaften. Warum die Ökonomie Moral braucht?* [Honest Business Making. Why the Economy needs Morality]. Munich: Piper Verlag.

Ladkin, Donna (2015). *Mastering the Ethical Dimension of Organizations. A Self-Reflective Guide to Developing Ethical Astuteness*. Cheltenham/Northampton, MA: Edward Edgar Publishing.

Laufer, William S. and Alan Strudler (2000). "Corporate intentionality, desert, and variants of vicarious liability," *American Criminal Law Review*, 37(4): 1285–1312.

Laustsen, Carsten Bagge and Jacob Dahl Rendtorff (eds) (2002). *Ondskabens banalitet. Om Hannah Arendts Eichmann i Jerusalem* [The Banality of Evil. About Hannah Arendt's Eichmann in Jerusalem]. Copenhagen: Museum Tusculanums Forlag.

Le Roy, Fréderic and Michel Marchesnay (2005). *La responsabilité sociale de l'entreprise* [The Social Responsibility of the Business Firm]. Paris: Éditions EMS.

Lebech, Mette, Jacob Rendtorff, and Peter Kemp (1997). *Den bioetiske vending* [The Bioethical Turn]. Copenhagen: Spektrum.

Leisinger, Klaus M. (1999). "Globalisering, minima moralia und die Verantwortung multinationer Unternehmen" [Globalization, minima moralia and the responsibility of multinational business], in Brij Nino Kumar, Margit Osterloh, and Georg Schreyögg (eds), *Unternehmensethik und die Transformation des Wettbewerbs* [Business Management Ethics and Transformation of Competition]. Stuttgart: Schäffer-Poeschel Verlag, 319–341.

Lenk, Hans and Matthias Maring (eds) (1998). *Technikethik und Wirtschaftsethik, Fragen der Gesellschaft*, [Technology Ethics and Business Ethics, Questions of Society]. Opladen: Leske + Budrich.

Lenk, Hans and Matthias Maring (2010). "Finanzkrise – Wirtschaftskrise – die Möglichkeiten wirtschaftsethischer Überlegungen" [Financial Crisis – Business Crisis – the Possibilities of Reflections in Business Ethics]. *Annual Review of Law and Ethics/Jahrbuch für Recht und Ethik*, 18. Berlin: Duncker and Humblot.

Lettevall, Rebecka (2004). "Kant og oplysningstidens kosmopolitisme" [Kant and the cosmopolitanism of the Enlightenment]. *Slagmark. Tidsskrift for Idéhistorie*, No. 41, Autumn.

Lindhardt, Jan and Anders Uhrskov (1997). *Fra Adam til Robot. Arbejdet, historisk og aktuelt* [From Adam to Robot. Work. Historically and Actually]. Copenhagen: Gyldendal.

Lipovetsky, Gilles (1983). *L'Ére du Vide. Essai sur l'individualisme contemporain* [The Epoch of Emptiness. Essay about the contemporary Individualism]. Paris: Gallimard.

Lipovetsky, Gilles (1991). "Les noces de l'éthique et du business" [The wedding of ethics and business]. *Le Débat*, 67: 145–167.

Lipovetsky, Gilles (1992). *Le Crépuscule du devoir. L'éthique indolore des nouveaux temps démocratiques* [The Dawn of Duty. The painless ethics of the new democratic times]. Paris: Gallimard.

Lipovetsky, Gilles (2006). *Le bonheur paradoxal. Essai sur la société d'hyperconsommation* [The Paradoxical Happiness. Essay on the society of hyper consumption]. Paris: Gallimard.

Lipovetsky, Gilles and Jean Serroy (2013). *L'Esthétisation du monde: vivre à l'âge du capitalisme artiste* [The aesthetization of the world: Living at the age of capitalism]. Paris: Gallimard.

Lockheed Martin (2005a). *Corporate Value Statement*. Lockheed Martin Corporation, Bethesda MD. http://www.lockheedmartin.com.

Lockheed Martin (2005b). *Ethics and Business Conduct. How the Ethics Process Works at Lockheed Martin*. Lockheed Martin Corporation, Bethesda MD. http://www.lockheedmartin.com.

Logsdon, Jeanne M. and Donna J. Wood (2002). "Business citizenship: From domestic to global level of analysis," *Business Ethics Quarterly*, 12(2): 155–187.

Lütge, Christoph (2014). *Ethik des Wettbewerbs. Über Konkurrenz und Moral* [Ethics of Competition. About competition and morality]. Munich: C.H. Beck Paperback, 6159.

Mac, Anita (2005). "Institutionalisering af nye værdier i virksomheder" [Social responsibility in businesses. From profix maximization to stakeholder dialogue], in Klaus Nielsen (ed.), *Institutionel teori. En tværfaglig introduktion* [Institutional Theory: An Interdisciplinary Introduction]. Copenhagen: Roskilde Universitetsforlag.

Mac, Anita and Jacob Dahl Rendtorff (2001). "Værdier og socialt ansvar i virksomheder. Fra profitmaksimering til interessentdialog" [Values and Social Responsibility in Business: From Profit Maximization to Stakeholder Dialogue], *Grus*, 65: 69–87.

MacIntyre, Alasdair (1981). *After Virtue. A Study in Moral Theory*. London: Duckworth.

March, James G. and Johan P. Olson (1989). *Rediscovering Institutions. The Organizational Basis of Politics*. New York: Macmillan/Free Press.

March, James G. and Herbert A. Simon (1958). *Organizations,* 2nd edition. New York: Wiley. [Oxford: Blackwell Publishers, 1993.]

Maring, Matthias (1985). *Märkte und Handlungssysteme. Zur wissenschaftstheoretischen Analyse eines systemtheoretisch-kybernetischen Handlungsansatzes im Rahmen von idealtypischen Strukturen* [Markets and Action Systems. For a philosophy of science analysis of a system theoretical, cybernetic approach to action in the framework of ideal typical structures]. Frankfurt am Main/Bern/ New York: Peter Lang.

Maring, Matthias (2001). *Kollektive und Kooperative Verantwortung. Begriff- und Fallstudien aus Wissenschaft, Technik und All Tag* [Collective and Cooperative Responsibility. Concept and case-studies from science, technology and ordinary life]. Munster: Lit Verlag, Forum Humanität und Ethik.

Maring, Matthias (ed.) (2009). *Verantwortung in Technik und Ökonomie, Schriftenreihe des Zentrums für Technik und Wirtschaftsethik* [Responsibility in Technology and Economics, Writings from the Center for Technic and Business Ethics]. Karlsruhe: Universitätsverlag Karlsruhe.

Maring, Matthias (ed.) (2014). *Bereichsethiken im interdisziplinären Dialog, Schriftenreihe des Zentrums für Technik und Wirtschaftsethik* [Field Ethics in the Interdisciplinary Dialogue, Writings from the Center for Technology and Business Ethics]. Karlsruhe: Universitätsverlag Karlsruhe.

Martin, Hans-Peter and Harald Schumann (1998). *Die Globalisierungsfälle. Der Angriff auf Demokratie und Wohlstand* [The Trap of Globalization. The attack on democracy and welfare]. Hamburg: Rowolt Taschenbuch Verlag.

Matten, Dirk and Andrew Crane (2005). "Corporate citizenship: towards an extended theoretical conceptualization," *Academy of Management Review*, 30(1): 166–179.

McAlister, Debbie Thorne, O.C. Ferrell, and Linda Ferrell (2005). *Business and Society. A Strategic Approach to Social Responsibility*. Boston/New York: Houghton Mifflin Company.

McCloskey, Deirdre N. (2006). *The Bourgeois Virtues: Ethics for an Age of Commerce*. Chicago: University of Chicago Press.

McCloskey, Deirdre N. (2010). *Bourgeois Dignity: Why Economics Can't Explain the Modern World*. Chicago: University of Chicago Press.

McIntosh, Malcolm, Deborah Leipziger, Keith Jones, and Gill Coleman (1998). *Corporate Citizenship, Successful Strategies for Responsible Companies*. London: Financial Times, Pitman Publishing.

McPhail, Ken and Diane Walters (2009). *Accounting and Business Ethics. An Introduction*. London/ New York: Routledge.

Milgram, Stanley. (1974). *Obedience to Authority: An Experimental View*. New York: Harpercollins.

Mintzberg, Henry (1994). *The Rise and Fall of Strategic Planning*. London: Prentice Hall.

Mintzberg, Henry (2004). *Managers not MBAs. A Hard Look on the Soft Practice of Managing and Management Development*. San Francisco: Prentice Hall.

Mirvis, Philip and Bradley Googins (2006). "Stages of corporate citizenship," *California Management Review*, 48(2): 104–126.

Mitchell, Ronald K., Bradley R. Agle, and Donna J. Wood (1997). "Toward a theory of stakeholder identification and salience: defining the principle of who and what really counts," *Academy of Management Review*, 22(4): 853–886.

Mølvadgaard, Kjeld and Ove Nielsen (2006a). "Social ansvarlighed i danske virksomheder" [Social responsibility in Danish companies], in Helene Tølbøll Djursø and Peter Neergaard (eds), *Social ansvarlighed. Fra idealisme til forretningsprincip* [Social Responsibility. From idealism to business principle]. Copenhagen: Gyldendal, Academica.

Mølvadgaard, Kjeld and Ove Nielsen (2006b). "Det sociale ansvar og det rummelige arbejdsmarked" [Social Responsibility and the inclusive Labour Market], in Helene Tølbøll Djursø and Peter Neergaard (eds), *Social ansvarlighed. Fra idealisme til forretningsprincip* [Social Responsibility. From idealism to business principle]. Copenhagen: Gyldendal, Academica.

Morgan, Gareth (1996). *Images of Organization*. London: Sage Publications.

Morsing, Mette (1991). *Den etiske praksis – en introduktion til det etiske regnskab* [The Ethical Praxis. An introduction to the ethical accounting]. Copenhagen: Handelshøjskolens forlag.

Morsing, Mette (2001). *Værdier i danske virksomheder. Skitse af et fænomen med mange ansigter* [Values in Danish Companies. Sketch of a phenomenon with many faces]. Copenhagen: Center for Corporate Communication, Handelshøjskolen.

Morsing, Mette and Christina Thyssen (2003). *Corporate Values and Responsibility. The case of Denmark*. Copenhagen: Forlaget Samfundslitteratur.

Morsing, Mette and Susanne C. Beckmann (eds) (2006). *Strategic CSR Communication*. Copenhagen: Jurist- og Økonomforbundets Forlag.

Nelson, Robert H. (2001). *Economics as Religion: From Samuelson to Chicago and Beyond*. Pennsylvania: Pennsylvania State University Press.

Nickel, James W. (1987). *Making Sense of Human Rights*. Berkeley: University of California Press.

Nielsen, Klaus (ed.) (2006). *Institutionel teori. En tværfaglig introduktion* [Institutional Theory. An interdisciplinary introduction]. Copenhagen: Roskilde universitetsforlag.

Nielsen, Mie Femø (2001). *Profil i offentligheden, En introduktion til Public Relations* [Profile in Public Space. An introduction to public relations]. Copenhagen: Forlaget Samfundslitteratur.

Nørby Committee (2001). *Nørby-udvalgets rapport om Corporate Governance I Danmark. Anbefalinger om God selskabsledelse* [Nørby Committee Report about Corporate Governance in Denmark. Recommendations on good corporate governance]. Copenhagen: Erhvervs- og Selskabsstyrelsen.

North, Douglass (1992). *Institutions, Institutional Change and Economic Performance*. Cambridge: Cambridge University Press.

Nussbaum, Martha (1997). "Kant and stoic cosmopolitanism," *The Journal of Political Philosophy*, 5(1): 1–25.

Paine, Lynn Sharp (1994a). "Managing for organizational integrity," *Harvard Business Review* (March-April): 106–117.

Paine, Lynn Sharp (1994b). "Law, ethics and managerial judgment," *The Journal of Legal Studies Education*, 12(2): 153–169.

Paine, Lynn Sharp (1997a). "Integrity," in *Encyclopaedia of Business Ethics*. Oxford: Basil Blackwell.

Paine, Lynn Sharp (1997b). *Cases in Leadership, Ethics and Organizational Integrity. A Strategic Perspective*. Chicago: Irwin.

Paine, Lynn Sharp (2003). *Value Shift. Why Companies Must Merge Social and Financial Imperative to Achieve Superior Performance*. New York: McGraw-Hill.

Painter-Morland, Mollie and René Ten Bos (2011). *Business Ethics and Continental Philosophy*. Cambridge: Cambridge University Press.

Parum, Eva (2006). *Strategisk kommunikation om ledelse. Et corporate og public governance perspektiv* [Strategic Communication about Management. A corporate and public governance perspective]. Copenhagen: Handelshøjskolens forlag.

Pedersen, Esben Rahbek (2006). *Between Hopes and Realities: Reflections on the Promises and Practices of Corporate Social Responsibility (CSR)*. Copenhagen: CBS. Ph.D Series 17.06.

Pedersen, Esben Rahbek (ed.) (2015). *Corporate Social Responsibility*. London: Sage Publications.

Pedersen, John Storm and Jacob Dahl Rendtorff (2003). "Værdibaseret ledelse – et svar på udfordringerne til offentlige organisationer og institutioner?" [Values-driven management – a response to the challenges to public organizations and institutions?]. *Nordisk Administrativt Tidsskrift*, 84: 163–185.

Pedersen, John Storm and Jacob Dahl Rendtorff (2010). "Balancing values and economic efficiency in the public sector: What can public welfare service institutions learn from private service firms," *Society and Business Review*, 5(3): 293–302.

Petersen, V.C. (2003). *Beyond Rules in Society and Business*. Cheltenham/Northampton, MA: Edward Elgar.

Philips, Robert (2003). *Stakeholder Theory and Organizational Ethics*. San Francisco: Berrett-Koehler.

Philips, Robert and R. Edward Freeman (eds) (2010). *Stakeholders*. Cheltenham/Northampton, MA: Edward Elgar.

Pietras-Jensen, Vinni (2005). "Corporate governance og virksomhedens regnskaber" [Corporate Governance and the Accounts of Businesses], in J.D. Rendtorff and Karin Buhmann (eds), *Virksomheders ledelse og sociale ansvar. Perspektiver på Corporate Social Responsibility og Corporate Governance* [Business Leadership and Social Responsibility. Perspectives on corporate social Responsibility and Corporate Governance]. Copenhagen: Jurist- og Økonomforbundets Forlag, 199–233.

Piketty, Thomas (2014). *Capital in the Twenty-First Century*. Cambridge, MA/London: The Belknap Press of Harvard University Press.

Pine, B. Joseph and James H. Gilmore (1999). *The Experience Economy. Work is Theatre and Every Business is a Stage*. Boston: Harvard Business School Press.

Pine, B. Joseph and James H. Gilmore (2007). *Authenticity. What Consumers Really Want*. Boston: Harvard Business School Press.

Popper, Karl (1957). *The Poverty of Historicism*. London: Routledge (reprinted 2013).

Porter, Michael E. (1980). *Competitive Strategy: Techniques for Analyzing Industries and Competitors*. New York: Free Press.

Porter, Michael E. and Mark R. Kramer (2003). "The competitive advantage of corporate philanthropy," in *Harvard Business Review on Corporate Responsibility*. Cambridge, MA: Harvard Business School Press.

Porter, Michael E. and Mark R. Kramer (2006). "Strategy and society: the link between competitive advantage and corporate social responsibility," *Harvard Business Review*, 84(12): 78–92.

Porter, Michael E. and Mark R. Kramer (2011). "Creating shared value," *Harvard Business Review*, January/February, 63–70.

Post, James E., Anne T. Lawrence, and James Weber (2002). *Business and Society, Corporate Strategy, Public Policy, Ethics*. New York: McGraw-Hill.

Powell, Walter W. and Paul J. DiMaggio (1991). *The New Institutionalism in Organizational Analysis*. Chicago/London: The University of Chicago Press.

Priddat, Birger (1990). *Hegel als Ökonom* [Hegel as Economist]. Volkswirtschaftliche Schriften 403. Berlin: Duncker and Humblot.

Priddat, Birger P. (2007). *Moral als Indikator und Kontext der Ôkonomie* [Morality as Indicator and Context of the Economy]. Marburg: Metropolis-Verlag.

Priddat, Birger P. (2010). *Wozu Wirtschaftsethik?* [Why Business Ethics?]. Marburg: Metropolis-Verlag.

Pruzan, Peter (1998). "Hvad er etik i erhvervslivet? [What is ethics in business?], in Kurt Boelsgaard (ed.), *Etik i dansk erhvervsliv – fremtidens lederkrav* [Ethics in Danish Business Life – the future requirements for leaders]. Århus: Jyllandspostens Erhvervsbandklub.

Pruzan, Peter (2001). "The question of organizational consciousness: can organizations have values, virtues and visions?" *Journal of Business Ethics*, 29: 271–284.

Rafalko, Robert J. (1994). "Remaking the corporation: The 1991 US Sentencing Guidelines," *Journal of Business Ethics*, 13: 625–636.

Rasche, Andreas and Dirk Ulrich Gilbert (2012). "Institutionalizing global governance: the role of the Nations Global Compact," *Business Ethics: A European Review*, 21(1): 100–114.

Rasche, Andreas and Georg Kell (eds) (2010). *The United Nations Global Compact. Achievements, Trends and Challenges*. Cambridge: Cambridge University Press.

Rasmussen, Peter Hagedorn, Søren Jagd, and Jacob Dahl Rendtorff (2006). *Fra værdiledelse til værdier i arbejdslivet*. Rapport til LO-projekt støttet af EUs Socialfond, Institut for samfundsvidenskab og erhvervsøkonomi [From Values-driven Management to Values in Work Life. A report to the Labour Union, supported by the Social Foundation of the European Union]. Roskilde: Roskilde University (RUC).

Rawls, John (1971). *A Theory of Justice*. Cambridge MA: Harvard University Press.

Rawls, John (1985). "Justice as fairness. Political not metaphysical," *Philosophy and Public Affairs*, 14(3): 223–251.

Rawls, John (1993). *Political Liberalism*. New York: Columbia University Press.

Rawls, John (1999). *The Law of Peoples*. New York: Oxford University Press.

Rendtorff, Jacob Dahl (1998). *Jean-Paul Sartres filosofi* [Jean-Paul Sartre's Philosophy]. Copenhagen: Hans Reitzels forlag.

Rendtorff, Jacob Dahl (1999). *Bioetik og ret. Kroppen mellem person og ting* [Bioethics and Law. The body between person and thing]. Copenhagen: Gyldendal.

Rendtorff, Jacob Dahl (2000). *Paul Ricoeurs filosofi* [Paul Ricoeur's Philosophy]. Copenhagen: Hans Reitzels forlag.

Rendtorff, Jacob Dahl (2001a). "Værdibaseret ledelse og etikprogrammer i amerikanske virksomheder. En diskussion af USA's 1991 'Federal Sentencing Guidelines for Organizations' og deres betydning for virksomhedens retslige og sociale ansvar" [Values-driven Management and Ethics Programs in American Business Companies. A discussion of the US 1991 'Federal Sentencing Guidelines for Organizations' and their significance for the legal and social responsibility of business]. *Grus*, no. 65.

Rendtorff, Jacob Dahl (2001b). "Religion i erhvervslivet. Den protestantiske etik efter sekulariseringen" [Religion in Business Life. The Protestant ethics after secularization], in Lisbeth Christoffersen (ed.), *Samfundsvidenskabelige syn på det religiøse* [Social Science Perspective on the Religious]. Copenhagen: Jurist- og Økonomforbundets Forlag.

Rendtorff, Jacob Dahl (2001c). "Fra bioetik til miljøetik og virksomhedsetik. Etiske overvejelser over marked, miljø, dyr og natur" [From Bioethics to Environmental Ethics and Business Ethics. Ethical reflections on market, environment, animals and nature], in Lars Danner Madsen and Mickey Gjerris (eds), *Naturens sande betydning – om natursyn, etik og teologi* [The True Significance of Nature – about views on nature, ethics and theology]. Copenhagen: Multivers.

Rendtorff, Jacob Dahl (2002a). "Globaliseringen, verdensmarkedet og virksomhederne. Kan virksomhedsetik styrke verdensretten" [Globalization, World Market and Businesses. Can Business Ethics strengthen World Law?], in Hanne Petersen (ed.), *Globaliseringer, ret og retsfilosofi* [Globalization, Law and Legal Philosophy]. Copenhagen: Jurist- og Økonomforbundets Forlag, 12–35.

Rendtorff, Jacob Dahl (2002b). "Values and organizational integrity: The function of integrity in achieving organizational excellence," *De Montfort Business Mastery Series* 1(2): 6–14.

Rendtorff, Jacob Dahl (2003a). "Værdibaseret ledelse og socialt ansvar. Aspekter af virksomhedernes gode statsborgerskab" [Values-driven Management and Social Responsibility. Aspects of the good citizenship of businesses]. *Økonomi og Politik nr. 3. Temanummer om virksomheders sociale ansvar.* [*Economics and Politics 3. Thematic Issue about the Social Responsibility of Business*], Autumn, 37–51.

Rendtorff, Jacob Dahl (2003b). "Basic ethical principles in values-driven management," in Jacob Dahl Rendtorff (ed.), *Værdier, etik og socialt ansvar i virksomheder – brudflader og konvergens* [Values, Ethics and Social Responsibility in Business – Tensions and convergence]. Roskilde: Center for værdier i virksomheder, 104–113.

Rendtorff, Jacob Dahl (2004a). "Værdier i den politiske virksomhed" [Values in the political Firm], in Christian Frankel (ed.), *Virksomhedens politisering* [The Politization of Companies]. Copenhagen: Forlaget Samfundslitteratur, 209–231.

Rendtorff, Jacob Dahl (2004b). "Det fælles gode og samfundsansvar i det økonomiske liv – er virksomheden andet og mere end et instrument til egoistisk profitmaksimering?" [The Common Good and Social Responsibility in the Economic Life – Is the company other and more than an instrument for egoistic profit maximization?], in Niels Jakob Harbo *et al.* (eds), *Det gode liv. Mere end dig selv* [The Good Life. More than yourself]. Århus: Philosophia, 187–213.

Rendtorff, Jacob Dahl (2004c). "Markedsøkonomiens nye ånd: værdiskift i det private erhvervsliv" [The New Spirit of the Market Economy: Valueshift in private business], in Brian

Mikkelsen (ed.), *Den konservative årstid. Betragtninger og visioner efter 2001* [The Conservative Season. Considerations and Visions after 2001]. Århus: Forlaget Hovedland, 228–241.

Rendtorff, Jacob Dahl (2005). "Corporate Governance og CSR i lyset af virksomhedsetik og stakeholderteori" [Corporate Governance and CSR in the light of Business Ethics and Stakeholder Theory], in J.D. Rendtorff and Karin Buhmann (eds), *Virksomheders ledelse og sociale ansvar. Perspektiver på Corporate Social Responsibility og Corporate Governance* [Business Leadership and Social Responsibility. Perspectives on Corporate Social Responsibility and Corporate Governance]. Copenhagen: Jurist- og Økonomforbundets Forlag.

Rendtorff, Jacob Dahl (2006a). "Corporate social responsibility, sustainability and stakeholder management," in Duro Njavro and Kristijan Krkac (eds), *Business Ethics and Corporate Social Responsibility*, International Conference Papers. Jordanovac, Zagreb, Croatia: Zagreb School of Economics and Management.

Rendtorff, Jacob Dahl (2006b). "Des principes de justice pour les parties prenantes" [Principles of justice for stakeholders], in *Décider avec les parties prenantes. Approaches d'une nouvelle théorie de la société civile* [Deciding with Stakeholders. New approaches for a new theory of civil society], Maria Bonnafous-boucher Yvon Pesqueux (eds). Paris: La Découverte.

Rendtorff, Jacob Dahl (2007). *Virksomhedsetik. En grundbog i organisation og ansvar* [Business Ethics. An Introduction to Ethics and Responsibility]. Frederiksberg: Samfundslitteratur.

Rendtorff, Jacob Dahl (2008). "The corporation as a good citizen: a case study of Lockheed Martin," *Tidsskriftet Politik*, 11(4): 48–59.

Rendtorff, Jacob Dahl (2009). *Responsibility, Ethics and Legitimacy of Corporations*. Copenhagen Business School Press.

Rendtorff, Jacob Dahl (ed.) (2010). *Power and Principle in the Market Place*. London: Ashgate.

Rendtorff, Jacob Dahl (2011a). "Institutionalization of corporate ethics and social responsibility programs in firms," in K. Buhmann, L. Roseberry, and M. Morsing (eds), *Corporate Social and Human Rights Responsibilities: Global, Legal and Management Perspectives*. London: Palgrave Macmillan.

Rendtorff, Jacob Dahl (2011b). "Corporate citizenship as organizational integrity," in Ingo Pies and Peter Koslowski (eds), *Corporate Citizenship and New Governance: The Political Role of Corporations*, Ethical Economy, Studies in Economic Ethics. Dordrecht: Springer, 59–91.

Rendtorff, Jacob Dahl (2012). "Cosmopolitanism and politics: double edges and tensions between human rights and justice" in Thomas Bustamante (ed.), *Human Rights, Language and Law: ARSP Beiheft* (Archiv für Rechts und Sozialphilosophie), Oche Onazi, Vol. II/131. Stuttgart: Franz Steiner Verlag, 11–23.

Rendtorff, Jacob Dahl (2013a). "Basic concepts of philosophy of management and corporations," in Christoph Luetge (ed.), *Handbook of the Philosophical Foundations of Business Ethics*. Dordrecht: Springer Science+Business Media B.V., 1361–1386.

Rendtorff, Jacob Dahl (2013b). "The history of the philosophy of management and corporations," in Christoph Luetge (ed.), *Handbook of the Philosophical Foundations of Business Ethics*. Dordrecht: Springer Science+Business Media B.V., 1387–1408.

Rendtorff, Jacob Dahl (2013c). "Philosophical theories of management and corporations," in Christoph Luetge (ed.), *Handbook of the Philosophical Foundations of Business Ethics*. Dordrecht: Springer Science+Business Media B.V., 1409–1432.

Rendtorff, Jacob Dahl (2013d). "Recent debates in philosophy of management," in Christoph Luetge (ed.), *Handbook of the Philosophical Foundations of Business Ethics*. Dordrecht: Springer Science+Business Media B.V., 1433–1457.

Rendtorff, Jacob Dahl (2014a). *French Philosophy and Social Theory. A Perspective for Ethics and Philosophy of Management*. Dortrecht: Springer.

Rendtorff, Jacob Dahl (2014b). "Risk management, banality of evil and moral blindness in organizations and corporations," in Christoph Luetge and Johanna Jauernig (eds), *Business Ethics and Risk Management*, Ethical Economy 43. Dordrecht: Springer Science+Business Media B.V., 45–71.

Rendtorff, Jacob Dahl (2015a). "The concept of equality in ethics and economics," in Peter Kemp and Noriko Hashimoto (eds), *Ethics and Politics. Éthique et politique: With a Third Part on Paul Ricoeur.* Vienna: LIT Verlag, 77–93 (Eco-ethica, Vol. 4), 212.

Rendtorff, Jacob Dahl (2015b). "Case studies, ethics, philosophy, and liberal learning for the management profession," *Journal of Management Education*, 39(1): 36–55.

Rendtorff, Jacob Dahl (2016a). "Ethics, economics and globalization: cosmopolitanism and the financial crisis," in G. Baruchello, J.D. Rendtorff, and A. Sørensen (eds), *Ethics, Democracy and Markets: Nordic Perspectives on World Problems.* Helsingfors: NSU Press, 283–303.

Rendtorff, Jacob Dahl (2016b). "Basic ethical principles as symbolic foundations and core values of European biolaw," *Ethics, Medicine and Public Health*, 2(2): 205.

Rendtorff, Jacob Dahl (2016c). "Peter Koslowski's ethics and economics or ethical economy: A framework for a research agenda in business ethics," *Nordicum – Mediterraneum*, 10(3), online, http://nome.unak.is/wordpress/volume-10-no-3–2016/conference-paper-10–3/peter-koslowskis-ethics-and-economics-or-ethical-economy-a-framework-for-a-research-agenda-in-business-ethics

Rendtorff, Jacob Dahl (2016d), "Responsabilité et l'éthique de l'environnement: Vers une responsabilité technologique, politique et économique pour un développement durable de la nature et de la société" [Responsibility and ethics of the environment: towards a technological, political and economic responsibility for a sustainable development in nature and society], in Peter Kemp and Norioko Hashimoto (eds), *Ethics and Environment/Éthique et environnement*, LIT Verlag (Eco-ethica, Vol. 5).

Rendtorff, Jacob Dahl (2017). "Corporate citizenship, ethics and accountability: the significance of the process of trust for corporate legitimacy in late modernity," in Güler Aras and Coral Ingley (eds), *Corporate Behavior and Sustainability. Doing Well by Doing Good* (Finance, Governance and Sustainability: Challenges to Theory and Practice Series). Abingdon, Oxon./New York: Routledge.

Rendtorff, Jacob Dahl and Peter Kemp (2000). *Basic Ethical Principles in European Bioethics and Biolaw*, Vol. I–II. Copenhagen: Centre for Ethics and Law / Barcelona: Institut Borja di Bioethica.

Rendtorff, Jacob Dahl and Jan Mattson (2006). "E-marketing ethics: a theory of value priorities," *International Journal of Internet Marketing and Advertising*, 3(1): 35–47.

Rendtorff, Jacob Dahl, Adam Diderichsen, and Peter Kemp (1997). *Social Development Between Intervention and Integration.* Copenhagen: Rhodos International Publishers (edited with Peter Kemp and Adam Diderichsen).

Ricoeur, Paul (1990). *Soi-même comme un Autre* [Oneself as Another]. Paris: Le Seuil.

Ruggie, John Gerard (2013). *Just Business. Multinational Corporations and Human Rights.* New York/London: W.W. Norton and Campany.

Salmon, Anne (2002). *Éthique et ordre économique. Une entreprise de séduction* [Ethics and Economic Order. An enterprise of seduction]. Paris: CNRS Éditions.

Samuelson, Paul A. (1947). *Foundations of Economic Analysis.* Cambridge, MA: Harvard University Press.

Sartre, Jean-Paul (1943). *L'Etre et le Néant. Essai de d'ontologie phénonomelogique* [Being and Nothing. Essay in phenomenological ontology]. Paris: Gallimard.

Schans Christensen, Jan (1992). *Ledelse og aktionærer. Seks essays om moderne selskabs- og børsret* [Leadership and Shareholders. Six essays about modern company and stock exchange law]. Copenhagen: Gad.

Schans Christensen, Jan (2004). *God selskabsledelse – dansk Corporate Governance set i sammenhæng* [Good Corporate Governance. Danish corporate governance seen in context]. Copenhagen: Forlaget Thomson.

Scherer, Andreas Georg (2002). *Multinationale unternehmer und Globalisierung* [Multinational Businesses and Globalization]. Heidelberg: Physica Verlag.

Scherer, Andreas Georg and Guido Palazzo (2008). *Handbook of Research on Global Corporate Citizenship.* Cheltenham/Northampton, MA: Edward Elgar Publishing.

Scherer, Andreas Georg and Guido Palazzo (2011). "The new political role of business in a globalized world: a review of a new perspective on CSR and its implications for the firm, governance, and democracy," *Journal of Management Studies* 48(4): 899–931.

Scherer, Andreas Georg, Guido Palazzo, and Dirk Matten (2014). "The business firm as a political actor: a new theory of the firm for a globalized world," *Business & Society Review*, 53(2): 143–156.

Schulze, Gerhard (1995). *Die Erlebnisgesellschaft. Kultursoziologie der Gegenwart* [The Experience Society. Cultural Sociology of the Present], 5th edition. Frankfurt am Main/New York: Campus Verlag.

Schulze, Gerhard (1999). *Kulissen des Glücks. Streifzüge durch die Eventkultur* [Scenes of Happiness. Wanderings through the modern event culture]. Frankfurt am Main/New York: Campus Verlag.

Schulze, Gerhard (2003). *Die beste aller Welten. Wohin bewegt sich die Gesellschaft im 21. Jahrhundert?* [The Best of All Worlds. Where is the society of the 21st century moving?]. Munich/Vienna: Carl Hanser Verlag.

Schwartz, Mark S. and David Saiia (2012). "Should firms go 'beyond profits'? Milton Friedman versus Broad CSR," *Business and Society Review*, 117(1): 1–31.

Schwartz, Peter and Blair Gibb (1999). *When Good Companies Do Bad Things, Responsibility and Risk in an Age of Globalization*. New York: John Wiley and Sons.

Scott, Richard W. (1995). *Institutions and Organizations*. London: Sage Publications.

Searle, John (1995). *The Construction of Social Reality*. New York: The Free Press.

Seele, P. (2014a). "Discussing Wirtschaftsethik with regard to 'business ethics' and 'economic ethics'," *Zeitschrift für Wirtschafts- und Unternehmensethik*, 14(3): 438–441.

Seele, P. (2014b)."Ökonomische Philosophie: Ein Plädoyer für die Rehabilitierung einer alten Disziplin" [Economic Philosophy. A plea for the rehabilitation of an old discipline], *Information Philosophie*, 14(1): 30–36.

Sen, Amartya (1987). *On Ethics and Economics*. Malden, MA: Blackwell Publishers.

Sen, Amartya (1999). *Development as Freedom*. New York: Anchor books.

Sennett, Richard (1998). *The Corrosion of Character: The Personal Consequences of Work in the New Capitalism*. New York: W.W. Norton.

Shaw, William H. and Vincent Barry (1998). *Moral Issues in Business*, 7th edition. Belmont, CA: Wadsworth Publishing Company.

Simpson, Justine and John Taylor (2013). *Corporate Governance, Ethics and CSR*. London/ Philadelphia: Kogan Page.

Sison, José G. (2008). *Corporate Governance and Ethics. An Aristotelian Perspective*, New Horizons in Leadership Studies. Cheltenham/Northhampton, MA: Edward Elgar Publishing.

Smith, Adam ([1759] 2002). *The Theory of Moral Sentiments*. Cambridge Texts in the History of Philosophy. Cambridge: Cambridge University Press.

Smith, Adam ([1776] 2000). *An Inquiry into the Nature and Causes of The Wealth of Nations*. New York: The Modern Library.

Solomon, Robert C. (1992). *Ethics and Excellence. Cooperation and Integrity in Business*. New York, Oxford: Oxford University Press.

Solomon, Robert C. (1999). *A Better Way to Think about Business. How Personal Integrity Leads to Corporate Success*. Oxford: Oxford University Press.

Søndergaard, Jens Teilberg (2003). *Ret, demokrati og globalisering. Om kosmopolitanisme og empirisme* [Law, Democracy and Globalization. About Cosmopolitanism and Empirism]. Copenhagen: Jurist- og Økonomforbundets Forlag.

Sørensen, Claus Vestergaard (2004). "Polis og Kosmos i den græsk-romerske verden" [Polis and Cosmos in the Greek-Roman world]. *Slagmark. Tidsskrift for Idéhistorie*, No. 41, Autumn, 39–55.

Sørensen, Mads P. (2004). *Den politiske forbruger* [The Political Consumer]. Copenhagen: Hans Reitzels Forlag.

Sørensen, Mads P. and Mikkel Thorup (2004). "Globalisering er ikke en etydig gåde" [Globalization is not a clear riddle]. *Slagmark. Tidsskrift for Idéhistorie*, No. 41, Autumn, 15–27.

Sparkes, Russell (2002). *Socially Responsible Investments. A Global Revolution*. London: John Wiley and Sons.

Steinmann, Horst (ed.) (1978). *Betriebswirtschaftslehre als normative Handlungswissenschaft. Zur Bedeutung der konstruktiven Wissenschaftstheorie für die Betriebswirtschaftslehre (Schriftenreihe der Zeitschrift für Betriebswirtschaftslehre, Band 9)* [Business management science as normative action science. About the significance of the constructive theory of science for business management science (Writings of the *Journal of Business Management Science,* Vol. 9)]. Wiesbaden: Betriebswirtschaftlicher Verlag Gabler.

Steinmann, Horst (1997). *Unternehmungsethik: Freiheit und Verantwortung in einer globalizierten* [Business Management Ethics: Freedom and responsibility in a globalized society]. Wirtschaft, Nürnberg.

Steinmann, Horst (2011). "Metaregulung der gesellschaftlichen Verantwortung der Unternehmen," [Metaregulation of the social responsibility of business], *Int. Strafrecht,* 179, 3.99.

Steinmann, Horst, and Albert Löhr (1994). *Grundlagen der Unternehmensethik* [Foundations of Business Management Ethics], 2nd revised and expanded edition. Stuttgart: Poeschel.

Steinman, Horst and Albert Löhr (1996). "A republican concept of corporate ethics," in Sabine Urban (ed.), *Europe's Challenges – Economic Efficiency and Social Solidarity*. Wiesbaden: Gabler, 21–60.

Steinmann, Horst and Bernd Oppenrieder (1985). "Brauchen wir eine Unternehmensethik?" [Do we need a business management ethics?]. *Die Betriebswirtschaft,* 45: 170–183.

Steinmann, Horst and Andreas Georg Scherer (eds) (1998). *Zwischen Universalismus und Relativismus. Philosophische Grundlagenprobleme des interkulturellen Managements* [Between Universalism and Relativism. Philosophical foundation problems of intercultural management]. Frankfurt am Main: Suhrkamp.

Steinmann, Horst and Andreas Scherer (2002). "Betriebswirtschaftslehre und Methodischer Kulturalismus. Was leistet das kulturalistische Programm zur Grundlegung der Betriebswirtschaftslehre" [Business management science and methodological culturalism. What does the culturalistic program offer for foundation of the business management sicence?], in: Mathias Gutmann, Dirk Hartmann, Michael Weingarten, and Walter Zitterbarth (eds), *Kultur – Handlung – Wissenschaft. Für Peter Janich* [Culture – Action – Science]. Weilerswist: Velbrück Wissenschaft Verlag, 149–181.

Steinmann, Horst, Georg Schreyögg, and Mitarbeit von Jochen Koch (2005). *Management. Grundlagen der Unternehmensführung – Konzepte – Funktionen – Fallstudien* [Foundations of Business Management – Concepts, Functions, Cases], 6th edition. Wiesbaden: Gabler.

Sternberg, Elaine (2004). *Just Business. Business Ethics in Action*. Oxford: Oxford University Press.

Stieb, James A. (2009). "Assessing Freeman's stakeholder theory," *Journal of Business Ethics,* 87: 401–414.

Suchman, M.C. (1995). "Managing legitimacy: strategic and institutional approaches," *Academy of Management Review,* 20(3): 571–610.

Sullyvan, Rory (ed.) (2003). *Human Rights and Business. Dilemmas and Solutions*. Sheffield: Greanleaf Publishing.

Sundbo, Jon and Flemming Sørensen (eds) (2013). *Handbook on the Experience Economy*. Cheltenham: Edward Elgar.

Taraborrelli, Angela (2011). *Contemporary Cosmopolitanism*. Bloomsbury Political Philosophy. London: Bloomsbury.

Terris, Daniel (2005). *Ethics at Work. Creating Virtue at an American Corporation*. Lebanon, NH: Brandeis University Press, University Press of New England.

Thielemann, Ulrich (2010). *Wettbewerb als Gerechtigkeitskonzept. Kritik des Neoliberalismus* [Competition as Justice Concept. Critique of Neoliberalism] (Habilitationsschrift). Marburg: Metropolis.

Thomsen, Steen (2004). "Holdninger til corporate governance i dansk erhvervsliv" [Conceptions of Corporate Governance in Danish Business Life], in Jens Valdemar Krenchel and Steen

Thomsen (eds), *Corporate governance i Danmark. Om god selskabsledelse i et dansk og internationalt perspektiv* [Corporate Governance in Denmark. About good corporate governance in a Danish and international perspective]. Copenhagen: Dansk Industri.

Thorup, Mikkel and Mads P. Sørensen (2004). "Uundgåeligt side om side – interview med David Held" [Inevitable side by side – Interview with David Held]. *Slagmark. Tidsskrift for Idéhistorie*, No. 41, Autumn, 27–39.

Thüsing, Gregor and Gerrit Forst (eds) (2016). *Whistleblowing: a comparative study*. New York: Springer international Publishers.

Thyssen, Ole (1997). *Værdiledelse* [Values-driven Management], 1st edition. Copenhagen: Gyldendal.

Thyssen, Ole (2009). *Business Ethics and Organizational Values: A Systems-Theoretical Analysis*. New York: Palgrave Macmillan.

Torfing, Jacob (2005a). "Institutionelle teorier inden for politologi" [Institutional Theories in Political Science], in Klaus Nielsen (ed.), *Institutionel teori. En tværfaglig introduktion* [Institutional Theory. An interdisciplinary introduction]. Copenhagen: Roskilde Universitetsforlag.

Torfing, Jacob (2005b). "Velfærdsstatens institutionelle forandring" [The institutional change of the welfare state], in Klaus Nielsen (ed.), *Institutionel teori. En tværfaglig introduktion* [Institutional Theory. An interdisciplinary introduction]. Roskilde: Roskilde Universitetsforlag.

Treviño, Linda K. and Kathrine A. Nelson (2014). *Managing Business Ethics. Straight Talk about How to Do it Right*, 6th edition. New York: John Wiley and Sons.

Ulrich, Peter (1993). *Transformation der ökonomischen Vernunft. Fortschrittsperspektiven der modernen Industriegesellschaft* [Transformation of the Economic Reason. Progress perspectives of the modern industrial society]. Bern/Stuttgart/Vienna: Haupt.

Ulrich, Peter (1994). "Integrative Wirtschafts- und Unternehmensethik. Ein Rahmenkonzept" [Integrative economic ethics and business ethics. A framework concept], in Forum für Philosophie Bad Homburg (ed.), *Markt und Moral. Die Diskussion um die Unternehmensethik* [Market and Morals. The discussion of business management ethics]. Bern/Stuttgart/Vienna: Haupt.

Ulrich, Peter (1998). *Integrative Wirtcshaftsethik. Grundlagen einer lebensdienlichen Ökonomie* [Integrative Economic Ethics. Foundations of a life-serving Economy], 2nd edition. Stuttgart/Vienna: Haupt.

Ulrich, Peter (2002). *Der entzauberte Markt. Eine wirtschaftsethische Orientierung* [The Disenchanted Market. A business ethics orientation]. Freiburg in Breisgau: Herder Verlag.

Ulrich, Peter and Thomas Maak (1997). "Integrative business ethics. A critical approach," *CEMS Business Review*, 2(1): 27–36.

Ulrich, Peter and Ulrich Thielemann (2009). *Standards guter Unternehmensführung: Zwölf internationale Initiativen und ihr normativer Orientierungsgehalt* [Standards for good Business Management: Twelve International Initiatives and their normative Orientation Content]. St. Galler Beiträge zur Wirtschaftsethik. Bern/Stuttgart/Vienna: Haupt.

United Nations (2003). *The Global Compact. Report in Progress and Activities. July 2002–July 2003*. United Nations Global Compact Office.

United Nations (2015). *The United Nations Millennium Goals Development Report*. New York: The United Nations.

United Nations (2016). *Guide to Corporate Sustainability*. United Nations Global Compact Office.

US Sentencing Commission (1995). *Proceedings of the Second Symposium on Crime and Punishment in the United States: Corporate Crime in America. Strengthening the "Good Citizen Corporation,"* September 7–8, Washington, DC.

Vallentin, Steen (2003). "Socially responsible investing – approaches and perspectives," in Jacob Dahl Rendtorff (ed.), *Værdier, etik og socialt ansvar i virksomheder – brudflader og konvergens* [Values, Ethics and Social Responsibility in Businesses – Tensions and convergence]. Center for værdier i virksomheder, Roskilde Universitetscenter: 114–121.

Vallentin, Steen and David Murillo (2012). "Governmentality and the politics of CSR," *Organization*, 19(6): 825–843.

Van Parijs, Philippe (1995). *Real Freedom for All: What (if anything) can justify capitalism?* Oxford: Oxford University Press.

Velasquez, Manuel G. (2002). *Business Ethics. Concept and Cases,* 5th edition. Upper Saddle River, NJ: Prentice Hall.

Verstraten, Johan (2000). *Business Ethics. Broadening the Perspective.* European Ethics Network. Core Materials for the Development of Courses in Professional Ethics. Leuven/Paris: Peeters.

Walzer, Michael (2004). "Governing the globe," in Michael Walzer, *Arguing about War.* New Haven, CT/London: Yale University Press.

Weber, Max (1904–1905). *The Protestant Ethic and the Spirit of Capitalism,* trans. Talcott Parsons, introduction by Anthony Giddens, London: Allen and Unwin, 1930. [Unwin Paperbacks, 1987.] Reprinted in MaxWeber. *Die Protestantische Ethik und der Geist des Kapitalismus* (1904–1905). In *Gesammelte Aufsätze zur Religionssoziologie,* I [Collected Works on the Sociology of Religion].

Werhane, Patricia H. (1999). *Moral Imagination and Management Decision Making.* The Ruffin Series in Business Ethics. Oxford: Oxford University Press.

Werhane, Patricia H., Laura Pincus Hartman, Crina Archer, Elaine E. Engelhardt, and Michael S. Pritchard (2011). *Obstacles to Ethical Decision-Making. Mental Models, Milgram and the Problem of Obedience.* Cambridge: Cambridge University Press.

Wheeler, David and Maria Sillanpää (1997). *The Stakeholder Corporation. The Body Shop Blue Print for Maximizing Stakeholder Value.* London: Pitman Publishing.

Wieland, Joseph (1989). *Die Entdeckung der Ökonomie. Kategorien, Gegenstandsbereiche und Rationalitätstypen der Ökonomie an ihrem Ursprung* [The Discovery of the Economy. Categories, Fields of Applications and Rationality Types in the Economy in their Origins]. Bern/Stuttgart: Haupt.

Wieland, Joseph (1993). *Formen der Institutionalisierung von Moral in der Unternehmung. Die amerikanische Business-Ethics-Bewegung: Why and how they do it* [Forms of Institutionalization of Morality in Business. The American Business-Ethics Movement: Why and How they do it]. Bern/Stuttgart: Haupt.

Wieland, Joseph (1996). *Ökonomische Organisation, Allokation und Status* [Economic Organization, Allocation and Status]. Tübingen: Mohr (Siebeck).

Wieland, Joseph (1999). *Die Ethik der Governance* [The Ethics of Governance]. Marburg: Metropolis. (5th edition 2007.) Metropolis-Reihe "Studien zur Governanceethik" Band 1.

Wieland, Joseph (2005). *Normativität und Governance* [Normativity and Governance]. Marburg: Metropolis. Metropolis-Reihe "Studien zur Governanceethik" Band 3.

Wieland, Joseph (2013). *Shared Value durch Stakeholder Governance* [Shared Value through Stakeholder Governance] (with Andreas E.H. Heck). Marburg: Metropolis.

Wieland, Joseph (2014). *Governance Ethics: Global Value Creation, Economic Organization and Normativity, Ethical Economy.* Studies in Economic Ethics and Philosophy. Heidelberg: Springer Verlag,

Williamson, Oliver (1989). *The Economic Institutions of Capitalism.* New York: The Free Press.

Wohlrapp, Harald (2012). "Für ein neues pragmatisches Denken" [For a new pragmatic thinking], in Jürgen Mittelstrass (ed.), *Zur Philosophie Paul Lorenzens* [About the Philosophy of Paul Lorenzen]. Münster: Mentis Verlag, 27–41.

World Commission on Environment and Development (Brundtland Commission) (1987). *Our Common Future. Sustainable Development in International Politics.* New York: Oxford University Press.

Wulf, Katharina (2011). *Ethics and Compliance Programs in Multinational Organizations.* Heidelbarg: Springer Gabler.

Zadek, Simon (2001). *The Civil Corporation: The New Economy of Corporate Citizenship.* London: Earthscan.

Zadek, Simon, Peter Pruzan, and Richard Evans (1997). *Building Corporate Accountability.* London: Earthscan.

Zadek, Simon, Niels Højensgård, and Peter Raynard (2001). *Perspectives on the New Economy of Corporate Citizenship.* Copenhagen: Copenhagen Centre.

Zimbardo, Philip (2007). *The Lucifer Effect. How Good People Turn Evil.* New York: Random House.

Index

For Product Safety Concerns and Information please contact our
EU representative GPSR@taylorandfrancis.com Taylor & Francis
Verlag GmbH, Kaufingerstraße 24, 80331 München, Germany